RAJNEESHPURAM

RAJNEESHPURAM

INSIDE THE CULT OF BHAGWAN
AND ITS FAILED AMERICAN UTOPIA

RUSSELL KING

CHICAGO
REVIEW
PRESS

Published by Chicago Review Press Incorporated
814 North Franklin Street
Chicago, Illinois 60610
ISBN 978-1-64160-472-7

Library of Congress Control Number: 2021950798

Typesetting: Nord Compo
Map design: Chris Erichsen

Printed in the United States of America
5 4 3 2 1

For Susan, the dreamer

CONTENTS

Part IV: Oregon, 1984

Part V: Oregon, 1985

Part VI: Flight, 1985

AUTHOR'S NOTE

IN THE SUMMER OF 1981, disciples of the Indian guru Bhagwan Shree Rajneesh descended into a bleak valley in Central Oregon to create a utopia for their master. Within a few years they had built a sophisticated commune from the ground up, complete with an airport, a hotel, restaurants, extensive farms, cutting-edge water treatment facilities, a public transportation system, and housing for thousands of commune members. And then disaster struck. The community vanished within a matter of weeks amid a bonfire of allegations about criminal conspiracies hatched in the commune's inner sanctum.

This book explores these events through the perspectives of disciples who were there, from all-powerful commune leaders to lay disciples who were happy to drive a bus or chop vegetables if it meant they could be close to their master's transcendent energy. It is not a comprehensive history of the Rajneesh movement or a biography of Bhagwan Shree Rajneesh. It is not the story of how a plucky group of Oregonians managed to topple the evil foreign invaders. It is a fresh examination of a perplexing chapter in American history, with an emphasis on the people at the center of it all.

This book is a work of nonfiction, drawn from hundreds of hours of interviews conducted with former commune members and people whose lives intersected with them, as well as a thorough review of commune records, criminal investigative files, deposition and trial transcripts, contemporary press accounts, archival news footage, disciples' memoirs, recorded oral histories, photographs, maps, and more. It relies primarily on objective, fact-based accounts and firsthand perspectives that can be corroborated with the historical record or other sources. Anything that appears within quotation marks comes from a written document or a video or audio recording. Dialogue in *italics* represents conversations or statements as original interview sources recalled them, unless otherwise indicated in the endnotes. I have changed the names of three individuals—indicated by the use of SMALL CAPS on first mention—and any similarity with the names of real people is strictly coincidental.

At its heart, this book is about the attraction to power in all its beguiling forms and how every utopia finds its victims.

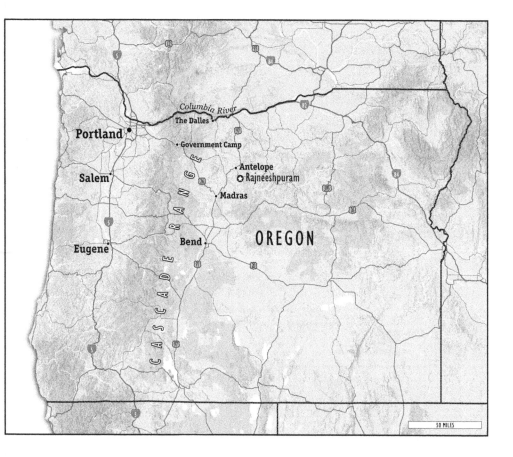

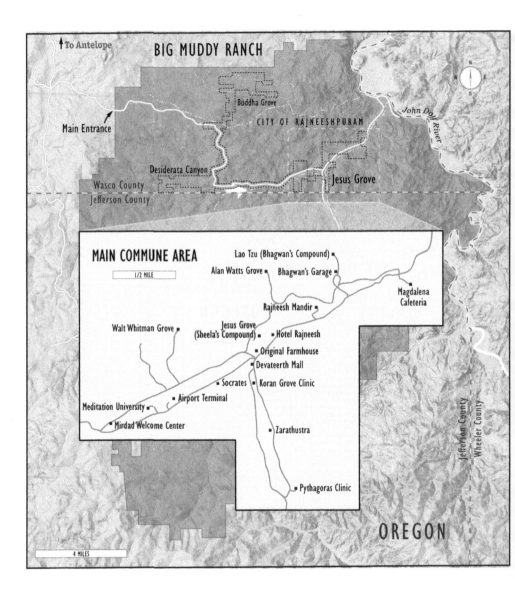

PROLOGUE

PETER STECK'S HOME LIFE WAS UNUSUAL, even before the people in orange pajamas invaded his castle. He was perhaps the only assistant city planner in New Jersey history to live in a turn-of-the-century mansion high on a ridge with unobstructed views of Manhattan. When he had first walked through the property's iron gates in 1978, he found Kip's Castle to be stately if not particularly beautiful, blending ancient and modern notions like crenellated roof lines, round turrets and square towers, a wraparound porch, and a breezeway tucked behind a columned arcade. The home's various owners over the decades hadn't invested much in maintaining or updating the property. The carriage house was a dilapidated wreck filled with raccoon droppings. Weeds choked out the extensive gardens that had once been maintained by the president of the American Dahlia Society. But the home's interiors were in decent shape, including an elegant solarium and a chapel with Tiffany-style stained glass windows.

Steck had jumped at the chance to rent five rooms on the third floor as he started his career as a planner for Montclair Township, a quiet bedroom community outside New York. He married his wife on the castle grounds, and they occupied the top story for the next three years.

And then the pajama people showed up in the summer of 1981, saying they had bought the castle. Steck had seen members of the group walking the Montclair sidewalks in their baggy reddish-orange clothing. He knew they ran a meditation center out of a downtown strip mall that sold books and tapes associated with their Indian guru. Now they were his landlords. The disciples seemed surprised to find tenants on the third floor and gently asked Steck to leave, but he'd signed a lease and knew his rights. Besides, the Stecks were about to close on a new home and move out on their own. They would all have to cohabitate for the next month.

While the disciples had kept a low profile in town for the past couple of years, purchasing Kip's Castle pinned them under the microscope. A local newspaper reported that their bald-headed, long-bearded guru, Bhagwan Shree Rajneesh, ran an ashram in India where his thousands of adherents had scandalized the community with their "free-wheeling sexual behavior." Montclair parents worried that their children might get swept up in a sex cult, especially as more and more orange-robed people were spotted roaming around town. "I saw girls kissing, with their arms around each other," one mother complained in another newspaper. "This is not normal, particularly for little kids to see." Even township officials expressed concerns about what might happen to the quiet bedroom community. "Yes, we're tolerant," the town manager said, "but we don't want to be known as the sex center of the East."

As Montclair's assistant planner, Peter Steck received a barrage of questions and concerns about the new occupants of the town's quirkiest old landmark. How could a cult occupy a single-family home in a residential neighborhood? How many people lived there? Why wasn't anyone stopping their renovations? Indeed, a mixed team of disciples and contractors were working around the clock to convert the thirty-room castle into a residence and retreat for fellow disciples. Steck watched with horror as they slathered white paint over the original curved bannisters and wood veneers, tossed the original doorknobs and fixtures into a dumpster, and laid down linoleum over the hardwood floors—as if they were going out of their way to destroy whatever charm the place once had. But, since the group seemed to be following the zoning regulations and the home wasn't entitled to any special protections, Steck would respond to callers that the disciples were acting within their rights. They could tear the whole thing down if they wanted.

His explanations didn't satisfy those who wanted the township to eject their strange new neighbors before they took root. While the guru was in far-off India, his disciples kept flooding into their little corner of New Jersey—and nobody could figure out why.

These simmering concerns threatened to become a bonfire when the local newspaper ran a warning from an Indian person familiar with the group's aggressive, controversial tactics: "Do not let them get the upper hand."

Other than a few run-ins in the basement laundry room, where everything had become stained with red dye, the Stecks and the disciples managed to live in peace throughout the month of May. But as June approached, the disciples began acting as if they were desperate to get the Stecks out of Kip's Castle, offering to move them for free, to buy them a washer and dryer, to put them up in a private home elsewhere. Nothing was worth the inconvenience of having to move twice, so the Stecks steadfastly declined.

On June 1, 1981, four days before the Stecks were to move into their new home, an anxious delegation of disciples appeared at their apartment door and begged them to stay out of sight throughout the day. Trying to remain good housemates, the Stecks agreed. Still, the commotion was too much to ignore. They saw and heard disciples scampering about the house and across the front lawn—cleaning, arranging, rearranging—as if trying to set a perfect tableau for some unknown visitor. Something momentous was about to happen, it seemed, and Peter Steck wanted to catch a glimpse.

As a hush settled over the crowd outside, he crouched on the floor near a third-story window and held up his small camera to the pane. He blindly snapped some photos of the fifty disciples on the grass quaking with anticipation, and a limousine crawling up the driveway, and a regal passenger in pristine white robes accepting his secretary's hand and placing his sandaled foot on American soil for the first time in his life.

PART I
NEW JERSEY, 1981

Ma Anand Sheela kneels before her master, Bhagwan Shree Rajneesh. *Photo courtesy of The Oregonian*

1 | THE GODMAN OF MUMBAI

MA PREM DEEKSHA'S STOMACH dropped when she received the call from India. She had expected to have additional weeks to complete her work but now learned that she had only days. The castle was a mess. She rushed through the property, berating the men and women who were supposed to be helping her.

With a robust frame and searching blue eyes, Italian-born Deeksha was regarded as a force to be reckoned with, the sort of person who could make a disciple's life hell if they didn't do exactly what she wanted. She had amassed an extraordinary amount of power at her master's glitzy ashram in India as the person who oversaw feeding the tens of thousands of visitors each year, and who directed all construction, cleaning, and maintenance projects at the property. Now her master had selected fearsome Deeksha to lead the vanguard transporting his Indian empire to the West. She had taken it as an honor, to be sure, but she had no idea the steep price.

Deeksha had spent the past ten years living within a mystical, sexually charged bubble where everything revolved around Bhagwan Shree Rajneesh. His image hung in a medallion around every disciple's neck, his photograph was displayed in every room at his ashram, and his philosophy permeated every aspect of his disciples' lives. Bhagwan's priorities had become Deeksha's. Even his way of thinking had become her own. But upon leaving the bubble to set up his home in New Jersey in May 1981, Deeksha had felt almost immediately untethered from her spiritual master. Part of it was just being outside that heady atmosphere and reacclimating to the modern Western world. As she dashed around New Jersey and Manhattan to buy supplies for his impending arrival, she struggled to imagine Bhagwan finding success in the United States. She worried that he was like an enchanting object at a foreign street market that became an ordinary trinket when placed on a shelf back home. A thing whose magic would evaporate as soon as it was removed from the place where it belonged.

But another reason Deeksha felt herself detaching from her master was her awareness of what exactly Bhagwan sought to accomplish in America, and how he and the people running his organization intended to get it done. When she learned that he would arrive in mere days, her concerns only deepened. Each day brought new clarity.

They were all headed for disaster.

I've been waiting for you.

The words still haunted her ten years after hearing them. Back then, in the summer of 1971, she was Mariagrazia, a young Italian woman raised in Switzerland and educated at boarding schools across Europe. She was a rebel and a seeker who had bristled at conventional, capitalistic Geneva with its banks and jewelers. Her extremely wealthy parents had encouraged her interest in Eastern spirituality and philosophy, which ultimately led Mariagrazia to the bustling city of Mumbai, India, during a postcollege, round-the-world tour. A family friend in town urged her to meet the fascinating guru Acharya Rajneesh, who had recently set up shop nearby.

I've been waiting for you.

Everything about the experience had been surreal. Instead of an incense-choked temple or a Himalayan ashram, this self-proclaimed enlightened being lived in a high-rise building in a vibrant commercial neighborhood. A tiny, birdlike Indian woman had greeted her at the door, dressed like a nun in an orange habit and robes, and introduced herself as Ma Yoga Laxmi, the personal secretary to the guru Rajneesh. She ushered Mariagrazia into a living room large enough to hold hundreds of people and lined with thousands of books encased in glass shelving. A wall of windows overlooked the building's lush front gardens and admitted a breeze from the Arabian Sea. A few Indians were waiting for a private audience with the acharya, the learned teacher.

This is your home. You've found me at last.

Laxmi admitted Mariagrazia to the inner sanctum, a room in the back that served as the guru's audience room and living quarters. Acharya Rajneesh sat on an orange easy chair in immaculately pressed white robes, with an embroidered towel folded over his lap. Just forty years old, the handsome Indian man had the motionless bearing of an ancient sage, with a long black beard, bald scalp, and enormous, hypnotic eyes. Smiling, he invited Mariagrazia to sit near his feet on the brown carpeting. In purring, thickly accented English, he asked some questions to make her feel comfortable: Why was she traveling? What was she looking for?

Maybe it was the setting. Maybe it was something more sublime. The longer they talked, the more she felt like she *knew* this man. Like she had known him forever, over the course of many lifetimes, and now they were finally reunited.

This is your home. You've found me at last.

Mariagrazia was taken immediately. She had never read Rajneesh's books, hadn't heard his lectures, knew nothing about his philosophy, but none of that mattered while sitting in his magnetic presence. When he told her to stay in Mumbai and return every day to see him, she canceled the rest of her travels. His energy was a drug, absolutely intoxicating, and she couldn't possibly walk away.

She visited the apartment nearly every day for the next couple of months. While some longtime Indian devotees might be turned away, Acharya Rajneesh always found time for a private audience with Mariagrazia from Switzerland, with her pale skin and curly brown hair that stood out among all the Indians. He gave lectures in Hindi each day in his spacious living room, and she didn't care that she couldn't understand what he said. She just wanted to marinate in his energy.

Reflecting on it later, she felt the guru had a unique ability to create a sense of intimacy with anyone who sat before him. Chatting with the learned man about her life and her deepest questions, Mariagrazia felt her natural skepticism and all her logical barriers dropping away. After a few weeks, she would have done anything for Rajneesh. And she had no doubts at all when he asked her the most important question of her life.

As Mariagrazia arrived in Mumbai in 1971, Rajneesh was wrapping up his life as a public guru who spoke to crowds of tens of thousands in public spaces around India. Gurus had only recently reemerged as a powerful spiritual force on the heels of India's midcentury independence from Britain. While traditional gurus were simple holy men who spoke on Hindu scriptures, a new breed in the 1960s incorporated an understanding of modern psychology, the skillful orchestration of the international press, and practical techniques to expand the consciousness, such as Transcendental Meditation. Some even performed feats of divine magic, like the guru Sathya Sai Baba, who conjured scented ash from his hands.

Acharya Rajneesh made a name for himself in India by staking out controversial positions in his public lectures, particularly on politics and organized religions. Being provocative seemed second nature to the man born Chandra Mohan Jain in 1931, whose family called him Raja or Rajneesh, meaning "king." According to his biographer Vasant Joshi, the charismatic and rebellious young Raja attracted a gang of boys who followed him around town pulling pranks and executing death-defying feats. He had been obsessed with death ever since he watched his beloved grandfather die in a wagon as they slowly trundled toward the doctor. Pushing other boys to their limits seemed to be a way for Raja to probe his own fears of death. He led them on dangerous late-night climbs along steep cliffs. He once pushed a friend who couldn't swim into the raging river to watch him struggle. Although Raja was exceptionally intelligent and a voracious reader, he was often in trouble at school for condescending to and challenging his teachers, all the way through college. After receiving his master's degree, he became a philosophy professor in the city of Jabalpur in central India.

Inspired by the modern guru movement, in the early 1960s Rajneesh began touring India to offer his own thoughts on religion, philosophy, spirituality, and politics. Wearing only a white cloth wrapped around his waist and another draped loosely over his torso, with his wild black beard and flashing eyes, Acharya Rajneesh cut a striking figure as he riled up crowds around the country with his incendiary words. He would criticize revered figures—Mahatma Gandhi, a "poverty worshipper," was a favorite target—and chide orthodox Hindus or anybody else who tried to impose religious strictures or other forms of oppression. His radical insistence on freedom and free thinking resonated with Indians who had only recently escaped the subjugation of their British colonial rulers. Rajneesh gained enough of a following by the mid-1960s to quit his teaching job and become a full-time guru. He also hosted popular ten-day meditation camps in rural spots around India, where he put into practice his belief that meditation is an essential tool to reach an enlightened state. "Meditation is the key; becoming totally aware is the result," he said. "Experiencing oneness with the whole is the reward."

Rajneesh skyrocketed to national notoriety in 1968 when he told a crowd of fifteen thousand people in Mumbai that sex is divine and that only by dropping shame and sexual repressions could one move into the higher state of being he called "superconsciousness." He kept returning to the theme of sex in his public lectures—a theme most gurus would never touch—which earned him a derisive nickname that would stick throughout the rest of his career: "the sex guru."

Despite all the attention and adherents he gathered on the road, Rajneesh was ready to settle in one place by the end of the decade. Beyond the indignities of travel, he felt stifled by the anonymous crowds he encountered at every stop. As he later described it, "It was always ABC, ABC, ABC. And it became absolutely clear that I would never be able to reach XYZ." He decided in 1970, at the age of thirty-eight, to plant roots in Mumbai and start a new phase of his work. He wanted to gather a group of people who would follow him to the edge of the cliff and jump.

Will you become my sannyasin?

Mariagrazia was more than ready to pledge herself to the supernaturally charismatic man who had taken her in from the spiritual cold. While she sat at his feet, Rajneesh dropped a beaded necklace around her neck and intoned her new name: Ma Prem Deeksha. He said it meant *unity with a master through initiation.* She became a lump of clay in Acharya Rajneesh's hands and couldn't wait to see what he would make of her.

At the time, Rajneesh had only recently started initiating disciples who accepted him as their master. He didn't want followers, he said, only people who chose to be with him because they loved him. In return for their devotion, Rajneesh promised to "awaken" his disciples by guiding them toward that highest state of consciousness called enlightenment. He called them "sannyasins," appropriating the term for the Hindu ascetics who could be seen all about India with their orange robes and begging bowls, having renounced the material world to dissolve their egos. Rajneesh thumbed his nose at such austerity, instead encouraging his "neo-sannyasins" to embrace the material world and enter "a great love affair with life itself." His disciples would pursue careers and remain productive members of society, never beggars or takers. They would meditate and love and laugh and take nothing seriously. They would enter and drop romantic relationships as they wished with whomever they wanted and enjoy guilt-free sex in all its varieties.

But he could only work from a blank canvas. In a ceremony that became known as "taking sannyas," new disciples shed their identities and became reborn at Rajneesh's feet. He gave them new names crafted from Sanskrit words meaning things like "love," "bliss," and "divine." All women received names that started with Ma, meaning "mother," and all men received names starting with Swami, meaning "master of oneself." He told them to dress only in sunrise colors (orange, red, purple, pink) to denote the dawn of their inner spirit. He also gave them a long necklace to wear called a mala, made of 108 rosewood beads representing the different forms of meditation and featuring a central pendant with Rajneesh's photograph. These were only external manifestations of their new identities—the real work happened within. With their master's guidance, his disciples would drop all the conditioning that had been heaped on them by governments, religions, schools, and families throughout their lives, dissolve their egos, and become self-actualized individuals.

As one of the first Westerners to come to him, Deeksha represented a minor tremor before a massive earthquake. The post–World War II counterculture movement had inspired many people from Europe, North America, and Australia to explore Eastern philosophy, medicine, meditation, and yoga. Books about Eastern spirituality became popular in the late 1960s and early 1970s, like Ram Dass's *Be Here Now*, which used eye-catching graphic design and snappy quotations to guide Western readers down the path to becoming a yogi, and Hermann Hesse's 1922 novel *Siddhartha*, which romanticized the spiritual journey east. Some seekers tried out meditation and yoga at their local "growth centers," but many others traveled east to find their own gurus. A famous example of this zeitgeist was the Beatles traveling to India in 1968 to live with the guru Maharishi Mahesh Yogi and practice Transcendental Meditation.

Acharya Rajneesh was one of many gurus initiating disciples in the early 1970s, but his profound understanding of the Western world made him unusually accessible. He was well informed about Western philosophy, psychology, and literature, having read, according to his estimate, over one hundred thousand books. He required no vow of poverty or silence or chastity, no renunciation of personal goods or relationships, no years of austere apprenticeship along the path to enlightenment. Becoming his sannyasin was incredibly easy. And, perhaps most impressive to those who arrived at his apartment without knowing much about him, he looked like a guru straight out of Central Casting, with his captivating eyes and benevolent smile.

Enough Westerners had arrived by 1972 that Rajneesh began to cater to them by offering the occasional English-language lecture. American disciple Ma Satya Bharti, a published poet and former speechwriter for presidential candidate Shirley Chisholm, became his unofficial English tutor when she arrived in Mumbai that year, spending long hours in his room gently correcting his grammar and pronunciation. The guru also expanded his reach beyond India by opening Rajneesh Meditation Centers in major cities in Europe, Australia, and the United States. He created this international network in a fairly hands-off way, sending Western disciples home with a name for the center and little other guidance. The centers sold books of his translated Hindi lectures, played audio recordings of his English discourses, and hosted meditation sessions, which all served to convert foreigners from spiritual browsers into dedicated sannyasins. By the end of the decade, Rajneesh's organization would claim more than five hundred meditation centers around the world.

Satya Bharti discovered Acharya Rajneesh in 1971 while chatting at a New York tea party with a jet-setting woman who had just returned from India and wouldn't shut up about her guru. The woman invited Satya to come to her house and try a practice Rajneesh had invented called Dynamic Meditation. Unlike traditional meditation, which requires one to calm the mind intentionally, Dynamic induces a trancelike state by first having the participants hyperventilate, then "go totally mad" by jumping, screaming, crying, or dancing, and then chanting the word "Hoo!" in fifteen-minute cycles. Rajneesh said the modern mind—particularly the "Western mind"—was too fast-moving and too agitated to enter meditation freely. Dynamic Meditation offered a solution that would bring the frantic mind to a halt and allow the participants to achieve real breakthroughs.

Satya had an explosive catharsis the first time she tried Dynamic Meditation. She felt as if she regressed to her innocent childhood consciousness and had to learn how to walk again. Raised in an upper-middle-class Jewish family in the suburbs, Satya had married at eighteen, borne three children, and found herself at age thirty a single mother freshly out of a loveless marriage. Inspired by her experience with the meditation, she hunted down books of Rajneesh's discourses translated from Hindi. When he spoke about people living in self-constructed prisons, she felt he was speaking directly to her. Through a Rajneesh Meditation Center in upstate New York, she became Ma Satya Bharti. Within a year, she relinquished custody of her three young children to her ex-husband and flew to India to be with her master.

I've been waiting for you, he said when Satya entered his room.

By that point, Acharya Rajneesh had cast aside his "teacher" honorific in favor of a grander name that represented his transformation from traveling guru to disciple-inducting master: Bhagwan Shree Rajneesh. "Bhagwan" (pronounced buh-GWAN) means "god" or "blessed one" in Hindi. The name alone caused some longtime Indian devotees to abandon him, repulsed by what they saw as an ego trip, but his Western disciples embraced it. As Satya saw it, Bhagwan generally struggled to form the intimate master-disciple relationship he desired with his Indian followers, who often had multiple gurus and didn't regard him as particularly extraordinary. Western seekers, on the other hand, had no tradition of casual guru relationships. Bhagwan was often the only guru they had ever encountered, and to them he *was* extraordinary. Many new arrivals to Mumbai would leave his room in the same way Satya Bharti had after her first private audience: so smitten by the serene, picture-perfect guru that they could barely walk down the hallway.

Bhagwan didn't overlook the fact that Western disciples had access to wealth that most Indians could never match. After spending months with him in Mumbai, Satya Bharti prepared to travel home in 1972 to visit her children. Bhagwan sent her off with a command: *Go back to America, and bring all the rich people you know to me.*

2 | OASIS IN PUNE

OLDER INDIAN WOMEN IN THEIR ORANGE SARIS had tutted when twenty-two-year-old Sheela Ambalal Patel Silverman first swaggered into Bhagwan's Mumbai apartment in 1972. Wearing blue jeans and a tight T-shirt, with her black hair in a chin-length bob, Sheela announced that she sought an audience. The guru's secretary, Laxmi, stood from her little desk near the entrance, unaware that she was meeting the woman who would dethrone her by the decade's end.

While Sheela waited in the living room, Bhagwan's early Western disciples Italian Deeksha and American Satya chatted her up. Speaking in somewhat broken English peppered with colorful American idioms, Sheela was quick to flash a pearly smile, quick with a sarcastic quip. Her impulsive, childlike energy struck Satya as a bit abrasive within the tranquil shrine.

Asked why she was interested in Bhagwan, Sheela spoke of her dying husband. When she was seventeen, Sheela's father had offered her the irresistible opportunity to attend college in the United States, where her older siblings lived. She left India in February 1968 and enrolled at Montclair State College in New Jersey to study watercolor painting and pottery in the fine arts department. There, she met and fell in love with a skinny, red-haired classmate a couple of years her senior who was studying physics. Marc Silverman had a scientist's mind and a seeker's soul, with a big heart and a corny sense of humor that tickled Sheela. They eloped in June 1969 and had a proper wedding in Montclair the next summer when Sheela's family visited from India. She was in and out of school while Marc finished his studies, and she worked various jobs to support her new family, including operating a hot dog truck. They would putter along the Garden State Parkway searching for busy construction sites where they could snag the lunch crowd, with Marc behind the wheel belting out his favorite old standards, like "Blue Moon." Construction workers would form long lines to grab a chili dog and shoot the breeze with the brassy Indian lady hawking them.

Everything about America excited Sheela. It was a land of promise, even for a young woman with dark brown skin and an Indian accent. She had no plans to leave her adopted home, no intention of moving back to India. But her plans were derailed in December 1972, during a fateful visit to India to see her parents. She stopped in Mumbai to see family and wound up sitting at Bhagwan's feet.

What are you looking for? he asked her.

Marc had been diagnosed with Hodgkin's lymphoma, a cancer of the lymphatic system, at age eighteen. Doctors had given him two years to live, but then cobalt therapy blasted the cancer into temporary remission. Still, Marc worried that he could pass in the blink of an eye, that at any moment he might simply stop breathing. He'd tried to end his relationship with Sheela before it got too serious, to save her from the pain of his inevitable death, but they pushed through it. Even after they were married, Marc continued to struggle with the cosmic unfairness of receiving a terminal diagnosis at such a young age. He hesitated to make plans beyond college, since he was uncertain how long he would be around.

Sheela thought Bhagwan might be able to help them. She hung around in Mumbai for a couple more days to speak privately with him about Marc and his disease and death. At Laxmi's urging, Satya and Deeksha tried to persuade her to take sannyas, but she refused. She spoke of meditators with a sort of dismissiveness, as if dedicating one's life to personal growth were a waste of time.

I can't take sannyas, Sheela had told Satya one day. *I'm a potter.*

Well, I'm a writer, Satya said, *and I'm also a sannyasin.*

*Yeah, but I'm a **serious** potter.*

So Satya and Deeksha were stunned when Sheela Silverman from America bounded out of Bhagwan's room one day with a beaded mala around her neck. She later said that he had bowled her over with his frank talk about death as the culmination of life, something to be anticipated with joy and not despair. When it finally arrives, he told her, death should be celebrated. Sheela felt that Bhagwan's attitude might ease Marc's anxiety and grief about his own impending death, if he were open to receiving it.

Watching Sheela fall in love with Bhagwan, Deeksha recognized a pattern she was starting to see among promising people who arrived at the Mumbai apartment. The guru would identify a new arrival's vulnerability, the thing that kept them up at night, and promise to fix it. It might be a bad marriage or a messy divorce, or a feeling that their parents had abandoned them, or strained relations with their children. It might be a feeling of powerlessness or a lust for power or a compulsion to be dominated. Whatever the exposed nerve may be, Deeksha saw Bhagwan eliciting it from the person at his feet and then pressing that nerve to get what he wanted. Sheela's raw nerve was her husband, who lived in fear of death, and Bhagwan offered a solution that required them to accept him as their master and become his disciples. He wouldn't entertain Sheela's objections, even when she insisted that she had no interest in meditation as the path to enlightenment.

When the time comes, he told her, *I'll push you in through the back door.*

Weeks later, Marc Silverman arrived in Mumbai and found himself enchanted by Bhagwan's philosophy. He decided to turn off his analytical mind and engage in what he called "a very insecure type of experiment" by taking sannyas and becoming Swami Prem Chinmaya while attending a meditation camp. "I have a fatal illness and am also therefore concerned with the fact of death. And I am afraid of death," he later wrote to his concerned grandmother. "Here, through meditation and Bhagwan's guidance, there is a possibility for me to overcome this fear. There is a way of knowing death before one dies, through meditation. I am here preparing for my inevitable death."

At the same meditation camp, Bhagwan gave Sheela her sannyasin name as well. Since the property hosting the camp was called Anand Shila—so similar to her birth name—Sheela Silverman was reborn as Ma Anand Sheela.

By early 1974, one year after Sheela took sannyas, Bhagwan's burgeoning movement was testing the capacity of his three-bedroom apartment. People were coming from the United States, England, Germany, the Netherlands, Australia, Canada, Japan, and South Africa to sit at his feet and receive his counsel. Early disciples had spread the word about Bhagwan throughout the world, and his translated Hindi lectures were becoming widely available for purchase. Readers were fascinated by the guru's frank talk about liberal sexuality and his ability to apply his expansive philosophies to their day-to-day lives. If they made contact with a local Rajneesh Meditation Center, Westerners were often encouraged to travel to India to meet the master himself. Those who stayed in Mumbai could participate in sunrise Dynamic Meditation on the beach, attend daily discourses in the guru's living room, receive the occasional private audience, and join his sporadic ten-day meditation camps in the countryside. Bhagwan developed special meditation techniques to address his disciples' particular problems. For instance, he told Satya Bharti to sit in her room and focus on her "sex center" while repeating his name in her head.

Bhagwan found other clever ways to keep his disciples occupied, including making extraordinary demands that seemed to probe how far he could push them. In the middle of winter, he sent Sheela and Chinmaya to meditate in the mountains of Kashmir, where they had no running water and could barely manage to write letters home because their hands kept freezing. He sent another crew of Western disciples to the middle of the Indian jungle and told them to convert a decrepit farm into a commune for him, although the conditions were so squalid that Bhagwan would never live there. He took an avid interest in the personal lives of the disciples who hung around Mumbai, asking where they were staying and who they were sleeping with. He seemed to relish pulling apart and pushing together couples, even instructing one young Scottish disciple to have sex with an older American woman, an act the disciple could only assume had some spiritual significance.

Disciples came to understand that these uncomfortable situations were "devices" Bhagwan employed for their spiritual growth. Taking a page from the Russian mystic and teacher George Gurdjieff, who had formed his own spiritual community in the early twentieth century, Bhagwan created situations that, he claimed, were designed to have a particular effect on his disciples. He didn't often specify what the device was, or what it was meant to do, or even confirm whether or not something *was* a device. Even today some current and former sannyasins consider their most challenging experiences to be devices that Bhagwan implemented to teach them something, which allows them to ascribe a spiritual significance to virtually any misfortune or hardship under his watch.

But devices and sunrise meditations weren't enough to capture the ever-growing community of disciples who wanted to be close with their spiritual master. After four years in Mumbai, it became clear to Bhagwan and Laxmi that they needed to establish an ashram where he and his disciples could live and meditate together. He'd made some vague moves over the years toward establishing an ashram in Mumbai, but the conditions were never quite right whenever Laxmi looked at properties in town—too humid, not airy enough, not big enough. By 1974, idle talk turned to rank necessity. Bhagwan's apartment could no longer contain the neo-sannyas explosion.

Laxmi found the perfect property ninety miles southeast of Mumbai in the city of Pune, an old hill station from the British Raj with a pleasant climate, excellent universities, and a lineage of spiritual masters who had lived there. With money from a wealthy Greek sannyasin, Laxmi purchased a Western-style mansion in a posh neighborhood called Koregaon Park, which was filled with gently decaying vacation homes built by India's nobility in the early twentieth century. After celebrating with hundreds of disciples on March 21, 1974, Bhagwan walked out of his Mumbai apartment for the last time and climbed into the back of a car strewn with garlands, chauffeured by his devoted secretary. A fifteen-vehicle procession accompanied him along the three-hour drive to Number 33 Koregaon Park.

Only a handful of people could live in the house, which Bhagwan dubbed Lao Tzu, and Laxmi set her sights on expanding the ashram grounds as quickly as possible. But expansion would cost money, and cash flow became a constant source of stress. Most of the businessmen who had propped up Bhagwan in Mumbai cut ties when their guru moved three hours away—a development that did not particularly bother Bhagwan, who felt that donations were unreliable and often came with strings attached. He wanted the Shree Rajneesh Ashram to be an industrious, self-sufficient community. Laxmi formed a new charitable trust called the Rajneesh Foundation, which she controlled as the managing trustee, to oversee Bhagwan's growing spiritual empire, and she began developing a business model that would provide the ashram with a steady source of income.

Fortunately, she had a free labor force at hand. Whereas in Mumbai disciples could flit in and out of Bhagwan's apartment, meditate on the beach, and do whatever they wanted with their free time, to live at his ashram they were expected to work, doing whatever Laxmi and her staff commanded, for which they received "free" room and board, and unlimited access to Bhagwan's pervasive energy. Laxmi organized departments to coordinate the dozens—and, eventually, hundreds—of ashramites responsible for food service, cleaning, maintenance, gardening, purchasing, accounting, press relations, and preparing Bhagwan's publications. Ashramites worked from morning to night, except for those fleeting moments when they could attend Bhagwan's daily lectures or receive an audience with the master. As the Scottish disciple later described it, "the card-playing, lime-sipping, lotus-eating days were over."

Ashramites were carefully vetted and had to be invited by Laxmi's staff. Anybody else who walked onto the ashram grounds was considered a visitor who had to pay for everything on offer, even attending discourse. Italian Deeksha became a driving force behind the ashram's ability to make money off people who passed through its gates. At Bhagwan's command, she took over the ashramites' canteen and the café for visitors, which she transformed into a sophisticated restaurant serving fresh-baked bread, minestrone soup, tofu and tempeh burgers, a rotating selection of desserts, and full Indian meals. With a small army of ashramites under her control, Deeksha became the go-to person for any building or maintenance projects. She would storm around the grounds with an entourage of disciples who would hop to clean whatever mess she noticed, fix whatever problems she saw, and revamp any rooms that struck her as shabby. If she wanted something done that Laxmi wouldn't pay for, Deeksha would simply tap into her own considerable wealth.

Originally just Bhagwan's home and garden, by the late 1970s the ashram had expanded onto contiguous properties to become a lush compound covering seven and a half acres. Those who had already taken sannyas at an international Rajneesh Meditation Center often felt a sense of coming home as they entered the grounds. The drama started the moment their taxi or rickshaw pulled up to the ashram's majestic teak gates, which were carved with beautiful flowers, framed by white marble, and lit by a crystal chandelier. Passing through the gates revealed a private oasis sealed off from the chaotic streets of Pune, flush with thousands of orange-robed people—mainly well-educated, relatively affluent white-skinned Westerners—meditating, eating, working, and laughing together.

Bhagwan gave daily ninety-minute lectures in canopied Buddha Hall, which accommodated thousands of people. Alternating each month between Hindi and English lectures, he would speak in multiday series on whatever topics captured his interest, such as the Zen tradition, Buddhist sutras, Sufi mystics, or Pythagoras. The themes served as mere starting points that might lead to him ripping apart Indian politicians and other gurus; mocking the Pope, Mother Teresa, and organized religions; telling long stories from his childhood; and dropping crude jokes pulled from the pages of *Playboy* that left his disciples roaring with laughter. Sometimes he would answer preselected questions from his disciples. ("Bhagwan, you are calling from the peak. I am lost in the echoing valleys. How may I come to you?") Speaking without notes, he demonstrated a mastery of spiritual and esoteric traditions, an incredible memory for books he had read years earlier, and a razor-sharp wit.

Disciples who showed up to the Shree Rajneesh Ashram hoping to spend time alone with the guru, as they had in his Mumbai apartment, were sorely disappointed. Bhagwan isolated himself in Pune, perhaps owing to the sheer number of people who now clamored to be near him. He would meet with small groups of disciples in a semiprivate audience called "darshan"; these were invite-only affairs that had to be scheduled through Laxmi's staff. At the appointed time each night, the invitees would gather near a wrought-iron gate separating his home, Lao Tzu, from the rest of the ashram grounds and pass along a curved foliage tunnel to the open-air auditorium at the back of the house. There, Bhagwan would greet new arrivals, say farewell to those who were leaving, and induct new sannyasins. Disciples at his feet could briefly ask questions and chat about their lives. He might lean forward and press his fingers against the third eye, on the forehead above the eyebrows, to read their energy.

A Canadian man who took sannyas and became Swami Prem Avinasha described his first time kneeling before Bhagwan at darshan as an entrancing but terrifying experience. "I looked into his eyes and felt myself going into a place of total acceptance and total love for who I was," he recalled. "After a minute or two, unbeknownst to me, this deep fear came up between us like a big iron gate, and I slammed it in his face, to my horror. I was rejecting him on an unconscious level, worried I would lose myself if I continued to look into his eyes." Avinasha came to understand that his fear was rooted in his misconception that a guru would solve all his problems. To the contrary, he realized that surrendering himself to the master was only the first step, and that he remained in charge of his own growth.

At darshan, Bhagwan often gave new arrivals a prescription of what they should do while at the ashram. For most visitors from 1975 onward, this meant a healthy slate of group therapy courses. Group therapy had become a phenomenon among Western psychotherapists in the 1970s, blending classical psychological theory with the human potential movement's experiential practices. Groups varied in technique and focus, but they all shared the general purpose of helping participants drop past traumas and conditioning to move closer to self-actualization. Among the most popular groups of the 1970s was encounter, which invited participants—ten to twenty people, often nude—to explore their personal problems and release past traumas through free-form, multiday sessions of talking, dancing, screaming, pillow pounding, role playing, truth telling, confronting, touching, massaging, and doing whatever the group leaders might contrive to stimulate growth and awareness. By 1974, the *New York Times* reported that millions of Americans had participated in some form of encounter therapy.

Turned on to groups by all the Western psychologists and therapists who had visited him in Mumbai, Bhagwan came to believe they could support his goal of deprogramming and deconditioning his disciples, particularly because they gave seekers a sense of agency in their path toward enlightenment. Groups became a huge draw for Westerners lured by the attraction of something modern and familiar under the auspices of an Eastern master. By the end of the decade, the Shree Rajneesh Ashram had become the largest growth center in the world, offering dozens of groups at any given time, from gentle introductory courses to more aggressive groups like tantra and the ashram's famous encounter groups. Although he didn't lead groups himself, Bhagwan encouraged his appointed group leaders to push physical boundaries, since he believed that violence could be a useful tool in achieving self-awareness. This led to broken noses, broken limbs, and even sexual assault in the ashram's padded rooms.

Some disillusioned disciples came to view groups as serving a purpose far darker than personal growth. Among the ashram's loudest critics was Richard Price, the legendary founder of the Esalen Institute in Big Sur, California, where encounter groups had first been developed. Price took sannyas and visited Pune in 1978, but he left disgusted after participating in Bhagwan's version of an encounter group. In a letter published in *Time* magazine, he described the ashram's encounter groups as "an abomination—authoritarian, intimidating, violent—used to enforce conformity rather than to facilitate growth. Broken bones are common, bruises and abrasions beyond counting. As such, it owes more to the S.S. than to Esalen." In a letter to the ashram, Price urged Bhagwan to consider "whether you are running a growth center or a concentration camp."

Indeed, some disciples would later suggest that Bhagwan used his groups as a tool in creating a culture of surrender at the ashram. Surrender was a necessary prerequisite for Bhagwan's work on his disciples, as he made clear in his tentpole pledge: "Surrender to me and I will transform you." People interpreted it in different ways, but the general concept was that disciples had to surrender their egos to become their fully actualized selves. "When you surrender to a master you take the first step in renouncing the inauthentic," wrote Satya Bharti in a 1981 book, "so that a space is created within you where your uniqueness can begin to grow, to flower. It's renouncing the false so that you can begin to discover the real: what you were meant to be, what you really are beneath all your conformities and conditionings." Many disciples understood that they were not surrendering to Bhagwan himself or his commands. The master was just a device, and the surrender itself was the transformation.

But others—particularly those who became disillusioned and eventually left the movement—came to believe that "surrender" meant dropping any critical thinking and submitting entirely to Bhagwan. To live at his ashram was to surrender to the entire experience as he dictated it. Dropping rational thought was a feature of his message throughout his time in Pune, down to the sign at Buddha Hall's entrance that read, LEAVE YOUR SHOES AND MIND OUTSIDE. Bhagwan made clear in his discourses that anybody who questioned or criticized him or any aspect of the community should leave. "Your votes will never be taken," he told disciples in 1978. "Whatsoever I decide is absolute. If you don't chose [sic] that way, you are perfectly happy to leave."

He enabled ashram leaders to push the concept of surrender down to the ashramites. Deeksha's kitchen workers would get a tongue lashing if they didn't cut the carrots in the way she had specified, even though she knew it didn't ultimately matter whether the carrots were chopped round or straight. They needed to drop their individuality and surrender to her instructions, as part of the larger surrender of their ego. When ashram workers sat at Bhagwan's feet to ask questions at darshan, a regular topic was Deeksha's competence as a boss, since she was known to shout at and ridicule the ashramites working beneath her. Disciples rarely found a receptive audience in Bhagwan for their complaints. "Deeksha is crazy!" he said in June 1979. "You may be far more intellectual, far more rational—but you have to surrender to Deeksha. Her craziness is her quality—that's why I have chosen her. I have got many more rational people: I could have chosen a Ph.D. who would have convinced you that he is right. But when you are convinced and you follow, it is not surrender. When you are not convinced at all, you see the apparent stupidity of a certain thing, and still you surrender, that is a great step, a great step of getting out of your past."

The underlying message was to just go along with things in Bhagwan's world, even if they seemed wrong. Reflecting on it years later, Deeksha felt that the ashram turned disciples into "zombies" who would do whatever they were told. Bhagwan was a powerful teacher and an enlightened master, and even Deeksha felt that she had to accede to his dictates if she wanted to enter a more awakened state. That meant shutting off her conscious mind and just accepting what she was told, and demanding the same from the hundreds of ashramites beneath her.

Groups became the ashram's cash cow in the late 1970s. A single group that lasted five to seven days cost around eighty dollars on average—$350 today— and Bhagwan would suggest up to ten groups for new arrivals, taken sequentially with perhaps a day or two in between. The gentler introductory groups could have as many as two hundred participants. By 1981, the ashram claimed that two thousand people each month took groups and that its twenty-four group therapy rooms were in almost round-the-clock use.

While individual groups were not prohibitively expensive for most, the accumulation of them added up fast. As many cash-strapped sannyasins would discover, there was no charity at the Shree Rajneesh Ashram, and nobody took a group unless they paid for it. If a disciple's savings dwindled away and they stopped paying for ashram services, they might be summoned to Laxmi's office and told to go home to save up for a later return. This would come as devastating news to disciples who believed that being close to their master and part of his community was all that mattered. Some did go home, working odd jobs that allowed them to return to the ashram with cash in hand. Others created cottage industries in Pune that catered to their fellow sannyasins, like making clothes, giving tarot readings, drawing up astrological charts, or baking cookies. Some women raised funds by camping out in the lobbies of swanky Mumbai hotels and performing sex work.

Drug running became a particularly well-known way to earn a large sum of money fast. Local dope dealers would use down-on-their-luck Western sannyasins as mules, instructing them to carry a briefcase back home in exchange for a big chunk of cash. It became a joke around the ashram that when men suddenly cut their hair and shaved their beards, they were obviously about to transport drugs to the West. Multiple disciples have alleged that the ashram coordinated with drug dealers to help them identify vulnerable sannyasins desperate for money. The scheme was engineered to make everybody a winner: the dealers got their drugs to the West, the sannyasins could return immediately to Pune, and the ashram received the proceeds from the deal as a donation.

And Laxmi knew better than to ask where the money came from. She carried out her business from Krishna House, a gleaming modern home with plate-glass doors framed in dark teak that served as her base of operations. Visitors would find Bhagwan's secretary in her corner office atop a throne-like yellow chair and flanked by young assistants who helped her run a burgeoning empire. But despite her perch of power and the world she had created for her beloved master, events were conspiring against Laxmi by the end of the 1970s. One of the young women who sat at her right hand had sensed an opportunity on the horizon that would allow her to perform a critical service for her master in a way that only she knew how.

Sheela was preparing to make her move.

3 | THE NEW COMMUNE

HAVING MADE HIS MARK on tens of thousands of disciples from around the world, by the late 1970s Bhagwan was looking ahead to the next phase of his work. He was interested in nothing less than changing humanity. In his morning lectures, he began painting an image for his disciples of the world-altering work he could only accomplish at a spacious new commune. The portrait was hazy at first. Bhagwan said it would be a mystery school where he could impart secrets of Taoism, Zen, tantra, yoga, and other traditions to his disciples, with a beautiful facade of five-star hotels and swimming pools for visitors while the real work happened underground between master and disciple.

Over the course of multiple discourses, Bhagwan expounded on his grand utopian vision for the "New Commune," where he would create a novel species he called the "New Man": a multifaceted being with all the objectiveness of a scientist, the sensitivity of a poet, and the deep spirituality of a mystic. He described this ideal person as a "Zorba the Buddha," blending the decadent joyfulness of Zorba the Greek with Buddha's spirituality.

Life at the New Commune would be free of all the traditional institutions and obligations that repressed an individual's growth. No more nuclear families or marriages, those ancient relics that only encouraged people to control each other. Couples would make no commitment except to love each other in the moment. Although Bhagwan discouraged his sannyasins from having kids—and in fact urged them to get sterilized and have abortions—any children at the New Commune would be raised by the entire community, allowing them to learn from many different role models. No more rat-race careers, no more working for a paycheck, and no more religions. Bhagwan's sannyasins would practice a form of spirituality that transcended labels, without any dogma or strictures. Everybody would live richly, working side by side with playfulness, love, and laughter, with no ulterior motive other than to support the community and each other. The New Commune would become Bhagwan's "Buddhafield," where he could share his enlightened energy with all of his disciples and, eventually, the entire world.

But he could only nurture the New Man on a vast property that would allow him the latitude to dictate the rules for a radical new society. The ashram in Pune was too small and too crowded for him to conduct this all-important work. As Bhagwan laid out this vision, the New Commune became a rallying cry among his disciples. Laxmi raised massive donations from the promise of securing a home in the hypothetical New Commune, before any land had been acquired. She and Bhagwan used the vision as a way to keep sannyasins engaged and focused on the next step in their master's work. Just imagine everything they could accomplish together if they gave enough, worked enough, and believed one hundred percent in Bhagwan's ability to transform the world.

Bhagwan tapped Laxmi to find a suitable place in India to build his New Commune, and she spent much of the late 1970s scouring the country, often leaving the ashram at 4:00 AM and trading five-hour shifts behind the wheel with her assistants. But whenever she found a place that she loved, some external force always managed to squelch the deal. Her chief antagonist was Indian prime minister Morarji Desai, the eighty-one-year-old archconservative who took office in 1977. Bhagwan would often trot out the specter of "dry, dull, dead Morarji Desai" as a punch line during his discourses to illustrate a stubborn, joyless, coldly ambitious person. The prime minister represented the old Gandhian Indian establishment that Bhagwan so publicly loathed.

The feeling of antipathy was mutual. Desai's government found various reasons to block Laxmi's land purchases, such as potential national security risks if the New Commune were positioned too close to the Pakistan border. When the ashram sent disciples to petition Desai personally for his support, he dredged up the many insults that Bhagwan had hurled at him over the years. ("You call me a urine-drinking prime minister, and in the same breath you want my help?")

Undaunted, Laxmi continued searching and continued striking out, either because Desai's government made the purchase impossible or because the sellers demanded exorbitant prices when they learned that she represented the chandelier-draped ashram in Pune. She made some progress in 1978 when she rented a crumbling old fortress in Saswad, a rural town twenty miles south of the ashram, and sent a small team of disciples there to begin renovations. Desai's government again intervened to ensure that the state government denied the approvals Laxmi would need to convert the property into an ashram.

For help, Laxmi turned to an old family friend, Indira Gandhi. The former prime minister was revving up for another run for office, and she agreed to help Laxmi if she won. But Gandhi shut out Bhagwan's organization after winning reelection in 1980, even with Laxmi camping out on her New Delhi doorstep for six months. When yet another land deal fell through in northwestern India in September 1980, Bhagwan's frustration boiled over at a discourse where he threatened to bring one hundred thousand "orange people" to the area within ten years, whether the community liked it or not.

In the midst of this fruitless search, Bhagwan insisted that Laxmi solve another problem that had dropped in their lap: their burgeoning tax bill. Desai's government had revoked the Rajneesh Foundation's nonprofit status, questioning why the foundation should be considered a charitable trust when it did not serve the general public and reaped huge amounts of money from what seemed to be commercial services and goods: group therapy, clothing, malas, food, lodging, and more. After receiving a barrage of tax edicts and unfavorable court decisions, the Rajneesh Foundation owed about $5.4 million (nearly $20 million today).

Frustrated by these setbacks, Bhagwan placed both problems—the land hunt and the tax disputes—squarely in Laxmi's hands and told her to stay away from the ashram until she solved them. In the meantime, he needed somebody to steer the ship in Pune.

Bhagwan had thrust Sheela away almost as soon as he had embraced her as a new disciple in Mumbai. This became a recurring theme for her first couple of years as a sannyasin. Bhagwan sent her and her husband, Chinmaya, to the freezing Himalayas to meditate. He then sent them to Sheela's hometown, Baroda, to open an experimental commune. When he opened his Pune ashram in 1974, they were among the first to live there, but months later Bhagwan shipped them off to New Jersey with instructions to open a meditation center near Chinmaya's hometown. The couple incubated the Chidvilas Rajneesh Meditation Center out of a railroad apartment in Garwood and took civilian jobs while trying to generate interest in Bhagwan, with Sheela working as a "barmaid," as she liked to call it, at the Red Caboose and red-robed Chinmaya working as a substitute physics teacher for the Newark School District.

In 1975 they were called back to the ashram to become permanent residents. Sheela worked as a receptionist in the Krishna House office, one of many smart, self-assured women in Laxmi's orbit. But she quickly distinguished herself with her insatiable interest in business and her ability to find money in a pinch. She was one of the rare ashramites who spoke Hindi, which also allowed her to help Laxmi deal with local businessmen and politicians. By the late 1970s, Sheela had become so valuable that Laxmi appointed her as one of her two main assistants, along with Ma Prem Arup, a tall, officious woman from a wealthy Dutch banking family. Arup handled the ashram's correspondence, received Western disciples, and managed the group therapy schedule, while Sheela dealt with Indians outside the ashram and helped Laxmi keep tabs on finances. For sport, Laxmi took great joy in pitting her two assistants against each other, favoring one and then the other, until their jealousy and hostility boiled over in explosive confrontations.

Throughout this time, Sheela always kept a hand in the Chidvilas Rajneesh Meditation Center back in New Jersey. It remained small compared to the other centers, little more than a storefront where curious locals could try out Dynamic Meditation and buy Bhagwan's books and cassette tapes. But Sheela quietly nurtured the center that she and Chinmaya had founded, filing new articles of incorporation for it in December 1977 and requesting tax-exempt status from the State of New Jersey a few months later. Chidvilas became the American distributor of Bhagwan's books, tapes, and videos, and by 1980 it was the international distributor. For Bhagwan and Laxmi, Chidvilas became known as a dependable source of cash and material donations, particularly for things difficult to find in India, like modern electronics. The center purchased a Rolls-Royce for Bhagwan and had it stretched into a limousine and armor-plated before shipping it to Pune—just to take the guru the few hundred feet across the ashram grounds from his home to Buddha Hall every morning.

With the dawning of the 1980s, Sheela was second only to Laxmi among the people running Bhagwan's community. She was respected and even feared by some, given her willingness to throw her weight around to get what she wanted. While Laxmi often tried to remain ignorant about where sannyasins found their money, Sheela was willing to get her hands dirty to ferret out a lucrative donation, investigate a scheme to make cash fast, or use unorthodox methods to protect the ashram. Satya Bharti witnessed her old friend Sheela coaching a sannyasin mother and her fifteen-year-old daughter to exaggerate claims against an Indian bureaucrat, urging them to testify in court that he would extend the girl's visa only if she performed sex acts on him. And Sheela reportedly funneled hundreds of thousands of dollars of ashram money to the United States for her brother in Chicago to invest on behalf of the Rajneesh Foundation, although some disciples believed he dumped the money into dope.

She often traveled with Laxmi while she was hunting for land or trying to solve the ashram's political, financial, and legal problems in New Delhi. But in 1980, Bhagwan asked Sheela to stay in Pune and leave Laxmi to sort out their problems on her own. According to Sheela, Bhagwan confided in her that he had lost confidence in his longtime secretary despite everything she had done for him over the past fifteen years at his side. He needed somebody dependable to step into her place running the ashram and the international Rajneesh organization. He had some familiarity with Sheela's practical skills, street smarts, and just-get-it-done attitude, since she had sometimes accompanied Laxmi on her daily visits to Bhagwan's home to go over the ashram's business.

With Laxmi away, Bhagwan told thirty-year-old Sheela that he wanted her to become his personal secretary. Prior to taking sannyas, Sheela hadn't managed anything bigger than a hot dog truck, and now her master was placing her in charge of his multimillion-dollar international spiritual empire.

She was eager to step into the role, but something important was holding her back from giving her full commitment to the man who demanded it all. It was a problem that would soon need to be resolved.

Being around her husband, Chinmaya, seemed to be a tonic for Sheela, according to those close to her. She could be stubborn and quick to anger, and yet he tempered her drastic mood swings. With his wry sense of humor, Chinmaya never let Sheela take herself too seriously or go off too far on an ego trip. She was softer and more open with him, seeking his guidance and listening to his counsel. As she amassed control at the ashram and came into her own power, some of Sheela's friends felt that Chinmaya was the last remaining check on her most vicious natural impulses.

Despite some good moments of health, Chinmaya's Hodgkin's lymphoma was always rearing its head, always introducing new complications. He started chemotherapy in 1977. Thinking he might have tuberculosis, doctors in India opened his chest to remove a lung but sewed him back up when he nearly died on the operating table. When his health took a sharp decline in the late 1970s, friends saw Sheela growing despondent. Her constant travel in India and abroad meant less time at Chinmaya's side. She begged Bhagwan to find somebody else to do her work away from the ashram so she could stay with her husband. He said no. At a darshan with the couple, Bhagwan urged them both to confront death with clear-eyed enthusiasm. "Just accept it and then it will disappear," Bhagwan told Chinmaya. "So what? One is going to die, so one is going to die. What can you do about it? Accept it, and simply by accepting it there is no problem in it. And then it will become a great experience." He turned to Sheela. "You accept it too."

By early 1980, Chinmaya was bed-bound in an air-conditioned second-floor room at Krishna House. He developed shingles, which caused him excruciating pain. No matter how dire his condition became, he refused to return to his parents' care in New Jersey. "I do think about going back, but I've left decisions like that in Rajneesh's hands," he wrote to his sister. "I would love to visit and see everyone, but I don't want to leave Bhagwan either." Sheela brought in different nurses from the ashram's medical center to keep him comfortable, but she sent them away as soon as they fell in love with their goofy, warmhearted patient. She finally found an inconspicuous Filipina American nurse practitioner who was fairly new to the ashram, Ma Anand Puja. Chinmaya liked her, and the women struck up a friendship almost immediately. It helped that Puja was willing to do anything Sheela asked. In the coming years, Puja would prove time and time again that she had surrendered to exactly one master, and it wasn't Bhagwan.

That summer, Chinmaya's condition had not improved, and the constant care he required created a noticeable strain beyond his sickbed. Sheela was shirking her duties, refusing to travel, insisting on spending time with her husband. Bhagwan intervened during a June 10 meeting.

"Now it is time," he told her. "Chinmaya can go—he is ready. Now there is no need for him to suffer anymore in the body."

Back among her Krishna House colleagues, Sheela tearfully reported what Bhagwan had said. Those who had recently seen Chinmaya didn't understand, since his health didn't seem any worse than usual. When Chinmaya learned the news, he, too, was perplexed. Still, he and his wife threw a champagne party in their Krishna House bedroom that raged late into the night, allowing him a chance to say goodbye to old friends.

Adhering to his master's final order, Chinmaya duly died the next morning.

"He never wanted to let me down," Bhagwan said. "He loved me tremendously."

A huge celebration of life erupted across the ashram for the rest of the day, as was the sannyasin way, with music, singing, and dancing. Chinmaya's body, covered with flowers, was laid in front of Bhagwan's dais in Buddha Hall. *He looks gorgeous, doesn't he, Satsie?* Sheela said to Satya Bharti as they stood over her beloved husband, swaying to the old songs he had loved to sing.

The abruptness of his death, as well as it coinciding with Bhagwan's orders, has long raised suspicions among disciples that Sheela killed her husband or assisted with his suicide, with the help of the nurse Puja. A close confidant, Krishna Deva, would later tell the Federal Bureau of Investigation that Sheela had confessed to him that she had injected Chinmaya with something that caused his death, with Bhagwan's blessing, which she described as a "mercy killing."

No matter how it happened, Chinmaya's death allowed Sheela to devote herself entirely to Bhagwan. Three days after the funeral, he called her into his room.

This chapter is finished, he said. *Now you bury yourself in the work.*

4 | EXEUNT

THEY CAME TO BHAGWAN'S ASHRAM for spiritual salvation. They came to discover themselves through group therapy. They came to escape their lousy families, lousy jobs, lousy lives. They came to enjoy a nice vacation and check out the pretty girls at the no-holds-barred sexual paradise. They came to sit in the presence of a man they believed to be the only living master.

By 1980, Bhagwan had become an international icon in places like Germany, England, and Australia, drawing swarms of people who wanted to be with him, with around fifteen hundred sannyasins living in and around the ashram on an ongoing basis, and additional thousands visiting at any given time. The Rajneesh Foundation claimed an international discipleship of two hundred thousand followers. (Deeksha, who claims she saw the ashram's records, would later estimate that the real number was no more than thirty thousand at its peak.) Despite all of Laxmi's property grabs, despite cramming as many ashramites as she could into any available space, the ashram was at maximum capacity with nowhere else to go. Bhagwan's fantasy of the New Commune had become a very real necessity.

Perhaps because Laxmi had struggled for so long to find property for the New Commune, perhaps because the need was so acute, Bhagwan was unusually receptive to a radical idea that his new young secretary laid at his feet.

Since meeting Sheela in the Mumbai apartment nine years earlier, Deeksha had developed a close, sometimes combative relationship with Sheela. They were peers in a way, both holding important and powerful positions within Bhagwan's realm. As Deeksha got to know Sheela better throughout their time at the ashram, she realized that Sheela's heart remained in America—that land of opportunity where she had felt so free and so optimistic about her future as a young immigrant. In moments of fancy, Sheela would tell Deeksha that she had this wild idea that Bhagwan should build his commune in America, not some musty old castle in the Himalayas. Deeksha never took it seriously. The thought of the wise mystic Bhagwan Shree Rajneesh ever leaving India was too absurd to imagine.

After Chinmaya died in June 1980, Sheela spent more time in the United States, both to console her husband's family in New Jersey and to buy goods for Bhagwan and the ashram. Deeksha joined her for one of these trips toward the end of 1980, during which Sheela's Chidvilas Center in Montclair feted them like royalty. Sheela took Deeksha on grand shopping excursions in Manhattan, where she flashed her credit card and told clerks she was the Princess of Baroda. She spent time lounging on the couch and watching inane American television shows. *Life is so much easier here,* she would say to Deeksha. *Everything is so difficult back in India.*

Returning to the ashram in January 1981, Sheela surprised everyone by announcing that she had married a New York banker affiliated with the Chidvilas Center, Swami Jayananda, while on the flight to India. Deeksha was baffled as to why Sheela had chosen to marry such a business-minded guy, seemingly on a lark, after losing her beloved husband of eleven years only six months earlier. But the pieces clicked together a few months later, when Bhagwan called her on her office phone line at the ashram.

Deeksha, what do you think about building the New Commune in America?

With Laxmi out of the way, Sheela had captured Bhagwan's attention with her suggestion that his future might lie in the New World, not the ancient. She told him about the US Constitution and its protections for religious minorities, which would allow Bhagwan to say whatever he wanted. By leaving India they could shake off all the old political and religious enemies who had antagonized them for years. America offered ample space to build the New Commune. To prove it, Sheela's new husband, Jayananda, provided glossy real-estate brochures featuring impressive tracts of land. And resettling in America would also give Bhagwan's organization access to extraordinary wealth in an unmined population of potential disciples.

Lured by the siren song of America, Bhagwan authorized Sheela to begin making the preparations to move him. She claims it took little persuasion—that she simply mentioned the idea and he told her to get it done. Once she had his approval, the pieces came together quickly that spring. The Chidvilas Center bought Kip's Castle on April 21, 1981, to serve as Bhagwan's temporary home while they searched for property for the New Commune.

They could have waited to move him out of India until they found suitable land, but Sheela says that Bhagwan wanted to leave as soon as possible because he felt increasingly constrained by the crowded ashram and his inability to move about freely. Deeksha understood that part of the urgency had to do with fundraising as well, since it would be far easier to coax donations out of American disciples if Bhagwan were already in their country, proving that the much-vaunted New Commune was no longer a pipe dream but something that would be happening in their backyard.

Bhagwan dispatched Deeksha to prepare the castle in New Jersey for his arrival. She landed in the United States on May 14, 1981, accompanied by a team of disciples who smuggled valuable items into the country, including solid-gold bracelets that had been made to look like cheap brass, an expensive watch, and the master tapes of Bhagwan's lectures. While she got to work on the Kip's Castle renovations, Deeksha received increasingly distressed phone calls from Sheela updating her on Bhagwan's visa. In early May, Sheela had applied for a six-month tourist visa for Bhagwan, claiming that he required urgent medical care. The US consulate in Mumbai was dragging its feet, despite her repeated performances at the office, where she would explain, through tears, that her delicate master was in constant pain because of a slipped disc in his back and that he required surgery that could be performed safely only in the United States.

Some of what Sheela told the consular officials was actually true. Bhagwan's health was, by most accounts, not good in the summer of 1981. Despite being forty-nine years old at the time, he looked and moved like a man decades older. After he hurt his back in February during a particularly nasty coughing spell, the ashram called in Dr. James Cyriax, a well-regarded specialist from London.

Dr. Cyriax reported that Bhagwan's asthma and diabetes could be treated with proper medications, and his back pain was a simple slipped disc that should cause only mild discomfort. Removing the disc—a laminectomy—would be an aggressive option to treat the ailment, but Dr. Cyriax didn't think it was necessary. If they decided to move forward with surgery, he advised them to take Bhagwan somewhere outside India.

Sheela provided the consulate with medical records from ashram doctors that glossed over Dr. Cyriax's visit and implied that he urged Bhagwan to get a laminectomy overseas. "It is obvious that his care will require great skills in radiology, anaesthesiology, surgery, nursing care, sterility and physiotherapy," Bhagwan's sannyasin doctor wrote. "The only place where all such skills are available together with the appropriate standards of technology, is the U.S.A. I have therefore advised the patient he should go there without delay before neurological progress makes the journey a total emergency." Sheela would later testify that Dr. Cyriax had told her, "At the rate it's going, he [Bhagwan] won't have much longer to live." ("Nonsense," Dr. Cyriax responded when a reporter told him about Sheela's testimony. "He wasn't as bad as all that.")

At the same time that Sheela was campaigning to get him out of India, Bhagwan vanished from public view altogether. From one day to the next he was gone—no more morning discourses, no more evening darshans. Through Sheela, the ashram learned that he was entering a new phase of his work— silence—by which he would communicate only through the heart. He launched a new form of public appearance: the morning satsang ceremony, where he would sit in silent communion with his disciples. Bhagwan had been preparing his disciples for the possibility of his silence for years, telling them that he would withdraw from speaking at the New Commune when they could receive his energy without words. Many saw it as exactly the kind of disrupting situation the guru loved to create. He wanted his disciples to be flexible, able to grow and adapt, never secure or complacent. His silence was just one more curveball.

Although the ashram maintained that it had a spiritual importance, Sheela says that Bhagwan gave her a far more pragmatic reason for his public silence. He worried that his words—inflammatory, divisive, and headline-grabbing— could become an obstacle to her work building the New Commune. His silence would offer her some latitude to get the job done.

By the end of May, the American consulate still hadn't moved on Bhagwan's visa. Sheela grew desperate for new ideas to get him out of the country.

In the early morning hours of May 28, an incendiary bomb went off inside a warehouse near Pune that stored Bhagwan's Hindi-language books, causing a fire that took three hours to extinguish. The ashram immediately blamed it on religious fanatics. According to Deeksha, this was a lie. Before she left for New Jersey, Sheela had outlined to her a plan to burn their warehouse and some other sannyasin properties as a way to both collect insurance money and create the impression that Bhagwan was the victim of religious persecution in his home country. Concerned that it seemed reckless, Deeksha claims, she mentioned it to Bhagwan, who not only knew about the plan but also told her to help carry it out.

Around the same time, a well-connected American disciple put Deeksha in touch with a lobbyist who would petition Secretary of State Alexander Haig regarding Bhagwan's outstanding visa application if they paid for his "consulting time." Within a twenty-four-hour period, the Indian firebombings took place, the lobbyist received his "consulting fee," and the American consulate in Mumbai granted Bhagwan a six-month tourist visa.

Sheela called Deeksha at Kip's Castle and told her to be ready for his arrival. Two days later, while disciples went about their work and their play at the Shree Rajneesh Ashram, Bhagwan climbed into the back of his armor-plated Rolls-Royce and vanished from their lives.

Deeksha watched from the gate at John F. Kennedy International Airport in New York as Pan Am Flight 001 from Mumbai arrived on June 1, 1981. The gate agents allowed her to board the 747 jumbo jet and wait with her master in the first-class cabin upstairs, while everybody else deplaned to pass through customs and immigration. Given Bhagwan's poor health and agonizing back pain, Sheela had persuaded immigration officials to check his paperwork on the plane.

Deeksha offered her support, but Bhagwan had no problem getting down the stairs and into the terminal. In fact, he walked with no obvious problems at all as they made their way through the airport toward the exit. He carried himself like a dignitary on a state visit, namasteing to everyone around him, surrounded by Sheela, Jayananda, and other fawning orange-robed disciples who cleared his path.

It should have been a triumphant moment, but the scene hit Deeksha as unbearably sad. She was accustomed to seeing Bhagwan in the lusty, enchanting world he had created in Pune, where he would appear under dramatic lighting to the sound of ecstatic music, looming over his disciples, who gazed up at him from the floor like he were a god. At JFK Airport, Bhagwan was surrounded by people whose lives didn't revolve around him. Americans in shorts and baseball caps watched with dull interest as the white-robed Indian man and his orange-clad retinue shuffled by. Nobody seemed to know who he was. Even worse, they didn't seem to care.

They had no guarantee that Bhagwan's success would transfer across the ocean. They had no guarantee that the tens of thousands of people who had dropped their Western lifestyles to spend time with an Indian mystic at his exotic ashram would answer a call to join him in Ronald Reagan's America. There was no certainty that Sheela could recapture the lush, energetic atmosphere that Laxmi had created at the Shree Rajneesh Ashram.

Leaving India was a major risk, and nobody felt the pressure more than Sheela, who had orchestrated the entire affair. Getting her master to America was easy compared to what would come next: fulfilling his utopian vision for the New Commune. Bhagwan had given her a small window in which to find the land, lay the foundation for his dream, and regather his community. If she failed, he would replace her just as swiftly as he had replaced Laxmi, even after all she had done for him. Some other brazen young sannyasin would step forward with promises of fame and riches in another country, and off he would go, leaving Sheela exiled in America, just as Laxmi had been forced to watch from the ground at the Mumbai airport while her master's plane had lurched into the sky.

But America also presented an opportunity for Sheela to create her own masterwork. Free from all the hangers-on and the starry-eyed meditators, she could shape Bhagwan's community into what she thought it ought to be. *She* would decide who deserved to have access to Bhagwan and who should be cast aside. *She* would decide who was hardworking and generous and submissive enough to merit a golden ticket to the New Commune. Everything there would be done to her exacting standards. If anyone didn't like it, they could leave.

Laxmi's ashram would be a cheap roadside attraction compared to what Sheela had in mind for Bhagwan's new paradise. The time had come for Ma Anand Sheela to prove herself.

PART II
OREGON, 1981–82

Downtown Rajneeshpuram during its first winter. *Photo courtesy of Toby Marshall*

5 | FOUNDATIONS IN THE DESERT

THIRTY-TWO-YEAR-OLD CALIFORNIA PSYCHOLOGIST Swami Krishna Deva had been witness to the sad, confusing days in Pune as it dawned on thousands of disciples that their master had left them all behind. At first, very few people realized that he had even left the ashram, and then nobody could agree on *where* he'd gone.

Even before Bhagwan left, the ashram had been abuzz with rumors that the New Commune was coming soon. Sheela had convened an all-ashram meeting in mid-May to announce that they would be moving north to Gujarat, with no sannyasin left behind—a red herring to keep them off the scent of the plans for America. When Bhagwan abruptly left on the last day of May, some disciples continued to believe that he was ensconced in a rustic Mughal castle in northern India, preparing for them to join him. But then, in early June, news reports emerged from New Jersey about the white-robed Indian man seen zipping down the Garden State Parkway in a new Rolls-Royce. The Chidvilas Rajneesh Meditation Center confirmed that Bhagwan was in the United States for medical treatment.

The master's oasis collapsed around Krishna Deva within weeks. Buddha Hall's massive tent was torn down and the marble floor ripped up and sold off, leaving only a concrete slab. The grounds became littered with discarded clothing, crates, luggage, unwanted personal items. The Shree Rajneesh Ashram would soon become a deserted plot of land, just a shell of the magical oasis Laxmi had created, staffed only by a skeleton crew of caretakers.

Krishna Deva—"KD," they called him—had come to love the place, but he hadn't loved Bhagwan when he first arrived at the ashram in 1978. At the time he hadn't read any of the guru's books or even visited the local Rajneesh Meditation Center in Los Angeles. Handsome, with a lean athletic build, sparkling blue eyes, and a gentle smile beneath a soft brown beard, KD was a nice Jewish boy from an upper-middle-class family in the Chicago suburbs. He had been a high school athletic star and then an honors student at the University of Southern California, where he became interested in psychology and the healing power of therapy. After receiving his master's degree and becoming a licensed counselor, KD juggled multiple jobs to stay afloat, including becoming a realtor and opening a group home for troubled boys in North Hollywood.

Like many psychologists at the time, he kept up with the latest trends in personal growth, which for KD included the human potential movement, Eastern philosophy, and more aggressive techniques like encounter groups. As he prepared to embark on an around-the-world trip in 1978, KD decided to stop by the Indian ashram where he heard they combined Eastern philosophy with Western psychology. It was to be a temporary stopover, but drawing close to Bhagwan's gravity well had a way of altering the trajectory of people's plans. Although he found all the long-haired people and their orange robes a bit ridiculous, KD was impressed by the quantity and scope of groups offered at the ashram, as well as its individual counseling program. He canceled the rest of his travel plans. There was nowhere more exciting he could possibly be. He took sannyas while at the ashram and was later appointed to be a group leader.

But then it all fell apart. With Bhagwan gone, the ashram sent foreigners home until the New Commune could be established. KD drifted back to California, hoping to live with a community of disciples while waiting for his next chapter with Bhagwan. As luck would have it, his sannyasin girlfriend happened to be among the chosen few who got to live at Kip's Castle. KD visited her in July 1981—a trip that would alter the course of his life.

Sheela and Deeksha stood in the middle of eighty thousand acres of sheer cliffs and dirt, trying to imagine it as a utopian paradise. Their frantic land hunt over the past two weeks since Bhagwan arrived in America had brought them to Central Oregon, of all places, and now the slow-talking rancher who had picked them up at the airport invited them to take in the panorama. If they bought the Big Muddy Ranch, *everything* they could see would be theirs. The smattering of sagebrush and scraggly juniper trees. The weed-choked creeks. The steep rocky hills boxing in the valley.

Sheela would later claim that she loved the desolate land from the moment she laid eyes on it, finding something beautiful in its rugged austerity. But Deeksha saw something else working in her old friend's mind: pressure.

As soon as he landed, Bhagwan had put Sheela and Deeksha under unrelenting pressure to buy property, prepare the New Commune, and regather his sannyasins. Originally he had given them a couple of months, but as the days ticked by he kept moving up the deadline. Every property they had considered—in Arizona, Colorado, New Jersey, Tennessee, Texas, upstate New York—had come up short. Whenever Sheela returned to Kip's Castle empty-handed, Bhagwan would tell her how disappointed he was. Just days earlier he had been ensconced in his luxurious Pune paradise, surrounded by thousands who loved him. Now they had stuffed him into the upper floor of a moldering castle in suburban New Jersey while Sheela failed to deliver what she had promised.

So Deeksha felt the heavy hand of their spiritual master squeezing from across the continent when Sheela declared, on the spot in Oregon, that she wanted to buy the whole plot of mud and rock and sagebrush. While Sheela and Jayananda negotiated a purchase agreement with the seller, Deeksha returned to New Jersey, where Bhagwan pounced on her for an honest assessment of this ranch that Sheela had raved about over the phone. She tried to be honest without undermining her friend. To its credit, the Big Muddy Ranch did seem to meet some of Bhagwan's criteria, including spectacular views, clean air, and remoteness. *Extreme* remoteness. The property was about 125 square miles, larger than the cities of Baltimore, Orlando, and Milwaukee, vast enough to encompass six Manhattans. It was certainly large enough to host several thousand sannyasins to live and work. And whatever they did deep in the valley would be invisible to people on the outside.

It's a nice piece of land, Deeksha told her master. *It has potential. But it will be very hard work and very expensive to turn it into the New Commune.*

Don't worry about the money, Bhagwan told her. *The money will come.*

Money was the least of Deeksha's concerns.

While visiting Kip's Castle in mid-July, KD learned a secret that had not yet been revealed to the broader sannyasin community: Sheela had just closed on eighty thousand acres in Oregon for $5.75 million, with a cash down payment of $1.5 million.

Rather than celebrate the advent of the New Commune, KD balked at what he thought was a ludicrous idea. While setting up his Los Angeles group home before taking sannyas, KD had battled with zoning boards, hostile neighbors, and intrusive bureaucrats. He understood the trials and tribulations of building something nontraditional and unpopular when all the rules were tilted against you. And, even worse, he knew about Oregon's stringent land-use laws.

Deeksha, too, had come to appreciate the difficulties in store for them in Oregon. After touring the property, she had consulted a lawyer at a large firm in Manhattan about their ambitious plans to build a sprawling community with a meditation university, hotels, schools, hospitals, farms, and housing to accommodate thousands of disciples from around the world. The attorney was flummoxed, especially when he learned that the entire ranch was zoned for one use only: agriculture. He told Deeksha that Oregon had some of the strictest zoning controls in the country. There was no way the state would allow them to build a mixed-use residential/commercial/industrial/agricultural commune for thousands of people on a piece of land designated only for farm use.

When Sheela returned to New Jersey with the purchase contract in hand, but before the closing, Deeksha had taken her to the same attorney, hoping he might persuade her to back out of the deal before it was too late. As the lawyer repeated all of his concerns, Sheela seemed disinterested, unbothered, and even annoyed that Deeksha was trying to throw a wrench into her plans. *We'll sort it all out when we get there,* she said. *We can say that we're farmers and then bring on more people. It'll all be fine.* Considering her a lost cause, Deeksha took the lawyer's concerns to the ultimate authority. Sitting in his Kip's Castle study, Bhagwan watched with an expression of sheer boredom as Deeksha prattled on about laws and regulations. She walked away from the meeting thinking that Bhagwan and Sheela either didn't understand the magnitude of the lawyer's warning or didn't care.

While visiting Kip's Castle in July, KD asked enough pointed questions about how they planned to get around the land-use laws to earn him a meeting with Sheela's husband, Jayananda, who dumped an Oregon zoning regulations book on his lap and told him to get to work. Yes, they understood they would have to be creative to get things done as Bhagwan wished, and that is why they needed all the smartest, most experienced disciples to help them.

KD's serendipitous experience in the niche topic of zoning regulations set him up for a key role within Sheela's inner circle. Unwittingly, he had taken his first step on a path that would lead him to becoming one of the most pivotal characters in the rise and disastrous fall of Bhagwan Shree Rajneesh's American utopia.

———————

The easiest way to get to the Big Muddy Ranch in its earliest days was to fly into Portland, in the verdant Willamette Valley running down the western part of Oregon, and drive due east along the Columbia River. Passing over the Cascade Range into Central Oregon was like entering a different world. The mountains stripped moisture from the Pacific Ocean winds and left little but beige high desert to the east. Tiny towns scattered across the plateau served ranches and dry-land farms, the only forms of agriculture that could survive in the arid climate. Turning south and driving higher into the desert, a visitor would pass through sleepy little Antelope, population forty, just a couple streets, two churches, a school, small frame houses, and a roadside café. A poorly maintained county road with hairpin turns and sheer-cliff drops made the final drive into the ranch's main valley bumpy, treacherous, and slow—up to an hour to travel just twenty miles.

Krishna Deva arrived at the Big Muddy Ranch on July 24, 1981, a week after Sheela closed on the property. He and the other couple dozen occupants had to make do with the few modern conveniences that were available—a single shared phone line, a simple sewage system that emptied into the creek, and enough electricity to support only a small family. The ranch's caretaker at the time of the purchase, Bob Harvey, had agreed to stay on as a salaried employee of the Chidvilas Rajneesh Meditation Center, and he continued living in the original farmhouse with his wife and two daughters. Some disciples lived in a decrepit bunkhouse next door, but Krishna Deva stayed on "Cat Piss Porch" attached to the farmhouse, where he slept alongside up to seven other men, their mattresses literally touching. ("No fucking," one new arrival was told as first he settled in on the porch. They didn't want to upset the Harvey girls.)

Once she realized that KD was a smart person who understood land-use issues, Sheela had tapped him to move to Oregon to study the laws so they could obtain as many building permits as possible. As a stopgap measure, they began to move in mobile housing units and stuff them with disciples. But even temporary trailers required permits, and for that they would need approval from the county government.

The Big Muddy Ranch spanned two counties. The bulk of the property was in Jefferson County to the south, but the most desirable land sat in Wasco County to the north, and that is where the disciples would focus their development in the coming years. Since the land was all unincorporated—meaning it wasn't part of any municipal area like a city or a township—it fell under county jurisdiction. Any permits would need to come from the county planning offices. KD thus began making regular treks one hundred miles north to The Dalles, a town of about ten thousand people along the Columbia River that served as the Wasco County seat. There, he worked to persuade befuddled officials that the disciples of a far-off Indian guru wanted to build a modest farming commune on their ranch.

Indeed, farming became the mantra in all their conversations with county commissioners and planning officials over the coming months, because farming was the only engine that would drive their ability to expand. Since the ranch was zoned for agricultural use only, they couldn't just start putting up dormitories and restaurants and hotels and meditation universities. But they could build housing for farm workers and a cafeteria to feed them, and a two-story pole building for their farm equipment, and a massive greenhouse for indoor farming. Krishna Deva would later confess that every building permit he sought for their "farm" in these early months had a "second underlying and false motive." Their pole building, for example, had offices on its top story that hosted hundreds of sannyasins whose work had nothing to do with farming. Their greenhouse was the largest greenhouse in the state, two acres in size, big enough to serve as an assembly hall for special occasions. In these early discussions with the county officials, the sannyasins said nothing about their intention to convert the ranch into the epicenter of the international Rajneesh movement or that it would eventually be home to thousands—perhaps even tens of thousands—of disciples. They also didn't say that Bhagwan would soon be entrenched there himself. As far as the public knew, he was staying in New Jersey.

With grandiose statements about their plans to reclaim the battered land, the disciples managed to secure permits to bring in fifty-three three-bedroom mobile homes across both counties and to build the farm-related buildings. Neighboring ranchers, though, were skeptical. With roots in the region going back centuries, some were very familiar with the Big Muddy Ranch and had firm opinions about what sort of farming it would support. They knew it had once hosted thirty thousand cattle and sheep grazing across the sprawling acreage, but that it had been abandoned for at least a decade before the Chidvilas Center bought it. Geologists had classified most of the ranch's soil as incapable of supporting crops and possessing almost no economic value. One local rancher pointed out that winter rains would turn the earth into muddy gumbo soil that would clog their machinery and cake around their feet until it became impossible to move. And whatever meager harvest they wanted to eke out of the desert certainly didn't require all the earth-moving machinery, prefabricated housing units, and people that kept passing through Antelope throughout the summer and into the fall.

Feeling helpless as the sannyasins infiltrated the valley and the county governments kept granting them permits, locals tipped off the press in August about the Indian "sex cult" that had moved in next door. A journalist from the *Oregonian*—the state's most widely read newspaper—trekked out to report on the "orange people" and their unusual settlement. The article that ran a few days later provided most Oregonians with their first glimpse of their new neighbors. Alongside a photo of Sheela staring into space with dull, tired eyes, the article described the sannyasins laying irrigation pipes, planting sunflowers, and installing up to three double-wide mobile homes per week in tribute to their master. Although it mentioned some of Bhagwan's controversies in India, the article focused primarily on Sheela's farming ambitions.

"This ranch has been abused for many years," she told the reporter. "Everyone took things out of the ranch but didn't put anything back to nourish the land. I want to turn it all green."

The journalist couldn't help but notice two Rolls-Royce sedans parked outside Sheela's home. Was it a hint that her enigmatic master would soon be arriving in Oregon?

"I haven't invited him," she replied, since they had not yet made enough progress in their work. "I want to show off to my master that I am following the steps that he's teaching."

By the time the article ran on August 30, 1981, Bhagwan had arrived.

6 | THE MIRAGE

WHERE ARE ALL THE TREES? Bhagwan asked Sheela as they drove along the ranch's dusty roads. His private jet had touched down in Redmond, Oregon, one hour earlier, thanks to a disciple's $20,000 donation to cover the cost of "a specially chartered aircraft to carry our Beloved Master to Oregon." Now they rode through the ranch's central valley, in an area they called Jesus Grove, where two limp streams converged on their journey to the John Day River at the property's far eastern edge. Sheela had placed her own home in this area, right in the middle of everything, but to get to Bhagwan's house they proceeded north along a winding road and then up a narrow driveway to a promontory offering magnificent views of the valley to the south. They called it "B Site," where a sannyasin crew had been working around the clock to finish Bhagwan's private compound in time. He had insisted in late August that it was time for him to leave New Jersey and join his people in Oregon, whether Sheela was ready or not. A flurry of work had ensued to lay the foundation, connect the utilities, landscape, and complete the interior.

Bhagwan's car arrived in front of the mishmash of trailers that would stand in for the mansion he had left behind in Pune. The exhausted crew had only just finished their work and assembled on the manicured lawn to welcome their master to his new home. Although the official story was that Bhagwan—still on his six-month tourist visa—was simply visiting the ranch, all of the disciples knew that the Buddhafield now had its resident Buddha.

When Ma Prem Deeksha gazed up at her master from her place on the freshly laid sod, she felt absolutely nothing. No benevolent grace emanating from his gentle smile. No supernatural connection like they had known each other in past lives. No energy whatsoever. Her love affair was over.

It had started with that uneasy feeling that gnawed at her stomach ever since arriving at Kip's Castle. The more she was away from Bhagwan, the more she felt her bond with him weakening. When he finally showed up in New Jersey, what she witnessed horrified her.

Like most sannyasins, Deeksha had been isolated from Bhagwan ever since he established his ashram seven years earlier. Even as a top ashram administrator, she had little personal contact with the guru and didn't realize how much international fame and the ever-increasing throngs of worshipful disciples had transformed him. At Kip's Castle, Deeksha and Sheela acted as his personal attendants, summoned into his private study at all hours to cater to his whims and serve as a passive audience for his late-night rants. On a couple of occasions, Deeksha saw Bhagwan's caretaker Ma Yoga Vivek pass him a glass of milk and four to six Valium tablets—a massive dose of the strong narcotics. This alone shocked her, but the delusions of grandeur that came out of his mouth were even worse. He said he was the messiah that America had been waiting for. He said he would become the power behind the president of the United States. He said he would one day rule the world. He uttered a phrase that became inscribed in Deeksha's memory because it so sickened her: *I will succeed where Hitler failed.*

Deeksha knew all about fascists. She had spent her early childhood in Italy under the shadow of Mussolini. Her maternal grandfather was a monarchist who attended military school with the king of Italy and who later became a high-level public official. Deeksha's family staked out an uncomfortable position as firmly anti-Fascist leading up to and during World War II, and her grandfather refused to pledge allegiance to Mussolini and the Fascists. The party had him arrested, forced him to resign, and terminated his pension. Family friends with similar views were tortured to death. And now here was Deeksha's spiritual guru, a supposedly enlightened master no different than Buddha or Jesus Christ, telling her he wanted to take up a fascist mantle, to succeed where Hitler failed.

On another night, Bhagwan told Sheela and Deeksha that he would teach them the greatest art of all: manipulating people to do your bidding. He said that Hitler was a genius, particularly when it came to orchestrating public opinion. He urged them to study Joseph Goebbels to learn how to maneuver people within his organization. (*Who is Goebbels?* Sheela asked.)

It seemed to Deeksha that Bhagwan was using these sessions to train his new secretary in the methods he expected her to use to represent him and his interests in America. The most important thing he had to teach Sheela, he said, was that everybody had a price—something they most valued, which was not necessarily monetary. The key to manipulating a person was to figure out their price and then find a way to give it to them. If Sheela could do that, he said, she could control them.

Isn't it incredible, Deeksha? Sheela would gush after they had left Bhagwan's study. *Do you realize how lucky we are to get this training from our master?*

Deeksha, though, was disgusted. She was even more repulsed by the obvious ways that Bhagwan manipulated *them*. He had become enamored with Rolls-Royce luxury sedans after receiving one at the Pune ashram. Sheela bought him another soon after he arrived in New Jersey, but then Bhagwan demanded a new Rolls-Royce with specific paint and interior colors. He kept prodding them until Sheela finally confessed that they couldn't afford to buy it, given all they had invested in Kip's Castle and all they planned to spend on acquiring the New Commune. Bhagwan had flown into a cold, concentrated rage. *When I tell you to do something, there is no room to question what I've asked. If you cannot fulfill what I require, then I will go.*

He didn't mean he would go from America. Deeksha understood that Bhagwan was threatening to kill himself—to "leave his body," as he often put it—if he didn't get the car. Sheela burst into tears, begging him not to do what he was implying, promising to get him the car.

Deeksha had a very different reaction.

Fuck you, she thought.

At another meeting in Kip's Castle before she had bought the Big Muddy Ranch, Sheela warned Bhagwan that some high-profile disciples were angry that he left them behind in India, with some even suggesting that Sheela had kidnapped him. She worried that they might drop sannyas and spread negativity, which could harm the New Commune's prospects—particularly her ability to extract donations from American disciples. After laying out her concerns, Sheela made a pledge that struck Deeksha as strange.

I'm ready to do anything for you, Bhagwan. Anything.

He arched an eyebrow and said, *Hmm?*, as if she had left the thought unfinished.

Even if I have to kill for you.

Bhagwan asked Sheela to name these negative sannyasins who would damage him if they ever left the movement. The list became more extensive the next day when Bhagwan himself added more names, which Sheela jotted down. Deeksha couldn't believe some of the people on the list. They were longtime, devoted sannyasins who had sacrificed everything—family, career, money—out of love for their master, and now he was considering them potential enemies. She hoped it was just idle talk and that Bhagwan and Sheela didn't really intend to harm anybody. But the next day, Bhagwan told Deeksha that for just $5,000 Sheela's brother could arrange to have a person killed in a way that made it look like an accident.

To dissuade him from these murderous thoughts, Deeksha tossed out other ideas, like buying off disaffected sannyasins by returning any donations they had given.

Bhagwan cut her off before she could finish. *No*, he said, *it's better for them to die.*

Deeksha felt that she was witnessing the closest thing to evil that she ever experienced: two people out of their minds on a power trip, high from the lusty thoughts of controlling the lives—and deaths—of so many people. (Sheela denies that she saw Bhagwan abusing Valium or that he trained her to manipulate people while at Kip's Castle in the summer of 1981. She also denies that she and Bhagwan created a list of sannyasins who would need to be murdered if they ever dropped sannyas.)

Sitting at Bhagwan's feet in Kip's Castle offered Deeksha an unvarnished glimpse into her master's soul. She wondered if he had always been that way and she hadn't noticed, or if living in luxurious isolation at his own temple had warped him. He was supposed to be an enlightened master who had transcended the mortal world, but he now struck her as a petulant but dangerous child. She tried to remember how she had gotten so enmeshed with such a man. What had she originally loved about him? How had he broken down her barriers and dominated her life for the past decade?

Everything came back in a new light, all the extraordinary abuses of his power that Bhagwan had heaped on Ma Prem Deeksha—on Mariagrazia—for so many years.

Before he ever touched her breasts, Bhagwan had warned the young Italian woman sitting on the floor of his Mumbai apartment in 1971 about the dangers of repressed sexual energy. Westerners' energy was trapped in their first chakra, he said, located at the base of the spine and the pelvic floor, and they had no idea how to release it. He, a tantric master, could employ techniques that would allow that energy to flow throughout her body.

Deeksha felt a little embarrassed to be talking about sex and her body with anybody, much less an older Indian man she had met just weeks earlier. And then when he cupped her breast with his hand over the top of her orange robe, she wondered how she had allowed herself to end up in this situation—alone with a stranger, uncomfortable, and a little repulsed. She tensed up, but she didn't resist. Bhagwan was gazing at her with soft puppy-dog eyes, giving the affect of a benign teacher who wanted nothing more than to help his floundering student.

His "tantric work" escalated with each session. One day, he rubbed his bare toes over the top of her robe, vigorously, to stimulate her clitoris. The whole time he kept his eyes trained on hers, those kind and gentle eyes. Deeksha tamped down her fears that he was doing it for his own pleasure. He was a spiritual master, after all, devoting his precious time to releasing her repressed energy. If he needed to touch her genitals with his hands, with his feet, so be it.

Within days of their first tantric session, Bhagwan told Deeksha to take off her clothes, lie down on the bed with her legs facing him, and close her eyes. She did it. He touched her bare breasts. Then he told her to focus on her breathing while he touched her genitals.

Masturbate, he commanded her on another day. She tried, although it was so awkward with him watching from his chair.

Session after session, Acharya Rajneesh pushed Deeksha to drop her barriers and surrender to him and his ministrations. Each time he tried something new, she froze up, even when he climbed on top of her and pressed his erect penis against her thighs. She felt him ejaculate between her legs.

It kept happening, every time she was alone in the room with him, throughout her remaining weeks in India in 1971. She never liked it. She never felt comfortable. But she compared it to a one-on-one session with a yoga master. He was a powerful man, a wise teacher, using ancient physiological techniques to help her.

Throughout it all, she never felt that Bhagwan was taking advantage of a young disciple who had surrendered at his command, who wore his picture around her neck, who had adopted the name he had given her, who called him master. Anything he did to her as she lay there naked with her eyes squeezed shut was for her benefit—surely not for his own carnal pleasures.

Other women who spent time at the Mumbai apartment in the early 1970s reported having "ultimate darshans" with Bhagwan where he massaged their breasts and genitals, told them to masturbate naked on his bed, or pressed his penis at their groins before ejaculating between their legs. An American disciple showed up at the apartment one day in 1971 crying, saying she had to get an abortion before her boyfriend returned to Mumbai because the baby belonged to Bhagwan. Laxmi gave money to Deeksha and asked her to take the woman to the hospital for an abortion procedure.

He touched some female disciples' genitals without taking it to the extreme that Deeksha and others experienced. The American writer Satya Bharti, for example, spent hours sitting with Bhagwan in his bedroom in early 1973—more time than perhaps anybody else, since she lived at the apartment and was helping him improve his English. During their sessions, Bhagwan would often rub his toes against her breasts. One day he knelt beside her and slid his hand down her robe until he was holding her vulva. He didn't explain what he was doing or why he was doing it. She assumed he was checking her chakras. He never did anything else to her, and when gossip swirled among the sannyasin community in Mumbai that Bhagwan was having sex with his disciples, Satya had laughed it off. It couldn't be true.

Around 1973, Bhagwan ended his tantric experiments in Mumbai, saying they had served their purpose. Deeksha suspected that Bhagwan was under pressure from the businessmen who supported him financially, who were embarrassed that their guru was developing a reputation for sleeping with his young Western disciples. Privately, Bhagwan told Deeksha that the work he had done on her body for the past two years had been successful. She was no longer sexually repressed, and her energy was flowing freely. But before she could walk out of the room, he confirmed the omertà governing his private work: She was never to speak of their tantric exercises to anybody, not even other disciples, since it could be twisted and used to take him down. For many years Deeksha kept this promise, refusing to answer even direct questions from people who had heard the rumors.

A couple of months after Bhagwan said he ended his tantric work, Deeksha received a long, scathing letter from a Japanese disciple who had run out of Bhagwan's bedroom one day, her robe torn at the shoulder, and right into Deeksha's arms, screaming that the guru had just tried to rape her.

He's the devil! the Japanese woman wrote. *How can you stay with this man when all he wants is sex? How can you stay with a man who abuses his disciples?*

Deeksha threw the letter away without responding. Bhagwan was right: people wouldn't understand his work.

Witnessing his Valium-fueled delusions at Kip's Castle had finally jolted Deeksha out of what she considered to be a decade-long fugue state. As soon as she understood who he was, she wanted out.

Around the time Sheela finalized the purchase of the ranch in July 1981, Deeksha met privately with Bhagwan to say that she wanted to take a break from sannyas.

You can't leave now, he told her. *You are on the verge of one of the biggest breakthroughs in your life.*

He knew Deeksha's price. She was a spiritual seeker who wanted to flourish at the feet of a master. Now she could see the manipulation at work, and she refused to play along. She tried not to criticize Bhagwan directly and instead complained that Sheela had changed since they arrived in the United States.

Don't worry about Sheela, Bhagwan said. *I need to use her ruthlessness to build my commune. Be patient. Soon she'll be gone and you won't have to worry about her anymore.*

But it wasn't just Sheela, Deeksha told him. It was the two of them together, all of the things she had witnessed in his study over the previous month.

Bhagwan and Sheela were walking a path that Deeksha could not take part in. *I can't do it*, she said, breaking down in tears. *I can't do it. I can't do it.*

Bhagwan commanded her to look into his eyes. She saw danger flashing in them. He said that she could not leave until she had completed one final task.

You will go to Oregon and help set up my home. You promise me that you will wait until I get to the ranch before you leave.

It was not a request.

On the day that Bhagwan settled into his New Commune, Deeksha packed her bags and prepared to leave him forever. She'd held up her end of the bargain. Seeing the old man in Oregon had only confirmed that she no longer felt anything for him except revulsion. The spell was truly broken.

Sheela caught wind of Deeksha's activity and popped into her bedroom. Deeksha explained that she was done with sannyas, done with Bhagwan, and done with Sheela. They could do whatever they wanted and she wouldn't interfere. She simply wanted to move on.

Sheela deployed her full powers of persuasion to get Deeksha to stay a bit longer, to give it some more time, to see how things would go now that Bhagwan was there.

I'm not asking for your permission, Deeksha said. *I'm leaving.*

But she couldn't go before addressing the list that Sheela and Bhagwan had created in their last days together in New Jersey. The list of high-level sannyasins who could harm Bhagwan were they ever to leave the movement. The list of people who might need to be taken care of—*eliminated*, Bhagwan had told Deeksha, not simply bought off—if they were ever to leave.

If I ever learn that somebody from your list has died, Deeksha warned Sheela, *I will go to the authorities.*

Sheela responded with words that would continue to haunt Deeksha in the days and months and years after she escaped the commune.

*But Deeksha, **you** are on the list now.*

7 | BETWEEN A ROCK AND ANTELOPE

IN THE FALL OF 1981, the town of Antelope was little more than a clump of trees along a lonely county road in the middle of the high desert, just a couple of intersecting streets dotted with modest one-story homes with struggling lawns. A road map listed it as a ghost town. Its forty residents were mostly middle-class retirees looking forward to a quiet stretch of life now that their kids had grown and moved away. It was the sort of homogenous, conservative place where one lived to get away from any hustle-bustle, controversies, or culture clashes. "Women stand in one group and the men stand in another," explained a resident. "That's the type of community it is, and we like it."

Antelope's problem was that it was the closest city to the Big Muddy Ranch, twenty miles away. The disciples dipped into town by necessity soon after arriving in Oregon. The ranch had only a single, unreliable phone line that wasn't sufficient to support their international mail-order business for Bhagwan's books and tapes. They opened two small business offices on commercial lots in town that gave them access to better communications and a place to receive deliveries.

Antelope's mayor, Margaret Hill, kept a close eye on these strange new people intruding into their quiet little community. A retired schoolteacher with an immaculate perm and huge glasses, Hill had been receiving tips from people in far-off places about the free-loving, law-flouting disciples, and she was among the first people to alert the press about the sannyasin invasion in Central Oregon.

When Sheela learned that Hill was giving interviews about all her concerns, she tried to smooth things over by appearing at Hill's home with some pamphlets about Bhagwan and his movement, hoping they might help the mayor better understand her new neighbors. But Hill set aside the pamphlets and told Sheela she wasn't interested in learning about the sannyasins. Instead, she wanted Sheela to understand the longtime residents of Antelope, who were set in their ways and didn't want anything to do with an Eastern cult.

But we are here, Sheela responded, *and we are going to stay.*

The sannyasins would later claim that the battle over Antelope originated with an idea foisted on them by a land-use watchdog organization that had taken an unusual interest in their plans for the ranch. The nonprofit organization 1000 Friends of Oregon had come into being right after Governor Tom McCall had enacted the state's comprehensive land-use program in 1974, with a mission to advocate for compliance with the new laws. The organization had only a handful of employees, including some staff attorneys, and it operated largely off donations and a network of pro bono lawyers. Its primary work was reviewing city and county planning and zoning guidelines and challenging noncompliance with the state's regulations, but it would also tangle with private landowners, as the disciples of Bhagwan Shree Rajneesh were soon to find out.

The organization had received alarmed messages from ranchers and Antelopians, including Mayor Hill, about the "sex cult" that seemed to be working on a major development on their farmland. The locals had been doing their research and learned about Bhagwan's longstanding desire to build a sprawling New Commune to transform humanity. As more mobile homes and more people arrived at the ranch throughout the summer and fall of 1981, it seemed to them that the county government was standing aside so the disciples could convert their agricultural property into the megacommune their guru had been promising for years. Their fears were only confirmed when Bhagwan arrived at the end of August.

The people of Central Oregon made strange bedfellows with 1000 Friends because citizens of the region had staunchly opposed the state's land-use regime as it was being debated in the early 1970s. As many Central Oregonians saw it, politicians in the populous, verdant Willamette Valley had no business telling people east of the Cascades what they could do on their undeveloped land. When the land-use law came to a vote, only nine of the thirty legislators from beyond the Willamette Valley voted in favor of it.

But stopping a common enemy proved to be reason enough for the ranchers to join forces with the land-use watchdog. They captured 1000 Friends' attention with a plea from one of the most famous men in Oregon, Bill Bowerman, the legendary track-and-field coach and the cofounder of Nike. Bowerman owned a ranch that abutted the Big Muddy, and he claimed to be concerned that the sannyasins' development might have an impact on his property.

Representatives from 1000 Friends contacted the sannyasins over the summer to remind them that their property was zoned exclusively for agricultural use and that they could put up buildings and bring in people only to serve that purpose. Sheela had little interest in what a self-appointed land-use watchdog had to say about their development. Ranch leaders continued snatching up permits from the county governments and putting up "farm buildings" to serve as the foundation for Bhagwan's New Commune. When they announced their intention to build a bindery on their ranch to publish ornate books filled with Bhagwan's prior discourses, 1000 Friends again intervened to insist that they couldn't build an industrial building on their land. The group's representative offered a suggestion: *If you need to build commercial or industrial buildings, go to Antelope.*

The idea of using the ghost town as a temporary host for the Rajneesh businesses had some merit, since it would allow them to keep their operations going while charting a course to develop their own property. Taking 1000 Friends' cue, the sannyasins bought some additional pieces of commercial land in Antelope in the fall of 1981, and they applied to the Antelope City Council for a permit to build their book bindery in town.

Commune leaders would come to believe that Antelope was a trap and that 1000 Friends of Oregon had led them straight into it. As sannyasin attorney Prartho Subhan later recalled, "We didn't want to go to Antelope. Nobody wanted to go twenty miles up a winding road to this little tiny community to build a book bindery there and deal with all the logistics there. But we started to recognize that we'd have our hands full of land-use issues, and that 1000 Friends guaranteed they'd make it difficult for us unless we went to Antelope."

Developing in Antelope seemed to be a workable solution for the disciples, the local ranchers, and 1000 Friends, at least in the short term. But the increasing sannyasin presence in town was the last thing Mayor Margaret Hill wanted to see. She sounded an alarm to a reporter for the *Los Angeles Times* that would prove prophetic in a matter of months: "We can easily be outnumbered. That's our fear."

By October, Sheela was stuck in a bind. After granting permits for fifty-three residential trailers and a couple of farm-related buildings, the planning directors for Wasco and Jefferson Counties signaled that they would not allow any more development on the ranch, perhaps due to the overwhelming public pressure to rein in the expanding sannyasin presence. The permits the disciples had received to date offered nowhere near the capacity Sheela would require for the massive influx of sannyasins that Bhagwan expected. But they could not just give up and move away. They had already invested too much money and effort. Bhagwan was living there. The sannyasin experiment in America would either succeed or fail in Central Oregon.

A novel solution began to percolate within Sheela's inner circle of coordinators. If 1000 Friends was so adamant that the sannyasins could develop only within an urban area, why not create a city on the ranch?

Krishna Deva would later claim the idea struck him as he got up to speed on the state's land-use laws. He learned that a group of 150 people living in an unincorporated area could petition the county to form a new city. Only 20 percent of voters in the area needed to sign the initial petition, and if the county approved it the community members would vote yea or nay in a special election. If it passed, the county would grant a charter for the new city.

Sheela loved this idea, since it would allow her to build Bhagwan's commune as he (and she) envisioned it, without having to placate far-off bureaucrats. A sannyasin-controlled city council could write its own building codes, grant its own permits, inspect its own buildings, put up its own police force, and receive state tax dollars. Most importantly, it could rezone the agricultural land for other uses.

Although the law required them to wait until they had 150 people living on the ranch, Sheela told KD to file the incorporation petition immediately, which he did in mid-October at the Wasco County courthouse. Borrowing from the Hindi language, the proposed city would be called Rajneeshpuram—the "city of Rajneesh."

———————

On the morning of November 4, a bus filled with celebratory sannyasins traveled north from the ranch along the high desert plateau before gradually winding down to the Columbia River, where The Dalles sprawled along the riverbanks. The city's wide streets and broad brick and wooden facades gave it the feeling of an old-fashioned western town, but the disciples weren't there for a shoot-out. They were there to issue a declaration of independence.

The bus deposited them outside the Wasco County courthouse, an austere four-story affair on a hill, with drab gray columns, beige terrazzo floors, and blond oak doors and bannisters. As disciples entered the largest courtroom upstairs, Sheela told her people exactly where she wanted them to sit. The three judges of the Wasco County Court—Rick Cantrell, Jim Comini, and Virgil Ellett—assumed their positions on the dais. Wasco County followed a quirky tradition of calling its county commission a "court" and its commissioners "judges," although they served no judicial function.

The future of Rajneeshpuram depended on how the judges voted at this hearing on the sannyasins' incorporation petition. If a majority voted no, the dreams of Bhagwan's city would die right there. First, the judges opened the floor to comments. The sannyasins played a slick videotape promoting Bhagwan's vision for a beautiful little town to support their farms and promising to rehabilitate the neglected land.

Many community members rose to speak against the incorporation, including attorneys from 1000 Friends of Oregon and people from Antelope. *Why do they need a city?* was the most common complaint. *What are they planning to do out there that they can't do in Antelope? Why did they buy a ranch if they planned to bring in so many people and do so much construction?* Some critics used their time to attack the sannyasins' characters and unspool wild theories. A religious zealot screamed that God was going to rain fire on the disciples and demanded that the judges stare into her eyes to see how serious she was. Ranch foreman Bob Harvey later told investigators that Sheela and Jayananda had asked the woman to come to the hearing, hoping that her unhinged extremism would make their opponents seem foolish.

Although they paid attention to all the rambling commentary, two judges, Rick Cantrell and Virgil Ellett, felt the decision was out of their hands. The district attorney had advised them that the incorporation law was cut and dried: if at least thirty people signed the petition, the county had to allow them to vote on incorporating their own city, simple as that.

The third judge was not so sure. Jim Comini had been deeply suspicious of the sannyasins ever since they arrived in the area. He'd toured the ranch in the late summer and was repulsed by the overly friendly disciples and the gourmet meal they served him. They hadn't helped matters by visiting his liquor store in The Dalles and ringing up extravagant purchases. He felt they were directing business his way to try to curry favor with him—which in fact had the opposite effect. And Comini didn't care what the DA had to say about the incorporation law. He was a county judge and he would vote his conscience. In this case, he empathized with the local ranchers, who maintained that the disciples had been lying to the county government for the past four months about their "farm" when they always intended to build a city.

In the end, Comini was the lone "no" vote on the petition. The court set a special election to take place in May, when the incorporation would surely pass since the only people voting would be ranch residents. The disciples were in a festive mood that night as they packed into a restaurant in The Dalles to eat, drink, and toast to the future of Rajneeshpuram. Comini joined them, hoping to keep a line of communication open. Sheela's husband, Jayananda, pulled him aside. *You know, Jim, you are the one we thought we had on our side all along.*

Comini bristled at this comment because he felt it confirmed what he had long suspected: that the sannyasins had tried to buy his political support by dumping money into his liquor store. It felt very dirty.

Jim Comini wouldn't need to worry about the sannyasins' patronage much longer. After the vote, disciples stopped visiting his liquor store, and when he did encounter them, they treated him like an enemy they were icing out.

Three years later, they would try to kill him.

8 | BETTER DEAD THAN RED

THE COUNTY'S DECISION IN NOVEMBER 1981 to allow Rajneesh-puram's incorporation to proceed galvanized local opposition. Anti-Rajneesh activists predicted that if the disciples got their own city, they would approve ludicrous construction projects, exhaust the region's water table, and bring in thousands more residents. The character of their quiet, conservative pocket of Oregon would be forever changed, and the devastating impacts on the neighboring properties would be irreversible. Attorneys for 1000 Friends filed a blitz of lawsuits and appeals on behalf of neighboring ranchers to try to stop the May 1982 incorporation vote from taking place. One explosive argument they levied was that the sannyasins had bribed Judge Rick Cantrell—a rancher himself—by purchasing cattle from him in the midst of the incorporation proceedings and paying well over the market value. This argument never landed, and Cantrell was ultimately cleared.

The most serious legal argument that 1000 Friends advanced was that Wasco County had failed to consider how incorporating a new city on a piece of ranch land would affect the state's land-use planning goals. It raised an important question that had never been decided in Oregon: Is incorporating a new city a land-use decision? The state's land-use regulations were silent on what should happen if a new city were created in Oregon. Similarly, the incorporation law made no reference to the land-use regulations.

Attorneys for 1000 Friends took this question to the Land Use Board of Appeals, a three-person tribunal with the power to review any land-use decision in the state. The sannyasins responded that the board had no jurisdiction over the question, because allowing a group of people to vote on incorporation isn't a land-use decision. On a more fundamental level, they argued that people in an unincorporated area should be allowed to govern themselves if they so chose. The concept of home rule was enshrined in the Oregon Constitution, giving cities broad authority to pass laws, enact taxes, and regulate businesses according to the will of their residents. The sannyasins would argue over the coming years that they should be treated like any other group of people who, over the course of Oregon's history, had banded together to form local governments.

While the board considered these legal questions in early 1982, the fate of Rajneeshpuram hung in the balance. Around the same time, the sannyasins reached a standoff with Margaret Hill and the Antelope City Council. Hill had circulated a secret memo to Antelope residents expressing her concerns about the hulking metal printing press the sannyasins wanted to build in town, two stories tall, ninety by one hundred feet, which she said would be "incongruous and unsightly in our little western town." Sheela accused Hill of conspiring with the city council in private meetings and warned that the sannyasins "will not stand by and be persecuted or have laws unfairly enforced against us." Nonetheless, the Antelope City Council refused to take any action on the printing press application and three other buildings the sannyasins wanted to put up in town. The impasse would have to be decided in court.

In the meantime, Sheela asked KD—who had received his real estate license in California—to begin snatching up homes in Antelope on behalf of the Rajneesh Investment Corporation, a subsidiary of the new nonprofit that governed Bhagwan's movement: the Rajneesh Foundation International. They also bought the only restaurant in town, a roadside café where locals could order steaks, hamburgers, and cold beer, and converted it into a vegetarian restaurant and store called Zorba the Buddha Rajneesh Restaurant.

For longtime residents, the distant, ominous Rajneesh presence was suddenly right in their faces, living next door. They began to suspect what was really going on. The next Antelope City Council election was scheduled for November 1982. The old-timers worried that the disciples were trying to move in enough people to take over the town's government, which would give them control over the zoning rules, the issuance of building permits, and—most concerning—setting the taxes and fees that residents would have to pay. They had no doubt that their new overlords would waste no time making the city so expensive and so unpalatable that they would be forced to move.

Before that could happen, the longtime residents came up with a Hail Mary effort to exterminate the red-clad menace infesting their town once and for all. They would commit municipal suicide.

On a cool, crisp day in April 1982, more than one hundred reporters and photographers from statewide and national outlets descended upon tiny Antelope. The press roamed the streets to grab sound bites from elderly residents and cheerful sannyasins. They snapped photos of bumper stickers with slogans like MONEY CAN'T BUY ANTELOPE HERITAGE and BETTER DEAD THAN RED. And they stationed cameras outside the Lincoln School, where Oregon secretary of state Norma Paulus was presiding over a special municipal election.

The Antelope City Council had announced one month earlier that it would hold an emergency election to decide a single issue: whether or not to disincorporate their town. If it passed, the city government would dissolve and Antelope would become an unincorporated part of Wasco County, subject to the county's control. Passage required only a simple majority of Antelope citizens. At the time they had announced the special election, longtime residents had the votes to succeed in killing off their little town.

But Ma Anand Sheela was not going to sit by and watch the only town within a thirty-mile radius get ripped out from under her. The local residents had correctly guessed the sannyasins' intentions with Antelope. They had been buying up residential property so they could take political control of the city government and bend it to serve their purposes. If the city dissolved itself, there would be no local government left for them to dominate come November. With Rajneeshpuram's fate still uncertain, given all the legal challenges, Sheela wanted to keep Antelope as both a hedge and a bargaining chip, should it become useful.

To ensure the city of Antelope remained in existence, the sannyasins exploited a vulnerability in the state's election law. Sheela called it a "little loophole." An Oregon voter's residence was determined by where they slept the previous night. This meant any Oregon resident could move to Antelope one day before a local election, spend the night there, and both register to vote *and* vote the next day. Provided the sannyasins could find enough housing in town, they had one month to swarm the place with ranch residents who would "live" in Antelope before the April 15 election.

Between March and April, at Sheela's direction, KD intensified his property-purchasing blitz in Antelope and stuffed houses to the legal limit with sannyasin voters. To encourage reticent sellers, they threw all-night parties near the homes of elderly residents, shone spotlights through their windows to try to scare them, and engaged in graphic public displays of affection—holding hands, kissing on the streets, or whatever else might cause the conservative residents to cringe. Sheela dispatched photographers to document the comings and goings of the local residents, supposedly to prove they didn't really live in town.

Krishna Deva employed even more aggressive tactics. An elderly couple who refused to sell their trailer court claimed that KD showed up and badgered them for nearly five hours. They finally signed the purchase paperwork he presented to them because they were so terrified by his conduct. The couple left town in two separate vehicles, traveling in different directions, to minimize the risk of being followed.

In the end, the sannyasins' election strategy worked. The disincorporation petition went down, fifty-five no votes to forty-two yes votes. Antelope would remain a city. Mayor Margaret Hill couldn't contain her bitter disappointment at a postelection news conference. "The city has lost its heritage as a little western town," she said. "We who have lived here a long time have lost our homes."

The day after the election, Krishna Deva told a reporter that some disciples *might* decide to run for Antelope city office come November.

———————

As the sannyasins continued notching up political and legal victories in early 1982, they began to experience intense and sometimes frightening pushback from Oregonians. In April, a mediator from the US Department of Justice, John Mathis, called the office of Oregon governor Victor Atiyeh to convey his concerns about the potential for violence in Central Oregon. Mathis worked in the Community Relations Service, which styled itself as the "peacemakers" at the Department of Justice, and he had recently met with Wasco County officials to try to understand the tense situation in Antelope that had received so much national press coverage. Mathis conveyed to the governor that the situation was "very explosive and could blow at any time." Without government intervention, he feared the sannyasins might be attacked, raped, or even killed.

Just before the disincorporation election, the Land Use Board of Appeals had agreed with the sannyasins that an incorporation is not a land-use decision, and it therefore rejected the 1000 Friends appeal and paved the way for the May vote to incorporate Rajneeshpuram. This decision, combined with the infuriating situation in Antelope, had sparked a call to action for many people around the state who felt that the government was caving to the pugnacious intruders and their outspoken captain, Sheela. The disciples had made clear that they would outspend, out-litigate, and bulldoze their way into anything they wanted. Anti-Rajneesh sentiment only increased when the disciples announced in April that they planned to hold a "World Celebration" on their ranch that summer for thousands of sannyasins from around the world.

A week after Mathis's warning call, the Jefferson County district attorney also phoned Governor Atiyeh's office to say he was "extremely agitated" by what he saw at meetings between sannyasins, Antelopians, and local ranchers. He said that "in his judgment, there is a distinct possibility of violence against followers of the Bhagwan."

The sannyasins' lobbyist, a renowned Oregonian named Bob Davis, who had attended the Jefferson County meetings, expressed similar concerns when the governor's chief legal counsel called asking for his frank assessment of the situation. Davis said he had "never perceived such an intensity of hatred as that exhibited at the meeting by the older residents, especially when they were not before cameras." Davis said that he and several of his sannyasin clients had been threatened with physical harm. A rancher approached him wearing a necklace of .30-caliber bullets and said that Davis had better have a gun if he ever showed his face in that part of the country again, while other people at the meeting cheered him on.

Despite all these reports of potential violence, Governor Atiyeh's legal counsel recommended that the governor remain disengaged from the Rajneesh problem. At most, he suggested, the governor could issue a statement expressing hope for an amicable solution.

Atiyeh did not even bother with that. Instead, he gave a radio interview in which he offered his first public comments about the sannyasins since they arrived a year earlier. "It would seem to me that, I'm thinking now personally, if I moved into a neighborhood and people didn't really like me, the best thing to do is to move out."

At the May 18, 1982, general election, ranch residents voted 154–0 to incorpo-rate the city of Rajneeshpuram. The Wasco County Court issued a proclama-tion of incorporation, designating August 10, 1982, for a city council election.

In the face of mounting opposition from the outside forces, Bhagwan and Sheela were about to have their own city.

9 | A SMALL FARM TOWN

MUD. MUD AND TRAILERS and tents—the ragtag collection of facilities for the people tasked with building Bhagwan's utopia.

Those impressions stuck with Swami Avinasha after his first visit to the ranch in March 1982. The thirty-two-year-old Canadian was one of the many disciples who had been stuck in a holding pattern since Bhagwan left the ashram in May 1981, all hoping to get the call to join their master at his New Commune. Avinasha was a deeply spiritual sannyasin who had stumbled upon Bhagwan Shree Rajneesh at a metaphysical bookstore in Toronto in the mid-1970s. He'd become transfixed by the mirthful, irreverent face staring at him from a book jacket, and upon flipping through the text he found that everything Bhagwan said resonated in a way that no other spiritual teacher had. He expressed such brilliance in his understanding of psychology, and he was so, so funny. Seriousness, he said, was the death of spirituality. Avinasha was hooked.

To meet the man who would become his spiritual master, Avinasha felt it was important to travel over land, at least as much as possible from Canada, so he flew to London and hitchhiked through France, Italy, Greece, the Middle East, Afghanistan, Pakistan (where he picked up dysentery and was almost murdered), and finally to Pune. Arriving at Krishna House weak and vulnerable, Avinasha was delighted when a beautiful young woman in the office said, *Hello, swami. Welcome to the commune.* He took sannyas—an experience that jarred him because he was so afraid of what he saw in Bhagwan's eyes—and after six months he returned to Canada and ran a successful

Vancouver meditation center. When Bhagwan moved to America, Avinasha went to Berkeley, California, to work at another center, hoping he might get called to the New Commune, wherever it might be.

As soon as Bhagwan arrived in Oregon, calls flooded in from the sannyasin diaspora asking to move to the ranch, but it lacked the facilities to support a sudden influx of people. Coordinators sent out word that nobody should come without an invitation. While waiting, many disciples were told to gather money by selling property, cashing in whatever they had in the bank, and collecting donations from family and friends. Building the New Commune would be a massively expensive endeavor, and the Rajneesh Foundation would need disciples to commit their labor as well as their financial resources to get it done.

While still toiling in California, Avinasha was among a select group invited to check out the beginnings of the New Commune, only eight months into its development, for a small celebration in March 1982. And that's where he saw the mud and the trailers and the rough-and-tumble conditions that sannyasins were living through in order to build their master's dream. It was *thrilling*. Back in Berkeley, Avinasha did what he could to impress the center's leaders, hoping that word might reach Oregon that he was a dependable, capable worker.

In its earliest years, the ranch mainly invited people whose skills would help them build the commune: farming, construction, heavy equipment operation, law, and people with lots of money at their disposal. Avinasha didn't hit any of those marks, but the First Annual World Celebration finally offered him an opportunity. Preparing for such a major event would require far more labor than the already overworked ranch population could manage. Avinasha was among the lucky disciples shipped in from nearby meditation centers to pick up shovels and get to work.

———

His first stop upon arriving at the Big Muddy Ranch in the spring of 1982 was the office trailer that housed Ma Yoga Vidya, a former IBM systems analyst whom Sheela had tapped to run "human resources" for the commune. She had gained Sheela's trust in the late 1970s as an assistant in the Krishna House office, where she oversaw the ashramite work force. A robust South African woman with a cascade of blonde curls, penetrating gray-green eyes, and a pointed chin, Vidya was widely seen as competent and confrontational.

Everybody at the commune worked, doing whatever job Vidya gave them. A lawyer might very well end up driving heavy machinery. A psychologist might peel potatoes in the kitchen. An executive could scrub toilets. Vidya wielded her power with an iron fist. Many people walked out of her office with stories of being heckled, yelled at, or made to feel "unsurrendered." She was prone to ejecting anybody from the commune who was deemed negative, which typically meant they had been overheard complaining about the living conditions, the food, their work assignment, or Sheela and her team of coordinators.

Despite Vidya's fearsome reputation, Avinasha found her to be sweet and kind with him on his first visit. She told him to settle in, relax, and check back in a couple of days to discuss what she needed him to do. After he had caught up with old friends from Pune and pitched his tent in a valley near the cafeteria, Vidya assigned him to work on the commune's construction team, a position he would hold for the next three years.

Building the commune was by far the biggest priority for lay sannyasins at the time. Construction workers were idolized in a way—much as group therapy leaders had been idolized in Pune—since they were the ones going out every morning and erecting their master's Buddhafield. The crews were a mix of men and women, most of whom had never picked up a hammer in their lives. Work sites became collaborative learning environments, where those with construction experience would become crew leaders and teachers, showing any new team members fundamentals such as how to use basic tools, how to operate a circular saw, how to put up a frame wall. Avinasha knew nothing about construction, but he was a quick learner.

Aside from the fifty mobile home units that the sannyasins brought in during the ranch's early months, the first major nonresidential building went up in September 1981: a two-story, pea-green, sheet-metal-clad warehouse far down the southern valley from Jesus Grove. They called it Zarathustra, after the ancient Persian prophet. To Wasco County officials, it was called a farm storage building, but in reality its first level was filled floor to ceiling with boxes of Bhagwan's books, and the upstairs was a five-thousand-square-foot jam-packed office space. Various commune activities would occupy the offices over the next four years, including tape editing and duplication, the legal department, and Vidya's personnel department. A former disciple later told reporters that while only about 50 sannyasins worked the farms during the first year, as many as 250 people worked in the Zarathustra offices.

The next major building, completed just in time for Bhagwan's fiftieth birthday celebration on December 11, was Magdalena Cafeteria, located on the northeast edge of the main valley and the nexus of most residential development at the time. "Maggie's" would become the center of sannyasins' social lives, where they could catch up with old friends, read newspapers tacked onto the walls, participate in community meetings, and enjoy a beer.

In the spring of 1982, Wasco County granted a permit for the sannyasins to erect what would become the largest building they would ever put up on the ranch, with a spiritual and cultural significance that would eclipse anything else. It was their gigantic "greenhouse," more than eighty thousand square feet in size, as large as two football fields, situated in a flat area northeast of Jesus Grove. When it opened in May, the structure had a two-tiered roof, colonnades along the sides, and soaring glass walls.

Bob Harvey, the ranch foreman who would leave the commune in January 1983 after a disagreement over his wages, later told investigators they need look no further than the location of the greenhouse to understand its real purpose. The ranch had precious little arable land, and yet the sannyasins had placed the structure on some of their most viable farmland and destroyed even more valuable land with ornate landscaping and a gravel road that circled the building. *Why not place it at the edge of a field,* Harvey asked, *or simply build it on a rock pile covered with some dirt, since it didn't matter what was underneath it?*

Indeed, the "greenhouse" would never serve its supposed purpose. Disciples later blamed it on a design flaw: the building was positioned such that it didn't get the right amount of sunlight to grow plants inside. Its site did, however, capture breathtaking views of the rugged landscape for people who happened to be, say, meditating on the greenhouse's two-acre floor. They named it Rajneesh Mandir—the Temple of Rajneesh.

Although work days were long and the weather could reach extreme temperatures, many sannyasins who were there in the early years felt enormous satisfaction, including Avinasha. He found that all of his construction work sites were joyful atmospheres, filled with camaraderie as disciples worked arm in arm to build the Buddhafield. And they knew they were the fortunate ones.

Thousands of other disciples were clamoring to be right where they were, close to their spiritual master.

Commune members received amenities that made life easier. While they were out working every day, a cleaning crew kept their bedrooms and bathrooms immaculate. They always had freshly laundered clothing. A free bus system provided transportation around the ranch. They received delicious, ample vegetarian food three times a day at Magdalena, and they could enjoy beers with friends and lovers at night. The commune provided them with clothing, toothpaste, deodorant, cigarettes, and condoms. Since they didn't need to worry about basic necessities, they could devote their full energy to their work.

Indeed, a mantra at the New Commune was "work as worship." The idea originated in Pune, where ashramites were told to surrender themselves to completing their assigned tasks as perfectly as they could, while dropping their mind to the point that they didn't need to think about what they were doing. At Rajneeshpuram, sannyasins were told to use their daily work as their meditation. In every mundane task, they were to be mindful, deliberate, centered, and aware. Jobs became known as "worship," and work departments became known as "temples."

On the morning of July 3, 1982, Sheela pulled up to her master's compound in a gleaming white Rolls-Royce sedan. Bhagwan emerged from his home, which he had again named Lao Tzu, dressed in an ornate white gown and stocking cap. Sheela drove him down the hill, through the security gates, and along one of the many private roads they had laid across the ranch over the past year. They reached their destination within moments: a porte cochere designed for the use of one man only, attached to the newly erected "greenhouse." With his hands pressed together in a namaste greeting and a radiant smile on his face, Bhagwan crossed the stage at one end of the massive hall, where thousands of sannyasins were clapping, cheering, and crying as a band struck up a vivacious tune.

He was there to kick off Rajneeshpuram's First Annual World Celebration. Bhagwan had remained in public silence after arriving in America, and at the festival he would preside over five consecutive days of satsangs—silent communions with the master—just as he had done toward the end of the

Pune ashram, where he would sit quietly on a padded throne while a live band played Indian music and his doctor, Swami Devaraj, read passages from his discourses. For most disciples, the festival offered the first opportunity in over a year to be in Bhagwan's presence. More than five thousand sannyasins had heeded the call and traveled from all over the world to express their love to their regal master on his grand dais, who was obviously delighted to be surrounded by his flock once again.

Even the disciples living at the commune had received scant access to the Buddha on the hill over the past year. He'd made brief public appearances only at his December birthday celebration and a March event to mark the anniversary of his enlightenment. Otherwise, the only way for commune members to see their master was to rush to the roads of Rajneeshpuram every afternoon to catch a glimpse of him driving by in one of the two dozen Rolls-Royce sedans the commune had acquired for him. Bhagwan hadn't driven for years in India, but in New Jersey he had insisted on getting behind the wheel of his new luxury cars and taking disciples on some hair-raising trips along the Garden State Parkway. His drive-bys at Rajneeshpuram became a routine for both Bhagwan and his disciples—his opportunity to escape his Lao Tzu compound for an hour or two every day and his disciples' chance to have a moment of silent communion with their master, palms pressed together and fingertips at their lips, as he passed by.

Festival visitors slept in hundreds of tents that had been placed around the ranch and were served by "temporary" utilities. Attorneys for 1000 Friends of Oregon had mounted a campaign against these facilities, which included fifteen new fire hydrants, a 250,000-gallon water storage reservoir, and a five-million-gallon-capacity sewage treatment plant, claiming they were obviously designed to serve an eventual city on the ranch. Although the land-use watchdog lost the case, its prediction would be proved correct.

The First Annual World Celebration allowed commune members who had been laboring for the past year the chance to reconnect with old friends from India and show off the fruits of their hard work. Visitors could see the impressive beginnings of the Buddhafield taking root in the long-neglected soil, and they could also take in a drastic culture shift within the ranch community. The trademark long orange robes from the Pune ashram were gone, replaced with practical clothing that suited their rugged environment: red jeans, work shirts, cowboy hats, and heavy boots. A sort of cowboy culture had emerged among the earliest disciples at the ranch, who were primarily male laborers; they shared Louis L'Amour novels and passed white lightning hooch around the campfire at night.

The festival's high point came on the final day, July 6, which they celebrated as Master's Day, a riff on the traditional Guru Purnima holiday in India for honoring teachers and gurus. As Bhagwan drove through the commune, a twin-engine plane showered his vehicle with the petals from fifty thousand roses. That evening, sannyasins sang and danced on Rajneesh Mandir's concrete floor while a raucous live band blasted hits like "Bhagwan, I Surrender to You," "Yes Bhagwan Yes," and "Love, Life, Laughter." From his easy chair, Bhagwan watched the proceedings with an amused smile.

One month after the festival came to a close, it was time for voters of Rajneeshpuram to elect their first city government. Although they needed the municipality for practical reasons, Bhagwan insisted to Sheela that there would be no party politics in his commune—something he had said back at Pune as well. They would treat the Rajneeshpuram government as a game. Disciples, who were generally uninterested in politics, were happy to play along.

Sheela tapped Krishna Deva, the California psychologist, to manage the ranch's first election. He had proved himself over the previous year by securing housing permits, spearheading the Rajneeshpuram incorporation plan, and persuading the people of Antelope to part with their homes. KD gave Sheela a list of potential candidates for office from among the commune members. She later gathered a small group to deliver the good news that Bhagwan had selected them to become city officials. One woman learned that her name would be on the ballot for city council as the designated loser, to make the election look credible. As each commune member picked up their precinct card in KD's office, he offered a "suggestion" about whom to vote for—leaving no question that they were to do as he told them. He had concocted a complex voter matrix to ensure the ballots came back with the precise results that Bhagwan desired. Everyone fell in line and the election went off as planned, except a city council candidate received one vote too many and found himself elected council president when he was not the man Bhagwan had intended for the role.

Once the council was in place, they voted on who among them would become mayor. Given the sannyasins' controversial stature in Oregon, the city's chief executive would assume a highly visible, highly strategic role in navigating Rajneeshpuram through turbulent waters. They needed a disciple who could become a respected face of Bhagwan's movement in America. But deciding whom to select required no debate among the council members, or even any actual voting, because the result had been preordained from the moment Bhagwan considered the list of potential candidates that Sheela had given him. The council duly appointed the man their master had chosen, a man Bhagwan considered to have a politician's smile. Everyone congratulated Mayor Krishna Deva.

KD's first major responsibility as mayor was drafting the Rajneeshpuram Comprehensive Plan, a document required by law that explained how the city would satisfy the state's land-use goals. It provided planners with an opportunity to articulate their vision for Bhagwan's experimental new city, which would exceed the land-use goals by creating a community living perfectly in harmony with nature.

Anybody who had spent the previous year listening to sannyasin representatives talk about their little farming community would certainly have been stunned to pick up the Rajneeshpuram Comprehensive Plan when its first draft was issued in late August 1982. The plan anticipated a population of twenty-three hundred people by 1987 and thirty-seven hundred people by 2002. Of course, a city that size would require a full urban infrastructure and all the necessities and conveniences that any comparable city would offer—particularly one that was so remote. Across seven hundred pages in three volumes, the plan described a diverse urban community with light industry (metalwork, clothing, cabinetry, crafts), commercial establishments (clothing and gift shops, grocery stores, bookstores, offices, a bank), tourist facilities (a hotel, a conference center, a restaurant, a service station, a coffee shop), an artists' colony of combined studio and living spaces, a religious retreat center with its own dining and housing facilities, a day care center, schools, health care facilities, a cultural center, and various permanent and transient housing options. The city would occupy just 3 percent of the enormous ranch, appearing on a map to be a strange jigsaw puzzle of three land parcels connected only by the county highway that meandered through the property. Most development would be centered around the Jesus Grove area, where Sheela lived, in the heart of the valley.

From the moment the Rajneeshpuram Comprehensive Plan became public, the days of "it will be a small farm town" were over. Bhagwan's vision of an expansive cosmopolitan settlement was laid bare. There could be no question that Rajneeshpuram was indeed the much-vaunted New Commune.

The Rajneeshpuram City Council unanimously adopted the plan on September 7, 1982, following days of presentations from Swami Deva Wadud, a handsome, Harvard-educated city planner from Marin County, California. Two months later, the Wasco County Court included Rajneeshpuram within the county's own comprehensive plan.

Still, attorneys from 1000 Friends of Oregon had not given up their challenges to the city. There would be many battles to come over the legality of Oregon's newest settlement. In the meantime, Mayor Krishna Deva and the Rajneeshpuram city government began to exercise all the awesome powers that come with a monolithic group running a city on property they entirely own. It was time to build, build, build, before anyone could stop them.

10 | MAKING IT LEGAL

WHEN A BEAUTIFUL WOMAN with a lilting, unplaceable accent arrived at the Houston, Texas, office of the Immigration and Naturalization Service in January 1982, agents were ready for her. Born in Chile to French parents, she had identified herself in visa paperwork as Maria Isabel Megret de Serilly, d'Etigny et de Teil de Chapelaine. When she had applied for her first visa extension in the fall, she'd seemed like just another foreign tourist stopping by the local INS office, hoping to stay in the country a bit longer. By the time she filed her second extension, the INS was well aware that she was better known as Ma Prem Isabel, a disciple of Bhagwan Shree Rajneesh who lived at his controversial commune in Central Oregon.

The INS had secretly opened an investigation into the Rajneesh organization in the fall of 1981, sparked by complaints from aggrieved parents that a foreign cult had swept up their children and was running immigration scams. After just one month working on the case, Portland INS investigator Tom Casey had formed some severe conclusions. "[Bhagwan] and/or his closest associates are opportunistic charlatans deriving a handsome income from his 'disciples,'" he wrote in an internal INS memo. "Although great efforts are made by these persons to present their group as peaceable and law abiding, writer believes that they could become very deceptive and intractable if it were to their advantage."

Among the red flags in Isabel's case, the INS wondered why she had traveled across the country to Texas when she could have gone to the INS office closest to Rajneeshpuram in Portland. After some digging, the service discovered that Isabel's Houston-based attorney had submitted at least sixty nearly identical visa extension requests for people at Rajneeshpuram over the preceding months. None of them stated the truth: that the applicants were sannyasins living and working at Bhagwan's commune in Oregon. When Isabel arrived at their office in January, the INS agents prodded both her and her attorney to explain what exactly was going on. The lawyer admitted that he and his wealthy father were both sannyasins and that he was representing foreign disciples for no pay. He withdrew from his representation, but that still left Isabel swinging. The INS denied her second visa extension request and ordered her to leave the country by April 5, 1982.

But she was far too valuable a resource to let slip away.

By 1982, hundreds of people were pouring into Central Oregon to tour the fascinating, highly publicized commune that had sprung up in the desert. The first disciple many of them encountered was Ma Prem Isabel. She served as the head of press relations for the commune, managing a small team of hostesses—"Twinkies," they were called—who acted as tour guides and public-relations flacks. With long black hair, high cheekbones, and a smoky voice, Isabel put a glamorous, cosmopolitan face on Rajneeshpuram for the many tourists and reporters who journeyed out to the ranch.

She had cut her teeth in public relations working for the Tahitian tourism board before traveling to Pune and taking sannyas in 1979. She became Laxmi's traveling companion, helping Bhagwan's old secretary put out political and legal fires and search for land in India. Isabel came to America in June 1981 on a tourist visa, having divorced her third husband, a British man, three days before she left India. She was again accompanying Laxmi, whom Bhagwan had invited to stay with him at Kip's Castle as an adviser—a role that did not suit Sheela, his new secretary, in the slightest. Sheela treated Laxmi so poorly that news of it reached Bhagwan, who hauled her in for a reprimand. She kissed his feet, sobbing and apologizing.

At Rajneeshpuram, Sheela made multilingual, articulate Isabel one of the commune's primary spokespeople. She would often to go in front of cameras to downplay concerns and reframe issues in her calm, deliberate voice. She was still in that role in March 1982, two months after the INS denied her visa extension, when the service announced a sweeping action against foreigners at the commune. Based on its investigation into suspicious tourist visa extensions—including the sixty in Houston—the INS denied seventy-nine visa extensions for foreign disciples and ordered them out of the country within ten days.

"They have not established they are bona-fide tourists," said Carl Houseman, the director of the Portland INS office. The commune members were working, which violated the terms of their tourist visas. The fact that everybody at the commune had a job—or a "worship," as they put it—and worked around the clock was no mystery: Sheela trumpeted it in newspapers and at public meetings. Isabel, a "tourist" in America, was often quoted in her capacity as the commune's press-relations agent.

"How do you define work?" Isabel said when asked for the commune's response. "Our work is our meditation. Nobody earns money. There is a very subtle difference."

Fortunately for Isabel, her own immigration status was no longer in immediate peril. Weeks before she was supposed to leave the country, she had traveled to Bend, Oregon, to marry Swami Prem Niren, a native Oregonian and a skilled corporate attorney who had given up his partnership at a Los Angeles law firm to devote his life to Bhagwan Shree Rajneesh. Niren petitioned the INS to grant his new wife a green card. Isabel was, for the time being, safely in America.

In September 1982, on a gorgeous fall day, Sheela united a longtime Indian disciple, Ma Aruna Bharti, with Rajneeshpuram's new mayor, Krishna Deva.

"Marriage is a three-ringed circus," she told the couple during the ceremony, "engagement ring, wedding ring, and suffering." Whenever she presided over a sannyasin wedding, Sheela would pepper her remarks with gallows humor about the dreaded institution. Bhagwan was famously derisive about marriage, saying it was just a means to control and oppress, but he wouldn't stop his sannyasins from getting married. They just had to go into it realizing that nothing in life is permanent and that "any commitment for the future is a destructive bondage."

Champagne flowed at the wedding reception, where guests ate a vegetarian feast and danced on the lawn near Sheela's home. Attendees included local notables like Wasco County judges Rick Cantrell and Virgil Ellett, who had voted in favor of their new city the previous year. A journalist for the brand-new *Rajneesh Times* newspaper snapped a photo of the happy couple, both wearing hulking floral garlands over their malas, with Rajneesh Mandir meditation hall looming far in the background. In the photo, KD's new wife has one hand flung up into the air and a huge smile. Wedged between the couple, Sheela beams at the camera.

KD, however, is not looking into the lens, or at his wife, or at Sheela, or at his wife's two young daughters standing in front of them. He's squinting into the middle distance over the photographer's shoulder, with a tight smile on his bearded face, like a man who isn't quite sure what he is doing there.

He had met the middle-aged Aruna while at the Pune ashram, where they became lovers despite the age gap and her existing marriage. Their romance persisted while KD moved back to America and got swept up in ranch affairs, with KD calling her and sending her love letters. After divorcing her husband in 1982, Aruna traveled with her two girls to Oregon, where she finally married the man she loved in a joyful ceremony officiated by Bhagwan's irreverent personal secretary.

At least, that's how Krishna Deva described his marriage in a sworn affidavit to get his wife's green card. He would later confess that the marriage was a fraud. He barely knew Aruna. He certainly was never in love with her. Sheela had hatched the plan as a way to get Aruna and her children—all Indian citizens—into America. Sheela and KD had scripted a romantic backstory, and the couple fabricated love letters as evidence. In reality, they lived completely separate lives at Rajneeshpuram.

At the time, KD and many other disciples believed that sham marriages were necessary to bring together the international diaspora to live in the Buddhafield. Foreign sannyasins would come into America on tourist visas, marry American disciples, and apply for green cards to stay permanently. Among sannyasins, there was little surprise that they would use marriage in this way since they had done the exact same thing at the Pune ashram, where Laxmi had arranged hasty marriages between sannyasins from the British Commonwealth and those from other places, which allowed the foreign disciples to stay in India.

While putting together her initial work crew at the ashram to travel to Kip's Castle in May 1981, Italian Ma Prem Deeksha claims she warned Bhagwan that the non-Americans on her crew might have immigration troubles. She had spent some time in New York before meeting Bhagwan in 1971, and she had learned that the number-one rule for foreigners visiting America was, as she put it, "Don't fuck with immigration." But Bhagwan had been unfazed, telling her to arrange the appropriate marriages between foreigners and Americans in advance to avoid any problems.

Still concerned they might get in trouble with immigration, Deeksha had consulted with her Manhattan attorney upon arriving in New Jersey. She described the way the sannyasins had used marriage as a tool for immigration purposes and said they would do the same thing in America. The attorney had stared at her in horror. *You'll end up in jail. Everybody who participates in this. You'll all go to jail.*

Deeksha says the lawyer later conveyed this same message to Sheela, who was unbothered. She also says she repeated the lawyer's concerns to Bhagwan. *Don't worry about the marriages,* Deeksha recalls him saying. *We can do that.*

The secretive Rumi Temple was located on the second floor of Zarathustra, the "farm warehouse" the sannyasins had built in their first months in Oregon. Under the auspices of commune president Ma Yoga Vidya, the department was tasked with arranging marriages between Americans and foreigners and helping to ensure that they stuck, without anything messy coming back to haunt the commune later. Some sannyasins have said this commune-organized service was only available to "somebodies" around the ranch—foreigners with valuable skills, connections, or access to wealth—whereas the "nobodies" had to find their own way to stay in America.

The Rumi coordinators would try to pair couples that seemed to be a good fit, at least on paper. American Swami Anugiten, for example, offered to marry his British girlfriend Ma Prem Savita, the Rajneesh organization's top accountant, so she could stay in the country. But since he had no college education, whereas Savita was a well-educated commune leader, Anugiten was told that Savita would wed somebody more suitable. She ended up marrying an American chiropractor with whom she had no relationship whatsoever.

Over time, Rumi grew into a sophisticated organization where sham couples would undergo drills to ensure they had their fabricated stories straight in case the INS ever asked them. Swami Sharan Ananda—nicknamed "Ernie" because he was so earnest—helped to run these coaching sessions in a large, open room in Rajneesh Legal Services. He would sit opposite a sham couple and grill them on mundane questions like "What color is your wife's toothbrush?" and "Does she wear pajamas or a nightie?" and "What side of the bed does he sleep on?"

All this coaching was necessary because the couples rarely knew each other, did not live together, and had constructed elaborate backstories to make their marriages seem legitimate. To facilitate the ruse, the commune kept two sets of records on where sannyasins lived—one that reflected actual residences and one that made it look like sham-marriage couples lived together. If INS agents ever requested such records, they would receive the fabricated set. The sham couples used their false addresses for all official purposes, including to register to vote, and they would even keep some clothing at their supposed residence in case of an INS raid.

With its April 1982 deportation order, the INS put the commune on notice that it would be placing foreign sannyasins under intense scrutiny in the months and years to come. The investigator Tom Casey had predicted at the beginning of the Rajneesh case in late 1981 that the INS would "find itself flooded with immediate relative and fiancée petitions by ashram members." He was right. Krishna Deva would later estimate that he knew of at least three hundred to four hundred sham marriages at Rajneeshpuram, and the INS would claim there were as many as five hundred.

————————

While the commune leaders began to take defensive maneuvers to protect their disciples from hostile INS inquiries, they had a much more pressing issue at hand in the fall of 1982. In fact, it was the only immigration case that mattered. If the sannyasins didn't prevail, everything they had built at Rajneeshpuram would become meaningless—a body with no soul.

11 | BHAGWAN TAKES A TRIP

ON A CRISP MORNING IN OCTOBER 1982, a young blonde woman in red clothing and a mala appeared outside the old Federal Building in downtown Portland with a broom. As people passed in and out of the building's rear entrance, she swept dust and dirt from the granite stoop and the sidewalk, clearing the way for a rolled-up red carpet, which she unfurled from the street to the doorway. A few other disciples arrived to help with the preparations, including Sheela, dressed in a fringed red cloak over a red-and-black plaid dress.

"Flowers?" she called to the growing gaggle of sannyasins. "Where are the bushes? Green bushes? What happened to the bushes I left here?" Metal buckets filled with colorful flowers appeared, and a dozen sannyasins carefully laid them along the carpet's edge while others used a Dustbuster and their fingers to clear off any offensive lint or dirt. "My master gets nothing but the best," Sheela told reporters capturing the bizarre scene for the evening news.

More and more sannyasins arrived in buses and cars from the ranch. Sheela arranged them along the red carpet. When there was nothing left to do, they stood there giggling at each other with anticipation. Any disciple with any stature at the commune seemed to be there: Mayor Krishna Deva, Sheela's husband Jayananda, Sheela's good friend the nurse Puja, spokeswoman Isabel. A young American sannyasin with arresting blue eyes, Swami Toby, played a lilting Indian melody on his flute that carried through the quiet city streets while Sheela made final tweaks to her perfect tableau.

A glistening white Rolls-Royce limousine finally glided up the street, with the City of Rajneeshpuram flag protruding from the hood—a white dove over a black dove—as though the car contained a visiting head of state. Sheela directed it into position along the red carpet and opened the rear door. A smiling Bhagwan Shree Rajneesh emerged, wearing a heavy gray robe with billowing sleeves and a thick black stocking cap. Although he was only fifty years old, his beard had grown entirely white and reached to his stomach. When he raised his hands together in namaste, his sparkling Cartier watch—rumored to be worth $150,000—slid up his arm.

Disciples closed in around Bhagwan as he walked the red carpet, all with their hands pressed together in a prayerful gesture, including Krishna Deva and Bhagwan's lawyer, Swami Prem Niren. Sheela guided her master into the lobby of the government building, where Jayananda waited in an elevator whose brass doors had been polished by a sannyasin.

Bhagwan was twenty-five minutes late for his interview with the Portland office of the Immigration and Naturalization Service. To her dismay, Sheela was not allowed to sit with her master while he gave his testimony. Instead, she waited in the hallway, anxiously chatting with reporters about why the US government should allow such a truly exceptional man to stay in the country forever.

The official story was that Bhagwan had been in horrible physical shape in India and required short-term medical treatment in America. But once he arrived in the country, he found that his condition had improved dramatically, even without the laminectomy and without seeing any non-sannyasin doctors. He realized that staying in America permanently would be good for his health. Once he fully recovered, he would be able to pick up all his religious duties again—the discourses, the audiences, all the public and private functions that he had fulfilled at his ashram in Pune before falling into silence more than one year earlier.

That was the official story, which commune attorneys had submitted to the INS along with his petition to become a lawful permanent resident. They also submitted paperwork requesting that the INS grant Bhagwan immigration preference because he was an internationally renowned religious teacher.

At a celebration to see Bhagwan off that morning at the Rajneeshpuram airstrip, Sheela had commanded all disciples to be one hundred percent positive so that the good vibes would help their master's case. Keeping him in America was her primary concern, more important than the battles with the small-minded Antelopians, more important than the squabbles with 1000 Friends of Oregon and county planners and bureaucrats. If Bhagwan were forced to leave, he would build his New Commune in some other country—and most likely with some other secretary at his side.

———————

"Did you like our master?" Sheela gushed before the INS examiner could begin to ask her any questions. After Bhagwan's interview, she had the opportunity to sit with the examiner, George Hunter, and provide information as the representative of the Rajneesh Foundation International, which was sponsoring Bhagwan's petition.

Sheela told Hunter the official story: Bhagwan's grave medical condition, the need to squire him out of India and into the healthy environs of Oregon, and his gradually improving health that would allow him to resume all his spiritual duties. She admitted that she had been the driving force that brought him to America. "I took a chance and I got lucky, hit the jackpot."

The interview seemed to be going well until Hunter threw Sheela a curveball: "When you visited the American Consulate on May 4, 1981, you told the consular officer, among other things, that the Bhagwan was possibly dying of cancer. Do you recall saying this?"

Cancer. Hunter had received a sworn statement from Joyce Smith, the consular official with whom Sheela had met repeatedly in May 1981 and who had ultimately granted Bhagwan's tourist visa. In her statement, Smith reported what Sheela had told her about Bhagwan's condition during her first visit:

> She said he was very ill and required medical treatment in the U.S. She said that he was possibly dying of cancer. I remarked that she might be overreacting due to the recent death of her own husband due to cancer. She admitted that was possible but said that the possibility that the Bhagwan had cancer had to be checked out urgently.

"No, I said my *husband* died of cancer," Sheela told Hunter.

"You mentioned nothing to the consular officer of the Bhagwan possibly having cancer?" he asked.

"No, nothing to do with cancer."

The possibility of Bhagwan having cancer hadn't appeared in any of the paperwork submitted to receive his visa, and it wasn't mentioned in any of his medical documentation. For George Hunter, Smith's memo raised important questions: Had Sheela lied about the severity of Bhagwan's medical condition to persuade Joyce Smith to issue a visa as soon as possible? And if so, what else had the sannyasins lied about?

———————————

Two hours after arriving, Sheela led Bhagwan by the hand back outside the Federal Building. As he reached his waiting Rolls-Royce, he turned around to give one more salute to his fawning disciples, only to discover that his secretary had dropped to her knees behind him and was pressing her forehead to the red carpet at his socked-and-sandaled feet. Laughing, almost as if he were embarrassed, Bhagwan bent over and touched Sheela's head.

His car pulled away with a gentle honk. The ebullient crowd clapped along to Swami Toby's flute music and cheerfully cleared away the flowers and the carpet and all the pageantry from their master's big day in Portland. The activity swirled all around Sheela, who remained on her knees, tears coursing down her round cheeks and onto the red carpet, as she watched her master disappear.

12 | TRUTH AND CONSEQUENCES

THE YEAR ENDED on an almost entirely positive note for Bhagwan and his disciples. They had laid the foundation for a major city on their huge piece of rural land, with the power to shape it according to Bhagwan's longstanding vision of the New Commune. They were also about to flex their muscles in Antelope after executing a coup de grâce at the November 1982 election, when they elected a slate of sannyasins to the city council and installed as the mayor Ma Prem Karuna, a stone-faced New Englander who coordinated the secretive Rumi Temple arranging sham marriages. Although she had previously given signals that they would abandon the ghost town as soon as they had their own city on the ranch, Sheela saw no reason to give up a perfectly good city into which they had already made a significant investment. Antelope could help to satisfy their long-term development needs in case they had legal problems at Rajneeshpuram, and the promise to withdraw from Antelope would serve as a useful piece of leverage in upcoming negotiations to get what they wanted on their ranch.

By the end of 1982, the sannyasins thus controlled not one city but two. Their success would come at a hefty price. As they amassed power, their antagonists would regroup and seek retribution. The coming year would be rife with political opposition, legal setbacks, and even violence from people who wanted to eject all the laughing, singing, lawsuit-slinging sannyasins from the state.

An apparent death blow arrived in the final week of 1982, when the INS denied Bhagwan's petition to stay permanently in the United States. The service determined that he was not a religious leader entitled to immigration preference, because he'd been in silence for most of the past two years. But even more troubling, the INS found that Bhagwan and his representatives had made false and misleading statements to secure his visa. The INS determined that Bhagwan had left India with the intention of staying permanently in America and that Sheela and others had exaggerated his medical condition. Lying to immigration agents was grounds enough to send him packing, and it could even lead to criminal consequences for the people who carried it out. Unless his attorneys appealed, Bhagwan would face deportation proceedings within thirty days.

It was the worst possible scenario for the future of the American commune. All the people, all the energy, and all the money they had poured into Oregon would amount to nothing if Bhagwan left the country.

But the master seemed to take it in stride. A reporter happened to be visiting him on the day the decision came out. "I had been expecting this all along," he said in his slow, melodious English. "This is the only way they could treat a Jesus or a Buddha."

PART III
OREGON, 1983

Bhagwan and his caretaker Vivek in one of his Rolls-Royce sedans during a drive-by at Rajneeshpuram. *Photo courtesy of Toby Marshall*

13 | RELIGION AT ITS HIGHEST

OREGON STATE SENATE PRESIDENT Ed Fadeley rose on his dais as thirty senators on the floor below him prepared for the morning's work. For the past 125 years, every senate session had opened with a religious invocation—an honor that Fadeley bestowed upon pretty much anybody who asked, since there wasn't much competition. A typical invocation came from mainline Christian clergymen, with the occasional American Indian representative who would deliver the blessing of the Great Spirit, or the group of Buddhist monks who blessed the assembly with incense and chanting. But the august chamber had never before hosted anybody like the exuberant woman in a maroon blazer and beaded necklace standing next to Senator Fadeley on the morning of March 23, 1983.

Fadeley spoke into his microphone. "The senate will be led in prayer this morning by Ma Anand Sheela. The full title is"—Fadeley paused at the unfamiliar word on the page—"*Ackareea* Ma Anand Sheela, personal secretary to the Bhagwan Shree Rajneesh and president of the Academy of Rajneeshism."

Fadeley retreated down one step on the dais, leaving Acharya Ma Anand Sheela to tower alone over all the legislators, clerks, and pages.

"In the name of Bhagwan Shree Rajneesh," she said, "I make this offering to the State of Oregon Senate." She handed Fadeley an ostentatious floral wreath cut from the Rajneeshpuram greenhouse and two boxes of champagne truffles crafted in the commune's kitchens, and then she began her invocation, ripped from one of Bhagwan's Pune discourses.

"Love is prayer groping towards god. Love is poetry born out of the sheer joy of being. Love is song, dance, celebration: a song of gratitude, a dance of thankfulness, a celebration for no reason at all. For this tremendous gift that goes on showering on us, for this whole universe, from the dust to the divine. Love is not what you understand it to be. Love is religion at its highest."

With her hands raised over her head like Eva Perón on the balcony of the Casa Rosada, Sheela sang a series of sustained syllables, a mantra borrowed from Buddhism. It was an unusually exotic sound for a Wednesday morning in the State Capitol building. After each swallowed-syllable phrase came to an end, Sheela offered a translation for the senators who didn't speak Hindi.

"I go to the feet of the Awakened One."

"I go to the feet of the commune of the Awakened One."

"I go to the feet of the ultimate truth of the Awakened One."

Throughout her prayer, the senators stood with their hands clasped, heads tilted down, respectfully silent. If they had any particular objection to Ma Anand Sheela offering a religious invocation in their hall, they kept it to themselves. But the public was not as sanguine after the *Oregonian* newspaper ran a quarter-page photograph of Sheela at the heart of the senate chamber with her arms spread triumphantly. Fadeley's office received phone calls demanding to know how it came to pass that Sheela was given such a visible, powerful honor in the capitol building. Fadeley defended himself by explaining the extent to which he had pushed back. First the sannyasins had asked to hold the invocation on the same day as a hearing in Bhagwan's immigration case, which would have served an obvious political purpose. They asked if their members could sing from the senate gallery, play musical instruments, and display Bhagwan's portrait in the chamber. They asked if disciples could walk through the chamber passing out champagne truffles during the invocation. Fadeley rejected all of these requests.

When Sheela rose before the Oregon House of Representatives one week later, everyone was on guard. The gallery was packed with journalists, lobbyists, public officials, and sannyasins eager to watch the unfolding spectacle. Representative Max Simpson had argued in the press that the House was "lending credence and publicity to a personality cult at a time its leader is embroiled in a lawsuit and faces deportation," and he alleged that the sannyasins were engaged in "an act of political mischief rather than an act of reverence." So many members protested that the House Speaker struggled to muster a quorum to open the session. When they finally had enough members in the room, Sheela stepped to the dais and began reading Bhagwan's words about God as the innermost core of each person. A half-dozen legislators walked out.

The people of Oregon were receiving their first introduction to the confusing, contradictory, brand-new religion known as Rajneeshism.

The year 1983 had kicked off with a burst of staggering news. Having just ordered Bhagwan to leave the country within thirty days, the INS abruptly reversed course in early January and reopened the guru's case based on a winning procedural argument from Swami Prem Niren, the dogged California attorney and Isabel's husband. During Sheela's interview, examiner George Hunter mentioned the statement he had received from US consular official Joyce Smith about Bhagwan possibly having cancer. Since Bhagwan's lawyers had never seen the statement, Niren argued that the Portland office had violated its own rules by using evidence that the petitioner had no chance to rebut.

Persuaded, the INS not only terminated Bhagwan's deportation order but also gave his attorneys a chance to present a full rebuttal of the December decision—including the determination that Bhagwan was not a religious leader because he was in silence. To prevail, the sannyasins would need to prove something that had seemed obvious to them: that Bhagwan Shree Rajneesh was an active leader of a religion.

One glaring flaw in their case was that Bhagwan famously loathed organized religions, having spent thousands of hours at his discourses in India ripping them to shreds. As he saw it, "religiousness" existed only while an enlightened master like Jesus Christ or Buddha was alive, when disciples could experience and savor all that supernatural energy. When the master died, the religiousness died with him. Ordinary people would then step in to create shallow, intellectual *religions* filled with dogmas and strictures used to control people in the name of the dead master. Religion was the "corpse of religiousness," Bhagwan had said. It might look like a living thing, but it had been dead for as long as the enlightened master.

INS examiner George Hunter had seized on these previous comments during his October interview, confirming that the guru had said that "the future of the world and the future of the church lie in diametrically opposite directions" and that the old religions should be destroyed to save the future of humanity. According to Sheela, Bhagwan's outside immigration attorney, Jeffrey Noles, urged her after the interview to fully embrace sannyas as a religion. Taking their master's lead, disciples had been inclined to describe sannyas with amorphous phrases like "a way of life." Noles said that wouldn't fly with the INS. He told Sheela to own Rajneeshism and even prodded her to develop something like the Bible or the Koran that she could put in the INS's hands as a holy text.

When she brought this monstrous idea to Bhagwan—that the notoriously antireligion master should dub his own movement a religion—he surprised her by smiling and saying, without hesitation, *OK, Sheela.*

On July 2, 1983, Bhagwan appeared for satsang in Rajneesh Mandir—the commune's "greenhouse"—before a throng of thousands of devotees. He had ditched his plain white garb for something more extravagant—a solid black robe with billowing zebra-stripe sleeves and a thick white stocking cap, launching an era of flamboyant fashion that would continue until his death. Still in silence, he sat on his throne, eyes closed, while his physician Swami Devaraj offered a dramatic reading from the Pune discourse series *Nirvana: The Last Nightmare* as a languid sitar droned from the rear of the hall.

After proving the previous summer that they could throw a huge festival without major complications, commune leaders had persuaded Wasco and Jefferson Counties to approve a six-week-long Second Annual World Celebration. Promotional materials invited visitors to come anytime from early June to mid-July, although the main festival program, when they expected the largest volume of people, would be the first week of July for Master's Day.

The ranch had been a chaotic whirl of activity in the months preceding the festival. Rajneesh Mandir had received a facelift, with painters working in relays to continuously spray the hall's roof with twelve hundred gallons of paint and another team laying linoleum across the two-acre concrete slab. A recently completed dam created a 360 million–gallon reservoir lake near the commune entrance, which they finished with sandy beaches, dozens of canoes along a wooden dock, and a floating pagoda from which festivalgoers could leap into the water. The dam itself was a sloping grass hill that featured an enormous rendition of the Rajneesh logo styled from colorful flowers and shrubs.

A temporary cafeteria went up in the south valley, equipped to serve up to six thousand meals per hour using vegetables from the ranch's own truck farm. The coordinator overseeing the food operations told the *Rajneesh Times* that she expected to go through 30 tons of yogurt, 100 tons of fruit, 20,000 gallons of milk, 10 tons of coffee, and 2 tons of chocolate chips during the festival. Her recipe for a spaghetti dinner included 3,600 pounds of noodles, 30 gallons of olive oil, 215 cases of tomato products, and 31 gallons of red wine.

To accommodate all the visitors, commune-crafted wooden platforms were distributed across the flattest parts of the valley, each bearing a tent large enough for up to four people. Campers received a foam mat, bedsheet, sleeping bag, pillow, and pillow cover. Orderly rows of tent platforms cropped up all around Rajneesh Mandir in the east and the airstrip in the west, and sprawled far down the southern valley beyond the Zarathustra warehouse and toward Jefferson County. Most guests stayed in the tents, but for more money they had the option of "mountain cabins"—tiny A-frame houses mounted on repurposed tent platforms.

With the Second Annual World Celebration, the commune began to approach the heights of Pune, that vertically integrated economy where a visitor's cash never needed to escape the ashram gates. Although the festival's basic admission fee of around $500 included housing and three cafeteria meals a day, new pay-as-you-go amenities at the heart of the ranch included a disco, a boutique, a bookstore, a beer garden with an open-air dance floor, and a long two-story mall hosting a restaurant, an ice cream parlor, and a pharmacy. The Rajneesh Meditation University offered meditation and group therapy in a cluster of trailers near the airstrip.

In the midst of the celebration, thousands of visiting disciples sat in Rajneesh Mandir for a special audience with Ma Anand Sheela. "I don't need to welcome you because he has already done that this morning," she said to cheers from the festival attendees. "But I can ask about the food. Is everybody having a good time?" She flitted from topic to topic, a little gossip here, a little news there, but she packed in a couple of major announcements. "For years Bhagwan has been talking about the possibility of creating a Buddhafield so strong that its positivity is capable of transforming the climate of the world. Now it has happened," she told them. "While you are here, drink as much of the positivity and richness as you can, so that when you return to your countries you can share it with everybody."

Sheela also announced that Bhagwan was in the process of dictating an extraordinary document that would explain his vision for what he called his "living religion."

"This is the first time that an enlightened master has put his religion into book form," she declared. "It is the first time that it has happened while the master is still alive."

While the team at Rajneesh Legal Services was busy in early 1983 documenting Bhagwan's claim to be a religious leader, Sheela gave Rajneeshism the sheen of a bona fide religion. Sannyasins suddenly began intoning the Hindi chant Sheela had uttered in the State Capitol—which they called "the gachhamis"—twice a day toward wherever Bhagwan was located. As the president of the Rajneesh Foundation International, Sheela would make public appearances in a costume that Bhagwan designed himself: silky red robes with the Rajneeshpuram logo embroidered on the front, a pearl or diamond mala necklace, and a red scarf affixed to her hair and trailing down her back. She became known, somewhat jokingly, as the "Pope of Rajneeshism." Dozens of commune members were named to the priesthood and allowed to preside over ceremonies such as marriages, funerals, and births.

As the immigration attorney had suggested, Sheela and Bhagwan began to work on a pocket-sized book with a red cover called *Rajneeshism: An Introduction to Bhagwan Shree Rajneesh and His Religion*. Bhagwan dictated the book to Sheela over three evenings. Across seventy pages, *Rajneeshism* spelled out the religious doctrine that had been anathema to him throughout his career as a guru. Drawing on quotations from his discourses, the book explained the purpose of meditation, how to worship, the concept of neo-sannyas, and various ceremonies. It also laid out a fussy clerical hierarchy—acharyas, arihantas, and siddhas—who could perform certain religious functions. All ministers had to meet a bulleted list of criteria, such as two years as a neo-sannyasin or two years practicing meditation.

Perhaps the most unusual part of Bhagwan's bible came at the end, when the guru predicted a grim fifteen-year span between 1984 and 1999 with unmitigated destruction of "every kind," including floods, earthquakes, volcanic eruptions, wars, and nuclear explosions. Tokyo, New York, San Francisco, Los

Angeles, Mumbai, and other major cities would be obliterated. The only way to escape the global holocaust was through Rajneeshism, Bhagwan explained, since his religion was "making the only worldwide effort to transform human consciousness so that man can die and a superman can be born out of his ashes." According to Sheela, Bhagwan wanted to include this apocalyptic post-script in *Rajneeshism* because all religious texts included the prediction of some future cataclysm that could be avoided only through religious devotion. "That's how you hang on to your congregation," is how she later described Bhagwan's thinking.

In a press release, Bhagwan underscored just how revolutionary his new religion was: "Ours is the only religion, the first religion in the history of the world. All the others are just premature experiments which have failed. And we are not going to fail."

Sannyasins at the ranch and abroad seemed to take these bizarre new develop-ments in stride. Many disciples had come to Bhagwan specifically because he was not a religion. He was an iconoclastic, free-wheeling guru who made fun of all those traditions and encouraged people to drop whatever programming that religious ministers had inflicted upon them. Now they were witnessing the creation of Bhagwan's own doctrine, his own clergy, his own church, in a spiritual mecca that he'd vowed would be free of such things. But even if they didn't like the idea of becoming part of a new organized religion, disaffected sannyasins at Rajneeshpuram didn't have many options beyond walking away. As with everything in Bhagwan's world, they were expected to surrender and remain positive.

Many took Rajneeshism for what it was: a political, legal, and public-relations tool. A devoted British sannyasin named Maneesha saw the religion as "just a gesture" that "almost certainly none of us took seriously." One day while flipping through a book that she helped publish, Maneesha was stunned to see that she was being credited as an acharya, with fancy initials after her name and degrees from the Rajneesh Meditation University alongside the legitimate degrees she had earned as a nurse. When a reporter asked Ma Prem Isabel about her own acharya title, she responded that she didn't really know what it meant. The flute player Swami Toby thought it was a joke when he learned that he was an arihanta. He had never taken any special courses, never received any sort of certification or training, never received a formal induction as a minister, and never was called upon to perform any rites.

Despite the campy humor to be found in all the new regalia and religious trappings, some sannyasins suspected that Sheela was playing a long game. When the journalist Frances FitzGerald interviewed sannyasins in the months before the advent of Rajneeshism, most told her that they would all leave the commune if their master died, since without his energy there was no Buddhafield. As FitzGerald put it, the sannyasins seemed to be building an expensive soon-to-be ghost town in the Oregon desert. But then Rajneeshism came along, offering a way to perpetuate Bhagwan's movement beyond his death and ensure that all the backbreaking work to create his commune would continue to have value after he was gone. And as the religion's pope, Sheela had assumed the pinnacle of power within this new institution that was designed to outlive her master.

The Second Annual World Celebration in July 1983 would be the largest-ever gathering of sannyasins, with the commune estimating that fifteen thousand people attended throughout its six weeks and that it brought in an estimated $12 million in revenue at a cost of $9 million. Although they could not have known at the time, the festival would also serve as the high-water mark for the commune's political and legal fortunes. Having spent their first two years in Oregon cowing their opposition and milking the law to their benefit, they were now poised to develop their community as Bhagwan had long ago dictated.

But everything hung on whether or not the INS would allow Bhagwan to stay in America. Throughout 1983, the disciples mounted a massive legal and public-relations campaign in defense of their master. His immigration attorney delivered evidence to the INS to substantiate the petition: three videos, fifty-one photographs, forty-eight pages of legal arguments, 628 pages of rebuttal evidence. The disciples later delivered another two-foot-tall stack of evidence. To apply some political pressure on the INS, they also organized large protests in support of religious freedom in major cities around the world—London, Zurich, Munich, Amsterdam, The Hague, Tokyo, Sydney, and Bonn, Germany.

A sannyasin delegation followed Vice President George Bush around Europe and tried to pass him a petition about Bhagwan's case. A convoy of cars, vans, and twenty-three buses deposited more than one thousand sannyasins in Portland for a parade, carrying signs and banners protesting the INS's religious bigotry (STOP MODERN CRUCIFIXION) and led by a garlanded flatbed truck bearing musicians and amplifiers. "We will fight to the last breath for religious freedom," Sheela declared at a press conference. They brandished Rajneeshism as both a sword and a shield to keep their master in the United States, but ultimately they could only wait to see what the INS would do with Bhagwan's application to become a permanent resident.

As Rajneeshism exploded across the world, a team of shrewd lawyers working for Oregon's attorney general was paying close attention. They were particularly interested in how the new religion seemed to infiltrate every part of Rajneeshpuram's government. And they were preparing to pounce.

14 | CHILDREN OF THE COMMUNE

DICKON KENT HAD COME HOME to horrifying news in the spring of 1982. A happy twelve-year-old living in Vermont, he had finally fallen into a comfortable spot over the past few months—new school, new friends, and even a girl he liked. But now his ecstatic mother in orange robes and beaded necklace sat him down on the couch to tell him that she had finally received the call. They were moving to Oregon.

As it sunk in that he would have to abandon the great new life he was building in Vermont, Dickon couldn't hold back his tears. *Why can't we just be normal?* he asked her.

When he was still a toddler in the early 1970s, both of his parents had gone on their own spiritual journeys. His mother's had taken her to India, where she became a disciple of Bhagwan Shree Rajneesh. She moved her five-year-old son from the English countryside to London to live communally with other sannyasins while she worked at a Rajneesh Meditation Center. Surrounded by photographs of Bhagwan and people who talked about little else, Dickon could hardly remember a time before the guru was an all-consuming presence in his life. When it became known that Bhagwan was in America, Dickon's mother moved with her son to a commune in Vermont so they'd be ready when the New Commune opened. Just as he acclimated to life as a regular American kid at a traditional public school, she dropped the bomb on him. His life was about to be thrown into chaos yet again.

They pulled up in front of the ranch's farmhouse in the spring of 1982, less than a year after the commune had been founded. Dickon was separated from his mother and sent to a nearby barn they called Howdy Doody, where he would live with other children.

He now belonged to the commune.

Bhagwan had often told disciples in Pune that children were an obstacle to spiritual growth, which was supposed to be the most important thing in their lives. He envisioned a generation of sannyasins without children, who could be totally devoted to him and his work. Plenty of parents took his disinterest in kids as an excuse to leave their own children behind. The writer Satya Bharti left her three children in New York so she could dedicate her life to Bhagwan, and she estimated that about one-third of the women who were closest to him had done the same thing. If disciples asked him whether they should have children, he invariably told them no, if they had any doubts. He also encouraged disciples to have abortions and get sterilized—particularly ashramites with important positions. The ashram's medical center performed vasectomies and tubal ligation procedures at no cost to the disciples, including on girls as young as thirteen.

Although he didn't want kids cluttering up his spiritual communities, Bhagwan knew that some disciples would have children, and he included them in his rhapsodic descriptions of the New Commune. In his utopia, children would belong to the entire commune, not to their parents, which he saw as the best way to raise them into well-adjusted adults. "The child need not get fixed and obsessed with one pattern of life," he said. "He can learn from his father, he can learn from his uncles, he can learn from all the men in the community. He will have a bigger soul."

In Oregon, Bhagwan put these words into action. Nuclear families were not allowed at Rajneeshpuram, and children generally lived apart from their parents. In the commune's first year, most preadolescents slept together in the Howdy Doody bunkhouse, where they had minimal adult supervision—a setup that one mother, an Australian named Bhasha, later called a "disgrace" and "pitiful." When she first arrived at Rajneeshpuram with her two toddlers in September 1982, she saw an infant sitting unattended in the dirt outside the farmhouse, pulling at his hair. The disciple who was supposed to be providing childcare hated children and didn't want to be there.

Bhasha refused to put her kids in the commune's childcare, despite pressure to conform. After she wrote a pointed letter to Bhagwan about the situation, the commune set up a dedicated bunkhouse and school for the children in Alan Watts Grove, a residential area in the canyon north of Rajneesh Mandir, and assigned experienced teachers to provide instruction during the day. Each night, two parents took a shift babysitting the dozens of preteens who lived there. Bhasha had no idea what the other parents did on their assigned nights, since there was no schedule, no rules, and no expectations—and that didn't bother her. "That's what we'd come for," she later explained. "I thought I'd come to share my kids. I wanted my kids to have a varied experience. That was the whole point of it."

Teenagers lived alongside adults in trailers throughout the ranch. Dickon shared a bedroom with five other girls and boys, while adults occupied the rest of the trailer. He had experienced so much chaos throughout his childhood that living communally with strangers, separated from his mom, seemed like par for the course. Besides, his trailer wasn't supposed to be a *home* in any traditional sense. Disciples worked such long days that they had little time to lounge in their residences, nor did they have televisions or cooking facilities. They used their trailers for little else but sleeping, bathing, and sex.

In his first year at the ranch, Dickon spent half his day in school, which he found to be confused and uninspiring. The commune employed unconventional educational methods, such as the day when Dickon and another girl were taken to Pythagoras Medical Clinic to watch a German disciple receive a gynecological exam. The doctor pointed out the labia, the clitoris, and other body parts to teach them female anatomy.

When he wasn't in school, he was working. All kids over the age of five worked for at least part of the day. The commune eventually created the accredited School Without Walls program, which allowed high school students to work full time in exchange for school credit. Dickon loved his job in Edison, the ranch's electronics department, where he worked alongside other teenage boys in a low-pressure environment, all striving toward one purpose. Although he never felt particularly attached to Bhagwan, the success of the community, which Dickon had grown to love, was an incredible motivation. Some nights he chose to work late at Edison because it was the only time he could have to himself. He would zip around the commune's roads on a bicycle late at night, listening to music on his headphones, experiencing a small taste of independence.

Nobody, including his mother, ever asked Dickon what he wanted to be when he grew up or whether he wanted to go to college. He never heard adults at the commune talking about the kids' futures. He wondered how they planned to repopulate all the highly educated sannyasin lawyers and doctors and accountants, since it seemed impossible that they would come from the ranks of the wild children of Rajneeshpuram.

A cycle kept repeating. Dickon would develop a crush on a girl his own age but then learn she was already dating somebody older. *Much* older, like guys in their thirties. "It was very common," Dickon recalled. "A lot of older guys were with younger girls."

The same was true with older women and younger boys. Dickon had his first sexual experience at age fourteen with a twenty-eight-year-old woman who lived in Bhagwan's household. He thought he was in love with her. Then he learned that she had sex with some of his teenage friends, like it was a game. The experience destroyed him. Even reflecting on it as an adult, he had complicated feelings about it. "It's hard to say I feel like I was taken advantage of or something, because at the time it was something I really wanted. But does that make it right? Does that make it not right?"

In Rajneeshpuram, adults who wanted to rape children found a place with plenty of unprotected kids and nobody who would stop them—not the commune leaders, not the adult bystanders, and not even the parents. Bob Harvey, the foreman who left the ranch in January 1983 after a pay dispute, told investigators that adults and children would come into the house he shared with his family and talk about their sexual exploits in an open and shameless way. Two men, including a disciple who cleaned Bhagwan's Rolls-Royces, bragged to Harvey about having sex with the same thirteen-year-old girl. Next door to the American writer Satya Bharti's bedroom, a history professor in his fifties shared his bed with an adolescent girl. The girl's parents seemed delighted that he was paying so much attention to her.

Dickon felt it was an open secret that adults and children were having sex at Rajneeshpuram—although it was barely a secret. Dickon maintains that the commune's leaders rarely intervened because they didn't see it as a problem—at least not a problem for the children. One night he attended a sexually charged, alcohol-fueled party in a trailer with adults and children. The children were later called into Jesus Grove, where Sheela berated them for participating in an event that could destroy the commune if people on the outside learned about it. To Dickon, she did not seem at all concerned about the children's well-being, only Rajneeshpuram's public image.

Bhagwan's long-standing philosophies about norm shattering, sexual freedom, and childhood sexual exploration had permeated his disciples' lives. He described the ages of seven to fourteen as an important period of sexual experimentation that prepared children for the next seven years, when sex would become attached to love. In the earlier phase, he wanted boys and girls to attend school together, swim together, share beds together, and be nude together, as a way to free them from harmful sexual repressions. He also wanted parents to train their young children how to have sex by allowing them to watch. "Make the place of your lovemaking a temple, so that the child from the very beginning starts feeling love is something sacred." He urged disciples to "make love a festive moment" and to allow the children to "dance around you while you are making love, sing beautiful songs around you, play on their small guitars, drums."

Another reason the sexual abuse of children could flourish at Rajneesh-puram was the profound sense of surrender that had been instilled in commune members. Everything within Bhagwan's community happened for a reason, they had been told, and their place was not to challenge. "There was a feeling that whatever happens in the community of our master is OK," Satya later explained. "It's the whole abdication of responsibility, which allowed us to put up with everything going on. You can fool yourself into believing anything if you suspend your critical judgment." Bhagwan taught them to be aware but non-judgmental, since something that seemed bad could actually be good. He once gave rape as an example. "It is not certain that raping the woman is certainly bad. Perhaps she was also waiting for it. Perhaps she was getting frustrated that nobody is raping her," he said. "All psychologists agree that a woman is raped because deep down she desires it." Even if the sexual abuse of children seemed wrong to adult sannyasins, noninterference was the expectation and the norm.

Satya Bharti refused to bring her kids to Rajneeshpuram because she felt the environment wasn't right. "If my own children were involved," she reflected, "I would have stood up and said no, you can't do this. But who knows? A lot of mothers and fathers didn't stand up."

15 | HORSE TRADING

IN MAY 1983, MA PREM KARUNA stood before a press conference she had convened at the State Capitol in Salem. She looked nothing like the stereotypical sannyasins in their early thirties with glowing skin, radiant smiles, and lithe bodies beneath their red garb. Karuna was a bit dowdy, with salt-and-pepper hair, heavy cheeks, and deep-set gray eyes. Holding a doctor of education from Boston University, the savvy New Englander had become vice president of the commune and then mayor of Antelope in November 1982. She also coordinated the Rumi Temple, where married couples rehearsed their phony answers to potential immigration questions.

And now Mayor Karuna was about to engage in an act of desperation before the gathered cameras.

The sannyasin-controlled Antelope City Council had recently proposed an $18,000 levy that would increase taxes and fees for all Antelopians, supposedly to improve services within the town. If enacted, it would drastically increase the amount that each Antelope resident would need to pay to the city. The proposed levy confirmed what the longtime residents had feared when they unsuccessfully tried to disincorporate Antelope the previous year. The sannyasins were trying to price them out of town.

But the levy didn't *need* to happen, Mayor Karuna explained to the assembled press. "We'd love to leave Antelope tomorrow and kill the [levy] on the way out," she said. But recent events had made it clear they couldn't simply walk away from town without first extracting some concessions. "We're going to be looking to Salem for some statesmen and stateswomen," Karuna said, "because we're developing very simple legislation which would solve the problem to the delight of everyone who lives in the area."

That same week, Sheela, Jayananda, and Krishna Deva had visited the office of Bob Oliver, the governor's chief legal counsel, to present a "scenario," as they termed it. If the governor would support legislation that explicitly stated that Rajneeshpuram was a properly incorporated city, the commune would call back all of its people from Antelope and sell all sannyasin-owned property in town. The legislature was at the time debating a land-use bill, and the disciples hoped to fend off any legal challenges to their city by receiving the state's endorsement in the new law.

Oliver knew it would never fly. Governor Atiyeh had previously described such deals as "an offer by someone who takes away your horse and cow, and—when you protest—offers you back your cow as a 'compromise.'" Indeed, soon after their meeting, the governor called the proposal a "blatant offer of trade," which was "the worst thing you can do to me." He would leave the fate of Rajneeshpuram to the courts, not engage in some sleazy horse trade with Antelope as the bargaining chip.

Undaunted, Jayananda blasted off a letter to nearly every local official:

> If the Oregon State legislature passes legislation this year effectively grandfathering Rajneeshpuram's existence as a city, Rajneesh Investment Corporation vows to put its properties in Antelope for sale and make all efforts to disengage from that city. It further pledges to make recommendations to the Rajneeshee community that no further development action be taken in Antelope; that all activities contemplated in Antelope be transferred to the city of Rajneeshpuram; and that the persons living in Antelope move to Rajneeshpuram as soon as possible.

The letter went to the three Wasco County commissioners, the district attorneys for Wasco and Jefferson Counties, the federal mediator from the US Department of Justice, Governor Atiyeh's top aides, and local ranchers and Antelopians, including former mayor Margaret Hill.

These very public offers were not conceived in a vacuum. They were provoked by a devastating court decision in March that threatened everything the sannyasins had built. Rajneeshpuram had sailed along in a fairly charmed way over the previous year, with the incorporation vote passing, the city installing its first government, and the community putting together an aspirational comprehensive plan that had received the blessing of the Wasco County Court. Every legal body to review the incorporation had allowed it to move forward, despite constant resistance from 1000 Friends of Oregon and local ranchers.

Opponents finally found a receptive venue for their arguments in the Oregon Court of Appeals. In March 1983, the court ruled that Wasco County's decision to authorize Rajneeshpuram's incorporation election was a land-use decision that should have gone through a rigorous process to ensure compliance with the state's planning goals. The court kicked the incorporation question back to the Land Use Board of Appeals, which had previously ruled that it had no jurisdiction over the question.

The situation worsened in May, when the state's ultimate land-use authority, the Land Conservation and Development Commission (LCDC), announced that at its June meeting it would consider a life-or-death question for the City of Rajneeshpuram. Buoyed by the court of appeals decision, 1000 Friends of Oregon persuaded LCDC to consider barring all new development at Rajneeshpuram, given the legal cloud over its incorporation. It was around this time that the disciples began using Antelope as a bargaining chip to try to secure some form of legislative protection for their city.

At their June 2, 1983, meeting, the LCDC commissioners were unpersuaded by 1000 Friends' arguments to block development at Rajneeshpuram. They would allow the sannyasins to keep building while the courts sorted everything out. Sheela lauded the commission for its "fairness, courage, and respect for the legal process" and for upholding "America's traditions of democracy and justice in the best possible way." But she changed her tune at the next LCDC meeting one month later.

"Are rules created for people or are people created for rules?" she demanded of the commission at its July meeting, barely able to spit out her vitriol because she was so angry. "Are Frankenstein created for people or people are created for Frankenstein?" The commission had just announced that it intended to adopt a framework that counties must follow in authorizing a new city, in an effort to avoid confusing situations like Rajneeshpuram and the years of litigation caused, at least in part, by the state's lack of guidance. Adopting a set of rules was not by itself problematic for the sannyasins. The problem was the rules' retroactive effective date: August 1981, three months before Wasco County had authorized the Rajneeshpuram election. The Land Use Board of Appeals was about to reconsider the Rajneeshpuram case in the coming month, and the disciples saw the retroactive rule as an effort to serve up the city's fate on a silver platter. If enacted, it would provide the board with a legal basis for declaring the city null and void, because Wasco County hadn't followed a procedure that did not exist at the time.

"The [land-use] goals were created for the people," Sheela railed at the commission, "to make their lives more comfortable. But what I understand now is that people's lives are not important." KD and the city's attorneys argued that there was no emergency at hand that required such an extraordinary measure and that the proposal was a blatant act of discrimination against the sannyasins.

Despite these arguments, the commission adopted the retroactive rules on a 4–3 vote. In the July meeting's wake, Sheela leveled her fury at 1000 Friends of Oregon, which she claimed had plotted behind the scenes with LCDC. "Thousand Friends should be named KKK," she told a reporter. "In the name of land use they are conducting a religious crusade against us."

But the sannyasins were not idiots, nor were they ever passive victims. The new rules included a loophole that allowed a county to grandfather in an existing city on rural land, considering factors such as the size and extent of commercial and industrial uses on the property. Rajneeshpuram immediately announced a $3.5 million building blitz that would include a new security building, a tourist reception center, a 62,000-square-foot factory, another cafeteria with outdoor seating for 15,000 people, an 8,000-square-foot recreation hall, and a 72-unit hotel with a 2.5-acre parking lot. To provide room for all this new construction, the Rajneeshpuram City Council approved a plan to annex 103 acres of additional ranch land into the city limits. City planner Deva Wadud claimed that all the construction would happen quickly so they could proceed under cover during the cold winter months. He denied that it had anything to do with further entrenching themselves on the land before the Land Use Board of Appeals applied the new retroactive rules to Rajneeshpuram.

The grueling building bonanza that would take place during the fall of 1983 would be the very last time the sannyasins had the power to do any further major development on their land.

16 | ROOM 405

THE SUN WAS JUST BEGINNING to dip behind the Cascades on July 27, 1983, when a yellow Volkswagen station wagon entered the ranch from Antelope. After passing the enormous reservoir and Krishnamurti Dam, the vehicle dipped into the flattest part of the valley, where the sannyasin settlement stretched out ahead. It drove past the Rajneesh Meditation University on the right and alongside the airstrip before reaching the commune's nexus, the Jesus Grove area, where it finally came to a stop.

Three men got out and walked into the welcome center, two White, one Black, all in their twenties or thirties, from their dress clearly not sannyasins. Despite the late hour, a hostess—one of the commune's famous "Twinkies"—was there to greet them, although she had to deliver the bad news that at 7:30 PM there wasn't anything for guests to do at the ranch. No more public tours, no meditation groups, and dinner had already been served. The men insisted they had cleared their visit in advance. They wanted to take a one-day meditation course starting the next morning.

The Twinkie called over to the meditation university, which had been erected ahead of the summer festival. Now that the thousands of festivalgoers were gone, the university was offering visiting disciples and curious civilians the opportunity to stay at the ranch for multiday spiritual courses. Although they didn't offer a one-day meditation course, the university said it would be OK to send the men over.

Next came the security protocols. On his entry paperwork, the man who seemed to be the leader of the trio wrote down his name: Stephen Walker.

The Twinkie didn't ask him for proof of his identity—one of many security gaps that would soon be remedied. He handed over his car keys so the security force could move the Volkswagen to an undisclosed parking area, where the guests would not be able to access it during their visit.

The moment of truth arrived when a member of the Rajneeshpuram Peace Force—the city's equivalent of a police force—came to search them, along with a German shepherd, Bear, who was trained to sniff for drugs. The officer glanced at their luggage but didn't dig into it. He glanced at their vehicle but didn't search it. When federal investigators asked the officer about it a few days later, he noted how odd it was that Stephen Walker and his companions didn't have much luggage, since Walker said they had driven up all the way from Los Angeles. They had only a couple of duffel bags.

Without their car, the visitors were at the mercy of commune transportation to get them around the sprawling property. A Rajneesh taxi drove them back to the meditation university near the commune's entrance, where they registered for the courses they would take the next day. When offered a choice between a tent and a room at the newly erected on-site hotel, they took the tent, at thirty dollars per person for the night.

Despite their long day on the road, all three men were up, exploring, moving about the ranch, late into the night. Disciples spotted them at 10 PM in the Rajneesh Tea Room drinking coffee and asking about the thing they had signed up to do at sunrise the next morning: Dynamic Meditation. An hour later, the Twinkie saw them using a ranch pay phone. And just before midnight, the peace officer noted them walking the barren roads that connected the distant buildings. A few minutes later, the taxi driver who had taken them to the university happened upon them. He urged the men to go to bed, since there was nothing to do at the commune at such a late hour.

Nobody saw Stephen Walker or his companions again that night. Nobody could say how long they wandered the dusty roads of Rajneeshpuram, or where they went, or what they did.

They were at Dynamic Meditation the next morning at the massive Rajneesh Mandir assembly hall, jumping around like mad men and chanting "HOO HOO HOO." Afterward, they walked the two miles back to the university, forgoing the free buses that could have driven them around the ranch. There wasn't much reason to walk, nothing really to see in that area except Sheela's private compound, surrounded by a barbed-wire fence.

When they finally made it to the university, they said they had forgotten something in their car. The disciple staffing the desk made a big to-do about it. If they wanted to go to their vehicle, they'd need to wait at the welcome center for somebody who could drive them out to the parking area. And, she added, they would be accompanied by a sannyasin guard.

The men did not go back to their car. At least, not with any sannyasin.

During a midday bus tour of the ranch, Stephen Walker was seen carrying a brown bag. Later that day, the men took a horse ride around the property. Something about the visitors put the sannyasin tour guide on edge. When investigators asked her about it later, she couldn't really describe it—it was just an instinct. She cut down her usual ninety-minute tour to one hour, without telling the men.

Early that evening, Stephen Walker and his companions and the duffel bags were on a bus back to the welcome center. They told the driver they had run out of money and it was time to get back to Los Angeles. The driver mentioned that the sannyasins owned a hotel in downtown Portland. If they were interested, the men could spend the night there on their way home.

Stephen Walker was interested.

As soon as the visitors were reunited with their car, they were gone. The threat they posed to the sannyasin community was not.

———

Before 1983, non-sannyasins could not have simply driven into Rajneeshpuram and expected to stay. Other than a short tour offered at set times throughout the day, the ranch had no public facilities and no accommodations to host visitors. Nor were the disciples very interested in having outsiders prowling about their property and scrutinizing their construction, their practices, or their immigrant-heavy labor force. But with the incorporation of Rajneeshpuram, the commune members had been able to issue their own building permits and get to work creating the resort-like facilities they had imagined in their comprehensive plan. As these new facilities were completed, the commune made itself more visible, more useful, and more accessible to outsiders.

Although there was plenty of money to be made in hosting visitors, another reason for these new facilities was public relations. The sannyasins' first couple of years in America had been rocky, to say the least, with many Oregonians viewing them as a dangerous cult that employed aggressive and deceptive tactics. Sheela and Mayor Krishna Deva saw that Rajneeshpuram could be their best marketing tool, allowing outsiders to experience all the miracles they had created in the desert and proving they had nothing to fear from their carefree neighbors.

The meditation university offered an introductory course called A Weekend Away from It All. For seventy-five dollars, a visitor could spend three days and two nights at the ranch, doing Dynamic Meditation in the morning, touring the facilities, learning sannyasin humming, singing, and dancing, and watching Bhagwan drive by in a Rolls-Royce. The university added longer courses lasting up to three months, with options such as bodywork, energy work, dance, encounter-group techniques, meditations, and more. University coordinators assured interested parties that there would be no pressure on them to take sannyas or wear sunrise colors.

At the same time they were inviting visitors to spend time at the ranch, the sannyasins were also opening businesses in Oregon that helped put a positive face on their movement. They also helped bring in money, which was a spiritual matter for the disciples of Bhagwan Shree Rajneesh, who expected them to be productive and profitable. The commercial expansion started close to home, in Antelope, where sannyasins had opened the Zorba the Buddha Rajneesh Restaurant in 1982. Inside, diners could order an avocado-and-sprout sandwich while thumbing through one of the many spiritual books on display. In October 1982, the commune made its first foray into Portland, with Zorba the Buddha Bakery downtown. The bakery was an outgrowth of the First Annual World Celebration, where the commune's kitchen had cranked out high-quality breads, cakes, cookies, and other pastries for more than five thousand people.

Two months later, they opened Zorba the Buddha Nightclub and Restaurant just blocks away from the Portland bakery. Built in a former Greek restaurant, the club served up Italian and Mexican food, a full bar, disco music, and live sannyasin bands. Sheela and Jayananda hosted the lavish opening-night party for three hundred invited guests—mainly political allies and business partners. Sheela's old rival from Krishna House, the no-nonsense Dutch woman Arup, took the stage to belt out a medley of up-tempo ballads. Sheela joined a belly dancer in gyrating across the room. The night ended with a disco dance party on the flashing floor, accompanied by syncopated strobe lights dashing off the mirrored walls as dry ice swirled among the revelers. The commune claimed that within a month of opening, the club had "taken off as one of the city's most popular entertainment spots," packing in 250 people on the dance floor on a typical Friday night.

In January 1983, the sannyasins showed how serious they were about establishing a foothold in Portland when they purchased the Martha Washington Hotel for $1.4 million. The historic building had 127 rooms, an expansive lobby, a lounge, a library, a rec room, a kitchen, and full dining facilities. Their main interest in having such a large hotel in such a prime location was to secure a base of operations for all their Portland businesses and to accommodate the sannyasins who worked in them. Since nobody wanted to be away from the Buddhafield for very long, the commune would cycle workers into Portland for a couple of weeks at a time. By the summer of 1983, the hotel had become an outreach and recruiting center for the neo-sannyas movement, offering evening meditations and Bhagwan's discourse videos five nights a week and a daylong meditation program on Saturdays.

While the Hotel Rajneesh was open to the public, one didn't often find non-sannyasins staying there. Perhaps they were put off by the relatively high room rates, or the commune's controversial reputation, or the perpetually smiling disciples in their red business attire and mala necklaces who greeted guests at the reception desk and filled their coffee cups and scrubbed their toilets. Or perhaps it was the guru's omnipresence. Photographs of Bhagwan hung throughout the lobby, his books were prominently on display, and songs celebrating him played over the sound system.

The man showed up by himself at the Hotel Rajneesh after midnight on July 29, asking if there were any rooms available. To the night clerk, he looked sort of sloppy: in his midthirties, with stubble across his face, wearing a wrinkled red T-shirt and jeans. He was carrying a single blue bag. He signed the registry as Stephen Walker.

He said he had to grab something from his car and came back a few minutes later with a brown bag. He told the clerk he'd be leaving soon to get something to eat. With his two bags, Stephen Walker rode the elevator up to Room 405.

The blast came half an hour later.

The night clerk raced outside, hoping to catch a glimpse of whatever had caused it. He scanned the buildings nearby, looked up and down the street, but he couldn't see anything. Then he hurried to the corner, where he saw two men standing near a mess of broken glass on the street. *Your hotel just exploded*, one of them said.

The clerk followed their gazes up. Smoke billowed out through shattered windows on the fourth floor of the Hotel Rajneesh.

The blast had awakened a hotel guest in Room 411. As he jumped up from his bed, he heard somebody shouting, *Help! Please help me!*

The smell of burning flesh overwhelmed him as he reached the hallway. He and another guest found the room where the man was screaming. Together they kicked in the door. To their immediate left, the bathroom door had been blasted off its hinges. A man lay on the tiles, covered in blood. The room reeked of gunpowder and was filled with dark gray smoke. They carried the man to the elevator and then the lobby. Along the way, they saw that his hair was melted, he had blood in his eye sockets, and he'd sustained wounds all over his face and chest. But the worst injuries were on his hands, which one bystander described as "demolished."

In the lobby, they laid him on the floor and covered his wounds with a sheet while they waited for an ambulance to arrive. The night clerk recognized the victim: Stephen Walker, who had just gone up to Room 405 with his two duffel bags.

Get me out of this building! Walker screamed from the floor.

Medical personnel arrived and transported Walker to the hospital. By that point, police officers, firefighters, guests, and hotel workers swarmed in the lobby. Many people went up to the fourth floor to check out the damage. The night clerk peered through the door of Room 405 and saw Walker's brown bag sitting on the floor. A police officer finally instructed everyone except emergency personnel to wait downstairs in the lobby, and a detective sealed off the room and the hallway.

Three officers remained on the fourth floor. They found a quiet spot around the corner to smoke and drink some coffee.

The second blast in Room 405 came one hour after the first.

And then came another.

Agents from the Portland bomb squad and the federal Bureau of Alcohol, Tobacco, and Firearms visited Stephen Walker at Emanuel Hospital shortly after he arrived. He seemed rattled, but stable, and had some difficulty hearing their questions. He clammed up and demanded a lawyer, but not before telling them that he had been a guest at Rajneeshpuram for the past two days. Officers seized his wallet and found a California driver's license that identified him as Stephen Paul Paster.

That night, detectives traveled to Rajneeshpuram and began to interview anybody who had seen Paster and his two companions while they were guests there. In the midst of their investigation, the Rajneeshpuram Peace Force chief begged them to ask Paster whether he had planted any bombs at the ranch, even though he had already invoked his right to remain silent. The commune's security force had been searching the grounds and hadn't found anything, but the visitors could have covered a lot of ground overnight at the ranch.

A bomb squad detective returned to the hospital and explained to Paster that human life was at stake, so he was going to continue to question him outside the presence of a lawyer. He urged Paster to reveal whether there were any more bombs planted at the ranch. The detective said their only goal was to deactivate any remaining devices and make the ranch safe. He promised not to charge Paster for any additional devices, as long as he disclosed them.

There is nothing planted at the ranch, Paster said. *You have my word on it.*

The investigation revealed that Paster had brought three pipe bombs into the Hotel Rajneesh in his two duffel bags. Each bomb had been packed with low-explosive material and armed with a quartz timer. He placed the first bomb underneath the twin bed closest to the bathroom and surrounded it with a sludgy homemade incendiary material known as fire fudge. He placed the second bomb inside the closet near the hallway door. And then he placed the third bomb in the bathroom medicine cabinet. The bombs under the bed and in the closet were apparently set up the way Paster intended, but he was in the process of arming the third bomb when it blew up in his face.

Police found the remains of the first pipe bomb—the one that had been placed under the bed—in Room 305, one story down. It had blasted a hole in the floor. Fortunately, the entire third floor was vacant. It's also fortunate that nobody happened to be in Paster's room when the second and third blasts occurred. The many people who walked in and around the area in the hour after the first blast had no idea that they were mere inches from an armed firebomb.

Paster lost six fingers and suffered permanent eye and ear injuries from the blast. State prosecutors charged him with three counts of first-degree arson. His wife flew up from California and posted his bond, just $2,000, and they disappeared before he stood trial. He later said that he fled the state because unidentified people had constantly followed him while he was out on bail. This was true. The commune had sent disciples to stake him out before his trial.

A year and a half later, law enforcement found Paster hiding in Colorado and extradited him back to Oregon. At his Colorado apartment, investigators discovered manuals for urban guerrilla warfare and instructions and materials for making improvised explosive devices. They had found similar items at his Los Angeles apartment, which a prosecutor described as a "bomb workshop."

After deliberating for one hour, a Portland jury convicted Paster of first-degree arson in October 1985. The prosecutor didn't offer a motive for the attack on the Hotel Rajneesh, although he did introduce evidence that Paster was involved with a violent fundamentalist Muslim sect, Jamaat Al-Fuqra, which had bombed two Hindu centers in Seattle while he was a fugitive in the Oregon case. At the sentencing hearing, a clinical psychologist hired by the defense testified that Paster had fallen out with his stepfather, whose neglect of Paster's Jewish religious education had supposedly led him to convert to Islam. "Religion became a real good way of acting out some of his anger and frustration toward his stepfather," the psychologist testified. She also suggested that Paster had transferred his anger at his stepfather to Bhagwan Shree Rajneesh, whom he considered to be a failed leader.

Paster ended up serving just four years of his twenty-year sentence, after which he moved to Pakistan, where he reportedly still provides explosives training to members of Jamaat Al-Fuqra. The two men who accompanied Paster to Rajneeshpuram were never found. Law enforcement never determined whether they brought bombs to Rajneeshpuram, and, if so, why they didn't plant or detonate them there.

The hotel bombing on July 29, 1983, had a profound impact on Bhagwan's beleaguered community. By extending themselves to outsiders, Bhagwan's disciples ended up closing themselves off even more. The front page of the *Rajneesh Times* called the bombing "the product of a pervasive atmosphere of prejudice that has been steadily increasing in Oregon and spreading out beyond the state's borders." After the bombing, Sheela drastically increased security at the ranch and the Hotel Rajneesh in Portland. All visitors would be subjected to rigorous searches of their persons, their property, and their vehicles. Guard posts went up from the "Top of the Ranch" closest to Antelope to downtown Rajneeshpuram to the John Day River, from which disciples watched for trespassers and monitored cars passing along the county highway. A new administrative center, the security temple, was created, with as many as 150 sannyasins trained to fight to the death if needed. And suddenly guns were everywhere at the ranch.

But the most invasive new security protocol would be invisible to nearly every disciple at the commune. Days after the hotel bombing, Sheela called in a furtive British sannyasin named Swami Anand Julian for a meeting. Julian ran the powerful Edison Temple and coordinated all electronics at the commune—televisions, video and audio recording, tape duplication, appliances, and whatever other odd projects might come up.

Sheela had a new odd project for Julian. Their enemies were serious about harming them, it was clear, and the commune needed a better way to protect its property, its people, and its resident guru. Sheela needed a spymaster.

17 | GOD VERSUS THE UNIVERSE

"CONGRATULATIONS ON SCREWING US, and good luck with your political career," Sheela seethed to the director of the Land Conservation and Development Commission in September 1983. The commission had just approved a decision from the Land Use Board of Appeals that applied the new retroactive rules to Rajneeshpuram. The board had determined that Wasco County hadn't followed the correct procedures—which hadn't existed at the time—when it allowed Rajneeshpuram to incorporate. The case would go back to Wasco County for another whack at the question of whether or not the city should exist. Sheela was furious at what she saw as a government conspiracy to destroy her community.

Wasco County's political landscape had changed significantly since the judges had approved Rajneeshpuram's incorporation two years earlier. The sannyasins had become loathed in Central Oregon for their aggressive rhetoric and high-handed maneuvers. When the county court took up the new legal challenge, there was every possibility that it would vote to wipe Rajneeshpuram off the map.

Before the judges could even consider the question, though, a judge on the Wasco County Circuit Court—a traditional judicial court, distinct from the Wasco County Court that ran the county government—halted nearly all development in Rajneeshpuram. Attorneys for 1000 Friends of Oregon persuaded the judge that the board's decision meant that the sannyasins had no authority to control development on their property. The injunction brought the commune's construction blitz from the past two months to a grinding halt.

A permanent injunction followed three weeks later. The circuit court ruled that Rajneeshpuram should be treated like an unincorporated area in Wasco

County while sannyasins appealed, meaning the county had complete authority over land-use decisions on the ranch. The injunction essentially froze the city of Rajneeshpuram as of October 1983. Whatever development the disciples had managed to cram into the previous year would remain in place, virtually unchanged, for the rest of the city's troubled existence.

As catastrophic as the injunction was, perhaps most alarming to the sannyasins was the betrayal it revealed. For the first time in the lengthy land-use litigation, officials from Wasco County had sided with 1000 Friends in seeking the injunction. Before that, the county had remained largely neutral when it came to Rajneeshpuram's fate, but county officials now seemed emboldened by LCDC's retroactive rules. The Wasco County planning director, Dan Durow, wasted no time in driving out to the ranch to conduct a full inventory of all the existing buildings and to photograph incomplete projects.

The commune struck back by threatening to sue the Wasco County Court for $80 million if the county interfered in its development plans or if the city's incorporation were determined to be illegal. "Quite simply stated," the claim read, "the county said go ahead and build it, and now years and millions of dollars later is saying, 'We made a mistake, but you will have to pay for it.'"

This perceived betrayal in the fall of 1983 would mark the beginning of a war between the disciples and the Wasco County government, one that would provoke commune leaders to strike with venom in the coming year.

Around the same time that the injunction was issued, a new antagonist stepped into the spotlight: Oregon attorney general Dave Frohnmayer. Over the preceding months, the attorney general's office had been paying careful attention to the very public rise of Rajneeshism, which the sannyasins had used to attack the INS for its treatment of Bhagwan's case. In June, a state representative had asked Frohnmayer's office to issue a formal opinion on the legality of the City of Rajneeshpuram receiving state funds when it seemed to be run, from top to bottom, by a self-described church.

Just two years into his term, Frohnmayer was seen as a rising star in Republican political circles and was widely expected to run for governor when Vic Atiyeh's term expired in 1987. A native Oregonian, Frohnmayer graduated magna cum laude from Harvard, attended Oxford on a Rhodes Scholarship, and received his law degree from the University of California, Berkeley. After serving three terms in the Oregon House of Representatives, Frohnmayer was elected the state's attorney general and took office in January 1981, six months before the disciples of Bhagwan Shree Rajneesh first descended into the valleys of Central Oregon.

Although Frohnmayer had minimal engagement with the sannyasins during their first two years in Oregon, the creation of Rajneeshism offered a perfect hook for the attorney general to take a closer look. The new religion may have helped to bolster Bhagwan's immigration case, but it also exposed a flaw in the conceit of a sannyasin-owned and sannyasin-operated municipality. The very first words of the First Amendment to the US Constitution prohibit the government from making any law respecting the establishment of religion. A clause in the Oregon Constitution bars the state from using money to benefit any religious institution. These clauses formed the legal foundation for Attorney General Frohnmayer's October 1983 opinion. Based on "known and assumed facts," he determined that the state could not lawfully send any funds to the City of Rajneeshpuram because it would only benefit the Church of Rajneeshism.

The crux of the problem was the way the Rajneesh organizations were set up and operated. With Sheela as president, the Rajneesh Foundation International (RFI) ran Bhagwan's spiritual empire—the commune, the book publishing and distribution, the festivals, and guiding meditation centers and businesses around the world. RFI was a nonprofit, tax-exempt organization known as "the Church." RFI had a wholly owned subsidiary, the Rajneesh Investment Corporation, that owned the $4.5 million mortgage on the Big Muddy Ranch and everything on it. Another RFI subsidiary was the Rajneesh Neo-Sannyas International Commune, which operated virtually everything on the ranch: the farming, cafeterias, restaurants, hotel, stores, transportation, and more.

The City of Rajneeshpuram threw a wrench into this corporate structure when it emerged in late 1982. The city, a unit of public government, was run entirely by sannyasins. It sat on property owned and operated by Church subsidiaries. Nobody could buy land in the city, and only invited disciples could live there. These facts set Rajneeshpuram apart from, say, Salt Lake City, where the Mormon church predominated but non-Mormons could still purchase property and live within the city limits.

Frohnmayer opined that a court would find that the Church of Rajneeshism and the City of Rajneeshpuram were one and the same. Any state funds going to Rajneeshpuram would thus be supporting a religion, in violation of the state and federal constitutions. But the most dangerous part of the attorney general's opinion came at the end. Although he hadn't been asked to reach this question, Frohnmayer noted that the mere *existence* of a city like Rajneeshpuram was unconstitutional. He promised to fully investigate the facts, verify the assumptions undergirding the opinion, and seek relief from a court if it all checked out.

The state representative who had originally requested the opinion was elated. "I believe this is the beginning of the end of Rajneeshpuram," he told his hometown newspaper.

He was right.

———————————

The threat of Frohnmayer's lawsuit was a bomb detonated in a minefield, creating yet another front in the sannyasins' ongoing war with seemingly everybody around them. Sheela rallied her staff to head off the case before the attorney general could file suit. Mayor Krishna Deva bombarded his office with notarized statements from key commune members—including Sheela and KD himself—trying to dispute the facts assumed in the opinion. A person reading the statements might get the impression that the City of Rajneeshpuram was an independent entity that just happened to be located on the Big Muddy Ranch. The affidavits went to great lengths to make clear that Sheela, the head of the Church, had nothing to do with the running of the City. Sheela swore that she "never attempted to influence any official of the City of Rajneeshpuram." KD similarly swore that the Church had never "interfered with nor tried to influence the City government," and that the City "operates as a separate entity from any other entity or corporation located within it."

Sheela, KD, and others would later confess that these were lies. Sheela in fact ran everything at the ranch, including the city government, and some disciples said this control went all the way up to Bhagwan himself. Krishna Deva had become mayor only because Sheela and Bhagwan had chosen him and because he rigged the city elections. As mayor, KD took his direction not from the voters but from his boss, Sheela, the Pope of Rajneeshism, who received her marching orders from the mystic on the hill.

If the investigators wanted to see a glaring example of Sheela controlling everything at the ranch, they need only have attended the Antelope School Board meeting two days after Frohnmayer issued his opinion.

The tiny Lincoln School in Antelope had become a flashpoint for local controversy in the fall of 1983. Although Rajneeshpuram sat within the Antelope School District, the commune's children had been receiving their education at the ranch. That left the Lincoln School in Antelope to the non-sannyasin residents, whose K–8 children attended school there and whose high school students were bused to the town of Madras fifty miles away. In September 1983, after some disputes over school levies, commune attorneys identified an obscure law that allowed them to eject all non-sannyasins from the Antelope School Board, which left only Rajneeshpuram city planner Deva Wadud in place. Wadud promptly fired all non-sannyasins working at the Lincoln School, replaced them with disciples, and announced that sannyasin children would now attend the school. He also declared that the school board would no longer pay to bus any students to Madras, since the Lincoln School would offer a world-class K–12 education.

This culminated in a standoff at the October 1983 school board meeting, held at Rajneeshpuram before a board that was now exclusively sannyasin, including Jayananda and Krishna Deva. A contingent of Antelope parents explained their concerns about having their students attend the new sannyasin-run school. Wadud, in a maroon sweater and close-cropped beard, became so furious at one mother's persistent questions about the decision to terminate busing to Madras that he slammed his gavel on the table and ordered her out of the room.

As tempers flared, somebody must have called Sheela. She stalked in and took a chair at the front of the room, right next to the school board, looking like she had just rolled out of bed in a dowdy pink sweatshirt and messy hair. She locked her dark-circled eyes onto the board members and leveled her fury at them for allowing the Antelope parents to waste the board's time with all their negativity.

"They don't know what superior education is!" she shouted at the board members, who stared rigidly back at her. "Margaret Hill was a teacher," she said, referencing the former mayor of Antelope, who was not in attendance. "Look at her face now. She looks retarded." Sheela next brought up some Antelope students who had complained about the Lincoln School takeover on the evening news. "I saw three students on the television," she said. "Not just parents were retarded, but students were absolutely retarded. They looked like"—she grunted and pretended to drool, her tongue lolling out of her mouth, a condition, she said, that was caused by the poor education they had received at the Lincoln School.

Finally, Sheela unloaded on an Antelope parent in the very back row who had recently said in an interview that sannyasins "control what little bit of life we have left." Two months before the meeting, the woman's husband had been removing a rifle from the back of his pickup truck when it discharged and shot him in the throat. He died at the scene, just outside Antelope, while his two sons watched.

"I tell you one more fact," Sheela said to the school board, in front of the crowd. "Her husband shot himself because he was screwing around with another man, if the board wants to know. She might want to tell her children the honest truth." A news camera panned to the widow in the back row, hunched forward, her mouth wrenched open in silent agony. Her sons took her by the arms and helped her out the back door.

A reporter later pressed Sheela on why she would make such a vicious public comment about a grieving widow when it had nothing to do with the school board's business. "Calling a spade a spade may hurt, but it opens the eyes, too. She should be honest with her own children. She's talking about children right now [at the meeting]."

Sheela looked into the camera. "I'm an honest person, and that has been taught to me by Bhagwan Shree Rajneesh."

Her ad hominem attacks would have little legal importance to Attorney General Frohnmayer and his staff. But Sheela did something far more damning before she stormed out of the meeting in a huff. "Answer from the board!" she barked, glaring at Deva Wadud and the other members. "Are you going to put up with this nonsense? I have meetings lined up. I have people waiting for me, and I'm wasting time. I would like the board to pass a resolution that any negative calls coming from anybody, they should not engage."

Sheela was not on the school board. She wasn't even a school district voter, as a foreign citizen. Still, the board unanimously passed the resolution that she had just dictated to them. It was exactly the sort of top-down control that the attorney general had referenced in his opinion two days earlier. The disciples tried to cloak themselves in the trappings of electoral and administrative power, but they took their orders from the pope.

Attorney General Frohnmayer filed his lawsuit on November 9, 1983, in the Wasco County Circuit Court, seeking a declaratory judgment that the City of Rajneeshpuram's incorporation was null and void as an unconstitutional merger of church and state. At the same time, the governor's office authorized state agencies to withhold funds from the City of Rajneeshpuram until the courts determined whether the city was legal—a move that infuriated Krishna Deva. "From the tone of KD's voice," attorney Bob Oliver noted to the governor after a tense phone call on this topic, "it is possible to surmise there may not be perfect harmony in the hierarchy."

The Frohnmayer litigation would span multiple state and federal courts and many procedural setbacks over the coming years. It was a remarkable thing: a state was trying to use the Constitution to wipe one of its own cities off the map—a city that had been duly incorporated by the official acts of an elected county government, a city with more than one thousand residents in 1983. The case would become an existential sword hanging over the necks of the sannyasins for the remainder of their time in Oregon, always leaving them just one court decision away from being obliterated.

Their hotel had just been firebombed. A judge had barred any development on their property. The attorney general, Wasco County, and the state's land-use regulators were all taking active measures to eliminate the city altogether. Sannyasin marriages were under scrutiny for an immigration fraud scheme, and the INS had already made clear its desire to eject Bhagwan Shree Rajneesh from America. The likelihood that sannyasins could overcome all of these major threats, from nearly every branch of law enforcement and regulatory control, was extraordinarily slim.

Against this backdrop in late 1983, a bold new commitment arose among Rajneeshpuram's top coordinators. Since everything on the outside seemed tilted against them, they would need to take exceptional measures to protect themselves, their commune, and their master. It was time to start fighting back—even if that meant bending or breaking the law.

"The whole state wants to screw around with the Rajneeshees," Sheela fumed during public testimony on their land-use battles in December. "It won't happen. The Rajneeshees will outsmart you."

PART IV
OREGON, 1984

The county road from Antelope into Rajneeshpuram. *© Ted Quackenbush / Wikimedia Commons*

PART IV

OREGON, 1984

18 | THE SPOOK

MA AVA, A YOUNG MEXICAN AMERICAN DISCIPLE from California, was tending bar at Zorba the Buddha Nightclub and Restaurant in Portland when a high-priority order came in. She mixed the cocktail and sent it to the restaurant upstairs. Later that night, she was surprised to find herself face-to-face with the Queen of Rajneeshpuram. Sheela had come downstairs to thank her for making what she called the best margarita she'd ever had.

At the time, Ava was just one of the many disciples who wanted little more than to live and worship in the Buddhafield and be close to Bhagwan. She'd stayed off the radar of the so-called Big Moms—the women who ran the largest departments at the ranch—and she certainly hadn't expected to come to Sheela's attention by slinging drinks a couple of weeks each month in Portland. But Sheela had a passion for quality cocktails, and now she had her eye on young Ava. From then on, anytime Sheela passed through Portland—which was often in 1983—Ava would rush to the bar to make her famous margarita for Bhagwan's personal secretary.

She became known as a utility player in Portland, serving as a cook, bartender, or whatever else the coordinators needed. And then Ava became *the* coordinator. For whatever reason, commune leaders tapped her over the summer of 1983 to manage the Hotel Rajneesh, making her the de facto boss of all Rajneesh industries in Portland and the hundred-plus sannyasins staffing them. She was twenty-two years old and had never managed anything.

Ava was at the Hotel Rajneesh in the early morning hours of July 29, 1983, when a loud explosion sent her rocketing out of her bed and down to the lobby, where she found a burned-up man on the ground with mangled hands. In the wake of the attack, she had to evacuate the building, coordinate with law enforcement, talk to the press, and later implement rigorous new security protocols for hotel visitors. For all this work, she received high praise from Sheela and commune president Vidya. Bhagwan even sent her a personal message telling her that he was proud of her, along with a wristwatch.

By early 1984, Ava's services were required at the ranch, and her days of commuting to Portland were over. She became the assistant to Ma Anand Puja, the licensed nurse practitioner who had tended to Chinmaya in his last days and who now ran the Rajneesh Medical Corporation. Around the same time, Ava received another bewildering work assignment: Sheela inducted her into an elite security force she had created to protect Bhagwan's life. Originally called "the 24," and then upped to "the 38," the group comprised sannyasins whom Sheela deemed to be the fiercest and most loyal people at the ranch, who would be willing to take the law into their own hands if necessary to protect Bhagwan.

And then Sheela asked Ava to buy an Uzi.

———————

Enemies, enemies, enemies. The sannyasins' enemies were circling the commune in early 1984, just waiting for their opportunity to crush the life out of Bhagwan's community. With the hotel bombing, the attorney general's investigation, the INS challenges to sannyasin marriages, and aggressive locals, a siege mentality was evolving among commune members, with Sheela stoking the fires of paranoia by warning them about spies infiltrating their ranks and government gunships that would swoop in to arrest Bhagwan. She made clear in public statements and at commune meetings that the sannyasins would not sit idly by while hostile forces tried to bulldoze them. They would fight back.

Before the hotel bombing, there had been only a couple of guns at the ranch: a shotgun in Sheela's house, a concealed pistol that Jayananda carried to protect his wife, and some guns that the Rajneeshpuram Peace Force had acquired for its officers. But after Stephen Paster firebombed the hotel, the commune's arsenal grew to include dozens of Uzis, Galil and AR15 rifles, .357 Magnum revolvers, tear-gas grenades, and riot guns with barricade-penetrating shells. The commune purchased these weapons lawfully via the Peace Force and through individual disciples, like Ava, who dutifully went to USIA Weapons in Portland and bought an Uzi for $300 under her legal name.

The number of sannyasins responsible for the commune's security drastically increased after the bombing. Anyone providing security—the city's small police force, the much larger Rajneesh Security team, and the exclusive "38" who were supposed to protect Bhagwan's life—received regular weapons training from an Israeli commando at a firing range so far from the main settlement that some disciples had no idea it existed until the press reported it. They practiced techniques like sneaking up on targets and using camouflage, and they rehearsed more complex tactical missions like what to do if Bhagwan's life were in danger.

To members of the various security forces, threats to the commune were not hypothetical. Locals had brandished guns at Sheela and fired guns near Bhagwan's convoy. Ranchers had shown up at public meetings wearing bullets around their necks. Angry deer hunters had shot at a security guard when he stopped them from trespassing. "Nobody is going to come in and destroy us," a Dutch sannyasin in Rajneesh Security told the Oregonian, "and we're not going to be like the Jews, you know, and just get slaughtered."

A show of force through weapons would help dissuade their enemies, but Sheela also insisted that the commune needed a better handle on what was happening within its borders. Days after the July 1983 hotel bombing, she tapped Swami Julian to become her spymaster. Julian was already the technology mastermind for the entire ranch, known to be an inscrutable, confident, meticulously organized disciple. With his slender frame, heavy bags under his eyes, and limp brown hair down to his shoulders, Julian looked like a shifty character from a spy novel. Some of the kids who worked with him in Edison Temple even called him the Spook, although they in fact worshipped him. He became a de facto father to some of the boys, perhaps trying to ensure they didn't have the same sort of rough childhood that he did growing up fatherless in an English mining town.

Julian was a fixture in Jesus Grove, one of the very few men to penetrate the uppermost level of the commune's management. He distinguished himself among Sheela's closest lieutenants as supportive of her wildest and most dangerous ideas. People who worked for him got the sense that he never wanted them to have the full picture of what they were doing or why—particularly as he became involved in the commune's security after the hotel bombing.

Stephen Paul Paster had walked among them, eaten alongside them, and meditated in their temple without anybody realizing the danger in their midst. That couldn't happen again. Sheela told Julian to select two people from Edison to form his undercover spy team. They would have to do their regular worship to avoid attracting attention, but in their "spare time" they would clandestinely help secure the commune. Julian chose two young men who had worked with him since Pune and whom he trusted. Swami Rajesh from Virginia was an electronics whiz who could do anything with stereos, radios, and wiring. French Canadian Swami Anand Michel had studied electrical engineering and psychology in Quebec and had worked as a Rajneesh computer programmer. Julian gave them a special room in the top floor of the Zarathustra warehouse to serve as their secret workshop for building surveillance devices and storing their books and equipment. While other Edison employees did their aboveboard worship in Zarathustra, like duplicating audio and video tapes, photocopying, repairing telephones, and programming computerized systems, Rajesh and Michel disappeared into their locked room and hatched covert operations. They fell into natural roles: Rajesh as the mission organizer and surveillance operative, and Michel crafting whatever gadgets they needed.

Julian told them—and Rajesh and Michel believed—that surveillance was essential for the safety of both the commune and Bhagwan. If people with ill intentions passed through the commune's open doors, the disciples needed a dedicated team to suss them out before they could launch an attack. Rajesh and Michel's initial assignment was to track and record suspicious people who visited the ranch, but their casual street surveillance soon gave way to more invasive measures.

Four months after the bombing, Julian sent Rajesh to the Alan Watts Grove residential area. The grove was littered with quadriplexes—large platforms that supported four small A-frame cabins around two shared bathrooms in the center. The commune's on-site factory cranked out up to seven A-frames per day on an assembly line. Each cabin included a single window, a heater and air-conditioning unit, cupboard storage space, and shag carpeting. They weren't exactly luxury living, but many disciples saw the A-frames as improvements over the tents and mobile homes that had marked the ranch's first year. Visitors to the ranch could also pay to stay in the "mountain cabins."

Julian directed Rajesh to go to an unoccupied quadriplex, Alan Watts A-4, and bug each of the four cabins there. He said it had something to do with ranch security, and Rajesh knew better than to ask questions. He pulled out wooden panels near the windows in each cabin, installed microphones on the beams behind them, and ran concealed wires from A-4 to another nearby quadriplex that would serve as the listening post for monitoring and recording the bugged cabins.

Immediately after Rajesh finished his rush job, three commune visitors spent the night in Alan Watts A-4. Two of them were known to be Sunni Muslims, and the third man had previously created a disturbance during one of Bhagwan's drive-bys. The next morning, a trusted Jesus Grove aide delivered a tape to Sheela from the listening post. The visitors had spoken in their room about bombing Bhagwan's Rolls-Royce during his daily drive. It confirmed to Sheela and her inner circle that eavesdropping on guests would need to become the status quo.

———————

Ma Sagaro worked long hours surrounded by nothing but neatly folded red clothing, but she could enjoy at least two things throughout her days: the beautiful sunlight that passed through the south-facing windows, and easy access to a small room nearby where she could smoke and gossip while taking breaks. Sagaro worked eleven-hour shifts in Socrates, a bland two-story office building on a private road near the ranch airstrip that housed multiple departments, including the computer department, purchasing, and the commune's clothing department. The exchange for the thirty-six telephone lines running out of the ranch resided in a building behind Socrates and adjacent to the smoke-and-gossip space they called "the old Xerox room."

Sunlight and socializing got Sagaro through her days, but those pleasures were stripped away just before the 1984 summer festival. One morning she arrived at work to find a wall where the doorway to the old Xerox room had once been. The only way to access it now was by entering through an exterior door behind Socrates. She was told the room was off-limits since Julian needed it to do some recording during the festival. And then Sagaro bumped into Julian himself, who told her to permanently close the blinds over the south-facing windows in her workroom. He didn't say why, and it wasn't her place to ask.

Still, Sagaro couldn't help but peek through the blinds from time to time and watch the handful of people who were granted entry to the old Xerox room after knocking on the exterior door. She heard music through the walls every day, at all hours. Repetitive music. Music that seemed designed to cover up whatever was happening inside.

It struck Sagaro as suspicious, but a lot of things in Rajneeshpuram were suspicious, and that didn't mean she would ever understand them.

In the ranch's earliest days, Julian had installed a recording device on the commune's main reception line to tape the threatening phone calls that came in. But before the 1984 Third Annual World Celebration, Sheela told Julian to expand their security measures to include monitoring all external telephone calls. Sagaro was spending her days alongside one of the largest illegal wiretapping operations in American history. Julian's spies ran wires from the ranch's telephone exchange through an electrical socket in the wall into the old Xerox room and back again. They set up tape recorders on tables in the old Xerox room to capture telephone conversations, but the operation became more sophisticated throughout 1984 and eventually included custom-built cabinets that housed voice-activated recording equipment. This setup allowed disciples staffing the listening room to monitor and record any phone calls coming in and out of the ranch via the outside lines, including all six pay phones.

To staff this round-the-clock operation, Sheela's aides at Jesus Grove selected a team of nearly two-dozen discreet, dependable sannyasins. Julian would sometimes initiate new monitors into the fold by talking in circles, never explicitly saying that the job was eavesdropping on telephone calls. But he always made the stakes clear: the commune was at risk, Bhagwan's life was in danger, and the escalating security concerns demanded these intrusive measures.

Staff in the old Xerox room were told what to listen for: anything that sounded threatening or menacing; any calls involving public officials, the press, or law enforcement; any calls with doctors, either sannyasin or not;

and anything involving a small group of wealthy California disciples at the commune who had become close to Bhagwan. If these topics came up, the monitors would preserve the tape and draft a summary for Sheela or one of her top lieutenants. Most conversations were of no interest, and the job was so boring that Vidya had to chide the monitors for failing to appear for shifts—which were in addition to their sixty-plus-hour workweeks in their regular jobs.

Bhagwan was aware of the wiretapping operation—he admitted as much when the public eventually learned about it—and some Jesus Grove coordinators believe Sheela shared with him information gleaned from recorded phone calls, particularly as it related to security threats. Many commune members suspected the phones were tapped because Sheela had repeatedly warned them that the government might be listening to their calls. Very few disciples realized that the people listening were the very same people who ate alongside them in Magdalena Cafeteria every night.

Around the same time that the Socrates wiretapping operation was being established, the commune's bugging operations expanded from the Alan Watts A-4 quadriplex to the Hotel Rajneesh on the ranch, which had gone up in time for the 1983 World Celebration on a flat piece of land across the creek from Jesus Grove. From above, the hotel looked like two hollow squares connected at one corner like a figure eight, each a two-story building with seventy units facing into central gardens with ponds and bubbling fountains. For well-off guests who weren't interested in the rustic Alan Watts mountain cabins, the Hotel Rajneesh provided amenities like room service, custom-built round beds, and televisions that played Bhagwan's Pune discourses.

At Julian's command, Rajesh and Michel bugged four rooms on the upper level of the hotel's Tarot Wing, installing multiple microphones in each living room and bathroom and running wires through the air-conditioning ducts to two rooms below, where Rajesh set up listening equipment. The operation would eventually seep into the hotel's other half, the Rajneesh Wing, where they installed more than twenty telephones with microphones that picked up conversations held in the room and phone calls.

The hotel staff knew that certain rooms were reserved for "special guests," but they were not told why. A call would come from Jesus Grove directing that a visitor be placed in one of the special rooms, and Rajesh and Michel would receive notice that somebody suspicious was coming who needed to be monitored. The spies would take turns staffing the hotel's surveillance post, where they listened to tedious conversations, sexual activity, long periods of silence, and snoring.

Julian had told his two spies that all their surveillance work was meant to protect the commune from outside violence, but throughout 1984 they realized their scope had creeped to include disaffected former sannyasins, journalists, politicians, and government agents. During a visit in the summer of 1984, John Mathis, the African American mediator from the US Justice Department, spent two days in the Hotel Rajneesh and had his conversations recorded under the code name "BLACK." A court reporter and a videographer who came to the ranch to record a deposition were monitored and taped at the hotel. Later that year, two newspaper reporters investigating Rajneeshpuram were recorded having an affair in the bugged Alan Watts quadriplex. The tapes went straight to Jesus Grove.

Despite all her concerns about enemies on the outside who might do them harm, in the spring of 1984 Sheela began turning her focus inward, to a place so holy that most disciples would never imagine it hosting anyone with ill intentions. She persuaded her closest allies that the biggest threat to their community was living mere steps away from their vulnerable master.

19 | THE ENEMY INSIDE

WHEN THE RAJNEESHPURAM CITY GOVERNMENT was first forming in 1982 and the possibilities for Bhagwan's community seemed endless, Ma Prem Hasya had managed to cross the one person she shouldn't have. That's how the woman formerly known as Françoise Ruddy—multimillionaire, jet-setter, ex-wife of *The Godfather* producer Albert S. Ruddy, doyenne of Beverly Hills society—found herself flipping burgers in Antelope.

Her problem was that she didn't need Rajneeshpuram as badly as almost everyone else who was there. Hasya had taken sannyas while touring India in the 1970s, after connecting with Bhagwan's philosophy of personal growth paired with ostentatious "yes you can" capitalism. The guru opened her mind about love, relationships, communication, and honesty, and he also helped her come to terms with the significant wealth she had accumulated after divorcing two extraordinarily rich men. "I had a bank account that can only be described as endless, perhaps 'fathomless' would be a better word," Hasya said in an interview with the *Rajneesh Times*. "In fact, I really didn't know that you had to put money into a bank account. I thought it was just there, always." Before Bhagwan, she felt empty when she bought an exotic car or a designer outfit. He gave her permission to enjoy her money.

Back in Beverly Hills, Hasya met up with other glamorous, wealthy sann-yasins, including a physician named Swami Dhyan John who had retired in his late thirties, and together they started an opulent Rajneesh Meditation Center in the Hollywood Hills. Their ability to make huge donations put them high on Sheela's radar, and in the summer of 1982 she invited Hasya and other disciples from Hollywood to move to the ranch, where they were given a nice trailer in an isolated part of the property, far from Jesus Grove. Rather than settle for the grim trappings that Sheela had selected for all commune housing, they brought in expensive furniture, elegant lighting, and original artwork. Rather than eat with their fellow commune members at Magdalena Cafeteria, they would hop in one of their personal luxury sedans every day and drive fifty miles to Madras for groceries. But after a honeymoon period, Sheela and Vidya brought down the hammer. If they wanted to live in the commune, they needed to work, just like everybody else.

"Well, we didn't want to work hard," Dhyan John later explained. "We didn't see any reason to work hard. And we didn't take sannyas and be with Bhagwan so we could go work twelve or fourteen hours a day. It seemed fine if you wanted to do it, but we didn't want to do it."

They resisted for as long as they could. Finally, Sheela said that Bhagwan had ordered them to merge with the commune. She split up the Beverly Hills contingent, sending them to live with strangers in regular commune housing all over the ranch, and she gave them "worship" assignments—jobs. Dhyan John became an accountant buried in an office trailer, Hasya a burger flipper at Zorba the Buddha Rajneesh Restaurant in Antelope.

They were miserable. Dhyan John later described how Hasya reacted to her worship: "Now here's a woman that has been married to a billionaire. . . . She never turned a hand in her life and never lifted a bag, and was, in my judgment, punitively sent to go out and cook hamburgers and became depressed and used to cry every night, and I mean for hours. She would go into her room and cry like a little three-year-old. She was totally traumatized."

Sheela caught wind of their negativity and hauled them in for a meeting, where she coined the appellation that would henceforth be applied to Hasya, Dhyan John, and any of their fabulously rich, rules-be-damned contingent from California. *The Hollywood Group*, she sneered.

They lasted only three months. By September 1982, the conflicts with Sheela and her lieutenants, the worship assignments, and the bleak lifestyle had all become too much. Hasya, Dhyan John, and the others returned to their pampered lives in Los Angeles, living communally in their meditation center and entertaining friends from the film community.

About a year later, in October 1983, Sheela phoned Dhyan John and formally invited the Hollywood Group back to Rajneeshpuram—an invitation they suspected had come from Bhagwan. They negotiated satisfactory terms. Dhyan John signed over the Hollywood Hills house to the Rajneesh Foundation International as a million-dollar donation and loaned nearly half a million dollars to various Rajneesh corporations. In return, Sheela said they could do whatever they wanted at the commune.

The Hollywood Group occupied A-frame homes in the Alan Watts Canyon north of the main valley and maintained control over their lives. Unlike every other commune member, who had to wake up at dawn to work at jobs they hadn't chosen and eat food they hadn't selected and hop on buses at whatever time they drove by, the Hollywood Group sailed above it all. Money talked at Rajneeshpuram.

Everything was fine until March 31, 1984, when Sheela united the leaders of two powerful factions who always danced just beyond her firm grip. Hasya looked radiant on her wedding day—a ridiculously wealthy woman in the prime of her life, with perfect skin, luminescent eyes, and a megawatt smile— with no idea the sequence of events that her nuptials were about to trigger. Her groom was British Swami Devaraj, Bhagwan's personal physician. A tall, lanky, Hollywood-handsome man with explosive blue eyes and a wild shock of prematurely gray hair, Devaraj had gained Bhagwan's trust back in Pune with his obsessive interest in every aspect of the guru's health and a willingness to experiment with new Western therapies and medications. At Rajneeshpuram, he was regarded as a person of high prestige since he lived in Bhagwan's home and was one of the few people with access to him.

And this access would become a problem, at least as Sheela—the wedding officiant—saw it. Most commune members had no interaction with Bhagwan, beyond quietly namasteing as his Rolls-Royce passed by each afternoon. He didn't speak publicly or host private audiences at his home, Lao Tzu. If disciples wanted to send him a message or question, they could write it down and drop it in a box at the cafeteria, and then Sheela would decide whether or not to share it with Bhagwan. Some commune members would later claim, falsely, that Bhagwan depended solely on Sheela for information about his community and the outside world. In fact, he had regular contact with members of his household staff, including his longtime caretaker Ma Yoga Vivek, his dentist

Devageet, and his personal physician Devaraj, who would sometimes pass along messages or questions on behalf of other disciples.

Hasya's marriage to Devaraj meant the glitzy Hollywood luminary had secured a direct line of communication to her master, independent of Sheela's control. And she knew the way to Bhagwan's heart, passing him catalogs filled with luxury items like million-dollar watches. When Sheela learned that Hasya was using a backdoor method to entice Bhagwan, she demanded that Hasya stop. As Sheela, Deeksha, and others in Bhagwan's close circle had noted over the years, the guru's taste for luxury knew no bounds, and he was generally unconcerned with how Sheela paid for expensive items or who would have to suffer as a result of the deficit in other areas. But beyond the financial concerns, Hasya's overtures sent Bhagwan a dangerous signal: I can give you something that Sheela cannot.

When Sheela intervened, Hasya pushed back, saying she simply couldn't say no to her master if he wanted something. Sheela responded that she *had* to learn how to say no.

This comment reached Bhagwan, who convened an audience with Sheela, Hasya, KD, and a few others. KD later told federal investigators that the guru had erupted at Sheela and threatened her job. While she mingled with whomever she wanted, Bhagwan said, he was stuck alone in Lao Tzu and needed things like expensive watches to keep him happy. If she didn't care about his happiness, he would replace her with other people who did.

Sheela promised to try to improve her relationship with the Hollywood Group, but KD knew it was a lie. She wasn't the type of person to forget that Hasya had ratted her out to Bhagwan and caused her such humiliation.

Around the same time that Sheela was going toe to toe with Hasya, she took a loud and pervasive interest in the medical care that Bhagwan was receiving from Swami Devaraj. She had long questioned the doctor's medical skills and judgment, and she was not alone. He had a reputation among disciples as an experimental physician willing to treat his patients with radical methods instead of following well-regarded, conservative standards of care. As KD put it, "If anyone needed competent medical attention, they would definitely not go to Devaraj." Another commune physician described him as "a nice guy, but a terrible doctor."

Although Sheela couldn't control whom Bhagwan selected to be his physician, she tried to stay informed about what exactly Devaraj was doing in his private sessions with the guru up at Lao Tzu. She had the nurse Puja keep tabs on anything that he ordered through the medical corporation. By the summer of 1984, Sheela was regularly fretting about Devaraj to her gang at her home compound in Jesus Grove. She told them that the doctor was experimenting on Bhagwan's body, pumping him with drugs, and allowing the dentist Devageet to administer far too much nitrous oxide—laughing gas—to the guru during his dental procedures.

Adding napalm to the fire, just before the Third Annual World Celebration kicked off in June 1984, Bhagwan told Sheela that he would leave his body— die—on Master's Day, July 6. Although he didn't specify the year, Sheela told her inner circle that she believed he intended to die on the coming Master's Day, in just a matter of weeks. She also suspected that Bhagwan would end his life with the help of his devoted doctor Devaraj, who, like Hasya, would never say no his master.

Some people close to Sheela found these allegations hard to swallow. Bhagwan's home was considered hallowed ground—a space charged with his supernatural energy—and most disciples treated the people chosen to live with him with great respect and even reverence. It was unthinkable that any sannyasin would harm Bhagwan, much less his physician. Among the skeptics was Ava, the promising young margarita maker who was becoming a utility player within Sheela's inner circle. One day she finally mustered the courage to voice her doubts.

Sheela said she could prove it. She played a tape-recorded conversation between Devaraj and his new wife, Hasya, in which they said nasty things about Sheela and other people running the commune—things so vile that Ava took it as damning evidence of their negativity. (At the time, she didn't question how Sheela came by a recording of a private conversation between two commune members.) Criticizing the people leading the community was no different than criticizing the community or even Bhagwan himself. Hearing the tape allowed Ava to see the fault line that Sheela had been setting up for the previous weeks: the sanctimonious people who lived and worked closest to Bhagwan on one side, and everybody else on the other. Sheela used similar tactics over the summer to persuade many of her top coordinators that Devaraj and other people living in Bhagwan's house were dangerous. What started as a simmering tension would soon explode into open conflict between Lao Tzu and Jesus Grove.

In the Rajneeshpuram civil war, "Lao Tzu" represented the very small group of people who tended to Bhagwan and lived in his home, while "Jesus Grove" was shorthand at the commune for the dozens of top coordinators and close aides who lived and worked in Sheela's bustling compound in the heart of the valley. At the top of the commune's hierarchy (aside from Bhagwan) was the "Holy Trinity": Sheela; Savita, the chief accountant; and Vidya, the commune president. A close fourth by 1984 was Ma Anand Su, a hard-nosed, raven-haired British woman who became president of the Rajneesh Investment Corporation and managed transportation and heavy equipment. Working beneath them were a couple dozen coordinators, almost entirely women, who ran departments such as the medical center, carpentry, construction, farming, cafeterias, accommodations, publications, and purchasing. Commune members would informally refer to coordinators as Moms, while the Big Moms, like Sheela, Savita, Vidya, and Su, ran the largest departments. Bhagwan said he wanted women running his commune because they were more intuitive and emotional than men, less intellectual and status driven.

Most disciples were happy to step aside and let Sheela and her crew run the commune, since they had little interest in politics or leadership. Sheela selected as coordinators people who were practical, hardworking, and not particularly spiritual. "I did not want people around me who were greedy for Bhagwan and his views, or for enlightenment," she later reflected. "They were ready to take responsibilities and work hard instead of wasting their time chasing dreams."

Some disciples on the fringes of power believed that the main criteria to be a coordinator at Rajneeshpuram was loyalty to Sheela above anyone else, even Bhagwan. The coordinators met each week in a large room in Jesus Grove to make major decisions—often freewheeling, jovial conversations orchestrated by Sheela as the ringmaster—after which each department would meet so the coordinator could pass down information to the general commune membership. One defector from Rajneeshpuram told a reporter that he never saw a vote taken or any meaningful discussion about any issue at a coordinators' meeting. Instead there were only "directives and scoldings with the implication that you're not working hard enough." An effort was made to make meetings seem collegial, but in reality every decision was handed down from the top.

Sheela controlled virtually every nook and cranny at Rajneeshpuram except for the interior of Bhagwan's house, which was his own domain, staffed by people with little affection for or loyalty to Sheela. Most commune members had no access to his private estate, which was the lushest place on the ranch, covered with a lawn so well tended it looked like a putting green and dotted with newly planted juniper trees. Graceful peacocks roamed the land, although some would meet grisly ends when they bumped into the electrified fence that Sheela had put up around the place. Security guards were positioned at the gate with rifles to ensure only approved guests entered the compound.

Sheela felt that Bhagwan had stuffed his home with snobbish "meditators" who would do anything he commanded, with little regard for the bigger picture. They might even kill him, if he asked. On top of that, Hasya and the Hollywood Group were using their Lao Tzu connections to fill Bhagwan's head with extravagances that Sheela could not afford. When she tried to interfere, he threatened to get rid of her.

But Sheela wasn't ready to give up yet. In June 1984, she launched her first offensive in the civil war, an effort to seize control of Bhagwan's household and exert her power over every inch of Rajneeshpuram—even the guru's inner sanctum.

When commune members became sick or required long-term medical attention, they were not allowed to recover alone in their homes, which were scattered all over the ranch and where they might infect their roommates. Instead, they would be admitted to the Koran Grove clinic facility in the south valley for "home care," allowing medical staff to monitor them and administer medication in one centralized location.

In late May, Sheela insisted that Hasya admit herself to Koran Grove to receive treatment for a chronic pain in her neck. After a few weeks, just as Hasya was preparing to leave the facility, a doctor diagnosed her with conjunctivitis—a contagious infection of the eye commonly known as pink eye. Since Hasya was married to Devaraj, who worked in close proximity to delicate Bhagwan, he was called in for a test as well. Sheela's close friend, the nurse Puja, ran the test herself and diagnosed him with conjunctivitis. She told the couple they would need to stay in Koran Grove until they recovered, so as not to infect anybody else. Puja didn't stop there, hauling in nearly everybody who lived at Lao Tzu for testing. They were all positive, she said. As the director of the Rajneesh Medical Corporation, she exercised her authority to force them to stay isolated in one cramped trailer at Koran Grove—Bhagwan's caretaker, his doctor, his dentist, and his cleaner.

When they were finally allowed to return home five days later, they found a delegation from Jesus Grove waiting to berate them for the disgusting condition of Bhagwan's house. They claimed to have spent the past few days scrubbing every surface and object in the compound since it was all so filthy, which only proved how little the Lao Tzu residents cared for their master. The meeting grew heated, and Bhagwan learned about it. He convened a summit that night between the Jesus Grove and Lao Tzu camps, including Sheela, where he pointed out the glaring rift between households and commanded them to coexist peacefully.

A couple of days later, to Sheela's absolute horror, Bhagwan took matters into his own hands by gathering a small group of disciples at Lao Tzu. One of the invitees described the motley crew as "like a cocktail party scene from an Agatha Christie book," with some longtime disciples from way back in Mumbai, some recent arrivals, and nobody from Jesus Grove except for Sheela. When they were all sitting at his feet, Bhagwan made the extraordinary announcement that twenty-one of his disciples had attained enlightenment, including everybody present in the room but Hasya, Sheela, and Bhagwan's longtime caretaker Vivek. More disciples would become enlightened sometime before Bhagwan died, and a third group would become enlightened sometime before they died. Bhagwan wanted all three groups to form committees that would promote his religion after he died. Under this construct, he explained to them, no one person would ever succeed him. No one person would assume all of his power and spiritual authority.

It was certainly a far cry from the Bodhi tree under which Gautama Buddha had attained enlightenment, or even the ethereal way in which Bhagwan himself had ascended from the mortal plane in 1953, when, after a long period of tortured questioning about God, the twenty-one-year-old college student had given up his spiritual search. As soon as he stopped looking for answers, Bhagwan later claimed, a new energy overtook him that lasted for seven days until it became unbearably intense. After midnight, he felt drawn outside to a nearby garden, where everything became luminous and all the plants vibrated with life. He sat under a tree for hours, although it felt like infinity. From that moment on, Bhagwan said, he had never been in his body, but instead had been hovering nearby, connected only by a very delicate thread.

In contrast, his twenty-one disciples discovered they were enlightened because Bhagwan told them so. He even gave them certificates. Enlightenment was now something for him to declare, not something his disciples could attain without his permission. With all the political turmoil within his commune in the summer of 1984, Bhagwan seemed to be thinking about hierarchy, control, and delegation. He seemed to be concerned about who would maintain his legacy when he was gone. He seemed to be anticipating his own death.

Sheela could not have seen it as anything but a stinging rebuke. Her plot to commandeer power from Devaraj, Hasya, and the Lao Tzu residents had backfired spectacularly. Multiple witnesses from Jesus Grove say that she manufactured the conjunctivitis epidemic as a way to clear Lao Tzu and intrude into Bhagwan's home. KD believed that she wanted to prove to Bhagwan that he didn't need the dangerous sycophants surrounding him and that her own people could provide much better care. Another member of Sheela's inner circle said that she cleared the house so her staff could dig through Bhagwan's medical records to discern what Devaraj was doing to him and how dangerous it might be.

But Sheela scored a far more practical win, even if she failed to drive a wedge between Bhagwan and his household staff. At some point in the summer of 1984—most likely while the Lao Tzu residents were exiled in Koran Grove— Swami Julian secretly swapped out all the telephones in Bhagwan's home with models similar to those used in the commune's hotel, which picked up not only telephone calls but also nearby conversations. He installed a microphone beneath the bed of Bhagwan's caretaker Vivek, and he placed another inside a small buzzer attached to Bhagwan's easy chair in his private living area that he used to summon Vivek. With signal amplifiers and long telephone lines, all of these listening devices fed directly into two bedrooms in Sheela's Jesus Grove compound with equipment to monitor and record nearly anything that was said within Lao Tzu.

The Lao Tzu bugging operation remained a closely guarded secret among Sheela's inner circle, and the fact that Bhagwan's room was bugged was even more confidential, with only a half-dozen or so trusted aides allowed to eavesdrop on him. Sheela has recently claimed that she bugged the home to protect Bhagwan and, incredibly, that he authorized her to do it—even the microphone in his chair, which recorded his intimate moments and private conversations. KD, who monitored Bhagwan's room, later told federal investigators that the guru was oblivious. Sheela would use information gleaned from the Lao Tzu listening operation to drag her closest intimates deeper and deeper into paranoid plots that were supposed to protect their master and their community.

Despite the setbacks in early June, Master's Day was quickly approaching. Devaraj was back at Bhagwan's side. If they wanted their master to survive July 6, Sheela told her close confidants, they would need to remove the doctor from the equation altogether.

At first it was just a minor case of diarrhea. Then Devaraj started to feel wobbly and uncoordinated, like he was having the physical symptoms of being drunk without any of the mental impairment. He brushed it off for a couple of days, even when people around him said he looked horrible. At dinner one night at the commune's restaurant, he became so uncoordinated that his wife, Hasya, had to pull him out of his chair and help him walk. Later, he became so dizzy that he couldn't stand up.

Seeing how rough he looked the next morning, somebody persuaded him to go back to the dreaded Koran Grove for a checkup, even though he had left conjunctivitis quarantine only a few days earlier. Watching with alarm as he staggered into the clinic, the medical staff placed Devaraj in a special bed for home care nursing services.

He was now in the hands of Ma Anand Puja. A licensed nurse practitioner of Filipina descent raised in California, Puja had been an obscure presence at the Pune ashram before stumbling into Sheela's spotlight while taking care of her husband, Chinmaya, in his final months. Sheela had ousted the ashram's medical coordinator and installed the young, relatively unknown nurse in her place. Sheela told the sannyasin doctors that Puja was brilliant and every bit as capable as they were, but the proof was not in the pudding. Some at the Pune medical center came to resent their new boss, who never treated patients and seemed to be little more than Sheela's eyes and ears. Some also came to believe that Sheela chose Puja for her subservient nature, particularly when it came to dispensing medication.

At Rajneeshpuram, Sheela tapped Puja to run the Rajneesh Medical Corporation, which came to include two clinics, a diagnostic laboratory, multiple offices, and a pharmacy. She ruled the medical center with an iron fist, leaving no room for error or deviation from her commands. "Everybody hated her," one doctor reflected. The medical center was an unusually serious and unhappy place to work for a commune that was supposed to be about love, life, and laughter. "Puja is a very secretive person," commune spokesperson Isabel later recalled. "She scurries around. She doesn't come into a room and say 'Hello.' She can spend twenty minutes there before you see her."

In addition to running the medical corporation, Puja's side job was serving as the private nurse to Sheela and her top coordinators. Oregon law permitted nurse practitioners like Puja to prescribe drugs—even strong opioids. Ma Ava, who worked as her assistant, said that Puja kept Sheela and other Jesus Grove coordinators supplied with Valium, oxycodone, and morphine, which she kept in a cabinet in her bedroom. Ava witnessed a couple of occasions when Sheela overdosed on drugs that Puja had given her and almost stopped breathing, requiring a doctor to administer lifesaving treatment.

The relationship between Sheela and Puja became ever closer throughout their time in Oregon. Puja played the role of Sheela's handmaiden, locked away in her bedroom doing who knows what, dressing and styling her hair like Sheela, carrying out her mistress's orders. Puja's lover Swami Toby would later speculate that she had found a family with Sheela and the women in her orbit, which perhaps served as an antidote to her turbulent childhood and a string of abusive relationships that had started at a very young age. "Serving Sheela was, in one way, Puja's whole motivation," said a sannyasin doctor. "When Sheela might make a passing reference criticizing her, Puja was totally destroyed."

Devaraj started feeling better after spending a couple of hours at Koran Grove. And then Puja arrived. She examined him and said he required an intravenous drip to keep him hydrated. Since he was already feeling good, Devaraj declined. But nobody could override Puja's medical decisions—not even a doctor, and not even Bhagwan's personal physician. They bickered back and forth until she won. She rolled an IV stand into his room and jabbed the needle into his arm. Later that night, Puja returned and injected something from a syringe directly into the drip. She told him it was vitamins.

Overnight, Devaraj's mild diarrhea became catastrophic. He described it as "full blown Turkish hotel syndrome, where you spend all night going back and forth to the bathroom, not sure if you want to vomit or have diarrhea." He developed a fever and started trembling. Arriving for her shift at Koran Grove that morning, Ava found Puja and Shunyo, a Harvard-trained physician and friend to Devaraj, frantically applying emergency measures. He was in septic shock and his blood pressure was dangerously low. After treating him with antibiotics, they managed to stabilize him.

When a friend from Lao Tzu stopped by that afternoon, Devaraj whispered his suspicion about what had caused his near-death experience: he believed that Puja had used a dirty needle in the IV she had administered the previous night. Shunyo performed a blood culture test and discovered the presence of *Citrobacter*, a genus of bacteria typically found in the intestinal tract or in fecally contaminated soil or water. Shunyo was baffled as to why *Citrobacter* would be in the bloodstream of a healthy person. Devaraj suggested that Puja must have wiped the IV needle on something contaminated with the bacteria.

Neither of them would levy such a serious allegation against a senior commune leader without proof. The doctors tucked away their suspicions and kept a close eye on the nurse with the crocodile smile who continued attending to poor Swami Devaraj.

I tried everything, Puja told Krishna Deva back in Jesus Grove, *and then I took the vase*.

Devaraj's condition had been improving too fast, she said. If she hadn't intervened, he would have been released the next day, gone back to Lao Tzu, and continued his experiments on Bhagwan. He might even have facilitated Bhagwan's suicide on Master's Day, as the guru had been cryptically suggesting to Sheela.

Puja told a similar story to her assistant, Ava. In a desperate effort to keep Devaraj in the clinic, she had grabbed a liquid close at hand—the dirty water from a vase of flowers—and injected it into Devaraj's IV drip. Puja told Ava that she had no intention of killing him. She simply wanted to keep him sick enough that he couldn't return to Lao Tzu.

To get him to Koran Grove in the first place, Puja and trusted helpers had been spiking his beverages with Dulcolax stool softeners and perhaps other drugs in the days preceding his illness. The morning after he was admitted,

Puja handed Ava a small envelope filled with a yellow powder, which Ava believed was crushed Dulcolax pills, and told her to sprinkle it over Devaraj's oatmeal. She did it, but she didn't know whether he ate it. Only later did she learn about Puja's flower water injection.

Puja confided in KD that the episode had terrified her. She had almost killed Bhagwan's personal physician. At the time, she still was not comfortable with the idea of murdering a fellow sannyasin to protect Bhagwan. That concern would soon vanish.

Under Shunyo's care, Devaraj slowly felt better. Within a few days he was well enough to sunbathe and smoke out on the Koran Grove balcony, but his full recovery took many more weeks. He remained ill throughout the Third Annual World Celebration in early July. This was particularly difficult because he played a prominent role during Bhagwan's satsang ceremonies, where the master would sit quietly while the commune band played haunting Indian tunes and Devaraj read passages from the guru's Pune discourses in his gentle British baritone. At the 1984 festival, recordings of Bhagwan's past lectures were played instead. Sheela and Puja had found at least one way to knock Devaraj off his pedestal.

20 | SHARPENING THE SWORD

THE PRESS CONVERGED ON THE RANCH in the last week of June to cover preparations for the festival. A Portland television station snagged Sheela for an interview, throughout which she lounged on a couch in Jesus Grove and answered questions in a subdued voice, while a crowd of aides hovered nearby and attended to her hair. The reporter talked to Sheela about the highs and lows of the previous few months.

In February the INS had handed Bhagwan a massive victory when it declared that he was a religious teacher for purposes of his application for permanent residency. All the mountains of evidence the sannyasins had submitted throughout 1983, the implementation of Rajneeshism, and their international protests against "religious bigotry" came together to help win the favorable decision. It did not by itself grant Bhagwan the immigration status he sought, but sannyasin attorneys crowed that he was a mere procedural hurdle away. Despite this bluster, the likelihood of Bhagwan being allowed to stay permanently in America was far from certain. The INS would only comment that Bhagwan's immigration case was "still pending." In fact, the agency would take no action on his application for the remainder of his time in the United States, leaving him in constant legal limbo.

One month after receiving the INS decision, the sannyasins scored another victory when the Oregon Court of Appeals sided with Rajneeshpuram on the question of whether their city had been legally incorporated. Krishna Deva called it a resounding victory that would allow the city to once again control its land.

146

But three days before the Third Annual World Celebration kicked off in late June 1984, the court of appeals reconsidered its earlier decision and reversed course, instead siding with Rajneeshpuram's opponents. The case would go back to Wasco County to determine the city's fate. Attempting to foster calm and stability within the community, KD promised an appeal all the way up to the US Supreme Court. "While the lawyers are arguing, and that could take years," he told the *Rajneesh Times*, "let's all enjoy the beautiful oasis which exists here at Rajneeshpuram."

The reporter interviewing Sheela summed up Rajneeshpuram's precarious legal status and suggested that 1000 Friends wanted to see the city dismantled.

"They are most welcome," she responded, her large brown eyes locked onto him and a tiny smile at the corner of her mouth. "I will personally see to it that our community will provide a feast for after their bulldozers have been painted red with our blood. I'll teach them how to paint the bulldozers red. I'll teach them how to celebrate afterwards. But I'll be dead."

Registrations for the Third Annual World Celebration never came close to the previous year's blowout. The commune expected fifteen thousand people to attend, but local officials monitoring traffic in and out of the ranch placed the number closer to eight thousand—about half the previous year's attendance.

A major factor driving the depressed registrations was the commune's efforts to domineer and centralize Rajneesh Meditation Centers around the world. European centers had done very well in the aftermath of Bhagwan's departure from India, since so many driftless sannyasins had returned to their homes and bolstered the meditation centers there. Foreign centers had commercialized by opening successful Zorba the Buddha restaurants and discos in places like Australia, Japan, and all over Europe, as well as specialized businesses drawing on their professional skills, like construction and computer-consulting firms. For all these businesses, the commune expected profits to be sent to the ranch.

Starting in 1982, Sheela and her coordinators began to put the squeeze on smaller centers around the world, instructing them to close and their members to coalesce into big communes in major cities. Having fewer, larger centers made it easier for the Rajneesh Foundation International to control what was happening in the international movement, including where any income from those centers and their businesses was going. But another result of this centralization was plummeting numbers among the discipleship. Many dropped sannyas altogether because they didn't want to relocate, and fewer centers also meant fewer opportunities to recruit new disciples. Sannyasins at foreign meditation centers blamed Sheela for this heavy-handed approach, but the instruction came from Bhagwan himself, as he later admitted, since he felt that smaller centers could be "crushed very easily." He dispatched Sheela to the various communes "to see that the religious work is carried out according to my vision" and ensure that all the facilities were exactly alike.

Although they were fewer in number, attendees at the 1984 festival experienced improved accommodations from the previous years. Guests would open their large tents to find four sleeping bags laid atop mattress pads, and custom-built shelves for luggage with hangers to either side of the entrance. At the foot of each sleeping bag sat a small cardboard box, compliments of the Rajneesh Medical Corporation, containing a couple of condoms, a bag filled with rubber gloves, and a brochure warning about the dangers of AIDS.

The festival also featured the implementation of an innovation from chief Rajneesh accountant Savita and her team of financial gurus: the Rajneesh Currency Card. Guests could open an account and deposit funds upon arriving at the ranch and never have to worry about cash for the rest of their stay, receiving a debit card to use at all the commune's accommodations—the stores, restaurants, hair salon, meditation university, and even the airport. "Cash-free is care-free!" Savita declared when the currency card was unveiled before the festival. By the time thousands of visitors poured into Rajneeshpuram that summer, the system had become fully computerized and the terminals were all linked electronically to a central server—an early use of online networking. It resulted in millions of dollars of cash flowing into the commune in the summer of 1984.

On the festival's first day, Sheela appeared in her pope robes and embroidered habit in Rajneesh Mandir, where she told disciples that journalists had been pestering her recently about what would happen when Bhagwan died. Although it was an obscene question to ask about a beloved master, she said she'd raised it to Bhagwan for his response.

"He definitely is going to survive twenty more years," she said with a huge smile on her face. Wild applause, cheering, and crying broke out across the hall. To drive up reservations, international disciples had been warned that

Bhagwan was suggesting he might die on July 6. *We don't know if he'll leave his body this year, but you'd better come just in case.*

But the good news came with a caveat. Bhagwan would survive for that long, Sheela warned them, only if his sannyasins expressed absolute, unshakeable positivity.

As energy from the Third Annual World Celebration began to fade in late July, Sheela and her team were left with a major problem that Bhagwan had dropped in her lap earlier that year. He had always monitored political and legal developments in Wasco County since arriving in Oregon. During her multi-hour meetings with Bhagwan at Lao Tzu each day, Sheela shared newspaper and television news clippings featuring him, Rajneeshpuram, and his movement. He would commend or criticize her performance in press appearances and "hit her hard" if she was being too subdued.

"She was falling below the standard. And I was continuously telling her, 'Don't be worried, we don't have anything to lose. We have the whole world to gain and nothing to lose. Be outrageous!'" Bhagwan later explained. "I have been sharpening her like a sword. 'Go and cut as many heads as you can.'" He was particularly interested in controlling the words that came out of her mouth, as his temporal spokesperson. "I had to teach her everything for three and a half years, two hours every day—what she has to say, what she has not to say. And she was repeating like a parrot, because it is not her experience. But she did well. As a parrot, she was perfect."

With his careful attention to news affecting the commune, Bhagwan knew by early 1984 that the sannyasins' political and legal fortunes were in jeopardy. Sheela, Krishna Deva, and a top lieutenant named Ma Shanti Bhadra (called Shanti B) have all said that Bhagwan grew particularly concerned when Wasco County officials betrayed them by siding with 1000 Friends of Oregon in seeking the injunction on construction. If the county got its way, the ranch would revert to unincorporated agricultural land, and the disciples might be forced to tear down or stop using most of their structures and drastically reduce the number of people living on the ranch.

Compounding matters, their meager political support on the Wasco County Court was about to disappear. In the fall of 1983, the Church of Jesus

Christ of Latter-Day Saints had sent the sannyasins' leading ally, Judge Rick Cantrell, on a long-term mission trip to Africa. Cantrell's replacement on the court, Ray Matthew, was no friend to the sannyasins. Another new judge who joined the court in 1983, Bill Hulse, was proudly anti-Rajneesh. That left Virgil Ellett as their only friendly vote on the three-person court—but even that support buckled in May 1984 when Ellett lost the Democratic primary to Jim Comini, the liquor store owner and former council member who had been the lone no vote on the incorporation petition in November 1981. (Comini had resigned from the court in 1982 in protest over the body's decision to grant a mass gathering permit for Rajneeshpuram's First Annual World Festival, but two years later he ran for the office again.) Ellett would serve out the rest of his term in 1984, but he would not be on the ballot in the November general election. Comini would face off against an anti-sannyasin Republican wheat rancher.

In any plausible electoral scenario, January 1985 would see three Rajneesh antagonists seated on the Wasco County Court, at a time when the fate of the sannyasins' community would be in the county's hands. But Bhagwan Shree Rajneesh and his secretary did not operate in the world of the plausible.

Voter fraud, voter fraud, voter fraud. Sheela repeated these words to KD throughout the summer of 1984, a mantra intended to spark creative ideas that might allow them to win the two county judge seats up for election in November. It became a virtual obsession between them. *Have you found a way?* she kept asking KD.

According to Sheela, Bhagwan placed her under constant pressure in 1984 to find a way to assume political control of Wasco County. He told her to brainstorm ideas and present them to him for his approval, which she says she did. Krishna Deva later told the FBI that Sheela and Bhagwan had discussed taking over the county government and that the guru had dictated a speech that a sannyasin candidate would give should they win the election. According to meeting notes that Sheela read to KD, Bhagwan's message was that sannyasins could not afford to be magnanimous until they occupied a position of power. Once they controlled the county, they would become more paternalistic toward non-sannyasins. And Sheela's lieutenant Shanti B similarly recalled that

Bhagwan had directed Sheela to seize control of the county and had dictated speeches for sannyasin candidates to deliver.

The pressure from Bhagwan seemed to overwhelm Sheela throughout the summer. Shanti B observed her acting manic at times and believed she was taking drugs to sleep, drugs to wake up. Sheela started calling daily meetings among her most trusted coordinators to press them for innovative ideas on how to win the county. It all came down to numbers. KD estimated they would need a solid bloc of five or six thousand votes to overwhelm the polls in a typical Wasco County election. At the time, they had around two thousand sannyasins at the ranch, and not all of them could vote. KD suggested some legal ways they might influence the election, like splitting the non-sannyasin vote by encouraging multiple candidates to run for office. This could leave room for sannyasin write-in candidates to sweep the two open seats.

But the more he chewed on the problem, KD came to believe that executing Bhagwan's directive would require drastic—and perhaps illegal—measures. One idea among the Jesus Grove brainstormers was to move one hundred disciples into the Wasco County seat, The Dalles, and have them each register to vote under five different identities, giving the commune a bloc of five thousand votes. KD persuaded Sheela to scrap the plan by May, pointing out that the deception would become obvious under any scrutiny.

Besides, a much safer idea had bubbled up around that time that would stack the odds in their favor. It even had the benefit of seeming legal. Under Oregon's generous voter registration laws, an adult who spent twenty days in the state before the election and who had an intention to stay was an eligible voter. If the ranch could bring in enough adult American sannyasins before the October voter registration deadline, they would have the numbers to over-whelm the non-sannyasin voters of Wasco County.

In May 1984, large advertisements began appearing in the *Rajneesh Times* newspaper, distributed weekly to sannyasins around the world, promoting a program that would allow disciples to live and work at the commune for three months, from September 10 to December 5, for just $250 a month. The only requirements were that the participants be American citizens who were eighteen years of age or older. The program was called the Buddhafield Experience.

The response was less than inspiring. By July, the commune opened up the Buddhafield Experience to *any* American adult—not just sannyasins. A press release trumpeted it as a "once-in-a-lifetime opportunity" offered in a "paradise on earth never before available in the history of mankind."

The commune sent out an invitation to all Americans to experience the magnificent Buddhafield for themselves. Sheela and her team waited to see if a few thousand people would take them up on the generous offer.

As the Buddhafield Experience got off the ground that summer, the Jesus Grove plotters were also mulling over a far darker strategy to win the Wasco County election. Rather than focus all their energy on increasing the number of supportive voters, they considered the other side of the equation as well: eliminating voters who opposed them.

21 | THE CHINESE LAUNDRY

THE WHITE SLAT SHED had been on the Big Muddy Ranch since long before the first sannyasin had ever set foot in Oregon. It sat between the original farmhouse and Sheela's sprawling Jesus Grove compound. Early on, someone had suggested that it looked like a rundown old place from a stereotypical Chinatown. They called it the Chinese Laundry.

First it served as a schoolhouse, but then Sheela moved the kids elsewhere, put a combination lock on the door, and gave control of it to her devoted handmaiden. Ma Anand Puja quietly turned the unassuming building into her private laboratory, complete with rat cages, petri dishes, a freeze dryer, and an incubator. Most people didn't know it existed, including other members of the Rajneesh Medical Corporation staff. Dr. Shunyo, who worked closely with Puja for years, learned about the clandestine laboratory only after she had left Rajneeshpuram forever.

One day in the summer of 1984, Puja summoned her lab assistant to the Chinese Laundry for a new project. She needed him to begin culturing salmonella bacteria in large quantities.

The request alarmed the young technician, since salmonella is danger-ous and highly contagious. When lodged in the intestines, it causes vomiting, diarrhea, and cramps for as long as ten days, and it can have severe health consequences for vulnerable people such as pregnant women and the elderly. Although the most common means of infection is through contaminated food, a carrier could easily transmit it to others through kissing. Culturing salmonella in the Chinese Laundry was a risk, even in a controlled laboratory setting, and

153

especially in a closed community of thousands of Bhagwan's beloved disciples, steps away from Sheela's own home.

But Puja wasn't the sort of boss who explained herself to her inferiors. Her lab assistant just did it.

What if people had the shits on Election Day? According to KD, Sheela came up with the idea during an election-fraud brainstorming meeting in the spring or summer of 1984. It triggered an intense period of research and consultation between Sheela and Puja on various ways they might make voters ill in The Dalles, which hosted the largest concentration of people in Wasco County. Keeping a significant number of anti-Rajneesh voters away from the polls could help tip the election in their favor. Puja decided to grow a contaminant in the Chinese Laundry, something with a predictable incubation period and that wouldn't be unusual to find in a medical laboratory setting. She toyed with the idea of using hepatitis, but ultimately she settled on *Salmonella* Typhimurium— a naturally occurring bacteria known to cause food-related outbreaks.

Earlier that year, the Rajneesh Medical Corporation had purchased some standard diagnostic samples from a Seattle company, VWR Scientific, including a medical-grade sample of S. Typhimurium developed from a particular strain classified as ATCC 14028. Inside the Chinese Laundry, Puja's lab assistant used a pipette to transfer a tiny amount of the sample bacteria onto a petri dish filled with a nutrient broth. He placed the dish in an incubator for a day or two. When it emerged, the liquid in the dish had grown brown and murky, riddled with millions of salmonella bacteria that had spawned in the warm environment.

The Chinese Laundry became a salmonella factory operating at full steam over the summer. The lab assistant would dump cultured salmonella in larger bottles to make room in the incubator for new cultures. One day, he handed his good friend Ava two large jars filled with the brown liquid and asked her to pass them to Puja. The time had come for a test run.

Mayor Krishna Deva walked into the Wasco County courthouse in The Dalles with a small bulge in his pocket in August 1984, three months before the election. He'd passed in and out of the bland building numerous times over the past three years to fight for Rajneeshpuram's incorporation and do battle with the county over building and festival permits. His business on this day was a private matter.

KD pushed through a blond wood door into the men's room on the first floor—a one-stall, one-urinal, one-sink affair. From his pocket he withdrew an eyedropper filled with a light brown liquid. He squeezed some out onto the urinal handle. He squeezed some more onto the sink knobs. He put some on the door handle. And then he left.

A few days later, after attending a hearing in The Dalles, KD stopped at the Portage Inn. It was the same restaurant where Sheela and Jayananda had thrown a lively Christmas party for public officials in their first winter at the ranch. KD arrived between lunch and dinner, when the place was fairly quiet, but some food was still out on the salad bar. When he was sure no one was looking, he uncorked a vial and poured brown, slimy liquid into a bucket of salad dressing.

When Puja had given him these substances and directed him to try them out, she'd warned KD to be careful while handling them and to wash his hands as soon as he was done. *You don't want to get the shits!* she said, laughing.

Later that month, Sheela, Puja, KD, and other commune leaders pulled up in front of Albertsons grocery store on the west side of The Dalles.

Sheela turned to Puja. *Let's have some fun.*

Oh boy, Puja chuckled.

They scattered across the store. Puja told KD she was thinking about injecting the brown liquid directly into some milk cartons. He tried to talk her out of it because he thought the tampering would be too obvious. Passing through the produce department, KD saw Sheela with a container up her sleeve, concealed in her palm, from which she was sprinkling brown liquid over the lettuce. Before leaving, they bought a box of Drumstick ice cream cones to share on the ride home. Puja giggled the whole way.

That night, the assistant manager of Albertsons' produce department made his wife guess which famous person he had served that day. Small, red-clad Ma Anand Sheela had been unforgettable.

The problem with all these efforts in August is that they didn't work. Nobody got sick, at least not in numbers large enough to come to their attention at the ranch. Sheela lashed out during meetings with her inner circle of trusted coordinators. Puja couldn't get her salmonella to work, and the Buddhafield Experience wasn't drawing the numbers of people they needed to win the election. Sheela pressured the nurse to figure it out.

Fate handed Puja some new test subjects at the end of August when two of the commune's fiercest political opponents hurtled straight into the spider's web.

Young Ava received a summons to Jesus Grove on the morning of August 29, where Sheela and Puja assigned her one of the odd jobs they liked tossing her way. She was always eager to make the Big Moms happy, even when they asked her to do things that made her feel uncomfortable. Her childhood had been tough, raised in a working-class Mexican American family in San Diego, with alcoholic parents whom she described as both loving and abusive. At age fifteen, she had latched onto Ram Dass's *Be Here Now* and began to explore spirituality, which led her to start taking yoga classes at the Utsava Rajneesh Meditation Center in Laguna Beach. A good Catholic girl, Ava tried to ignore the dark-eyed man glaring down at her from a photograph on the wall during her classes. He looked to her like the Antichrist.

After six months of yoga, she finally read some of Bhagwan's books and found herself taken by the master's brilliant words. He offered answers to spiritual questions that Catholicism had never been able to give her. While in college, Ava traveled to India to visit the ashram, where she was dazzled by all the loving people she met in their beautiful orange robes. She took sannyas with the master himself, who dropped a mala necklace around her neck, touched her third eye, and spoke to her about her new life. Ava came to believe that Bhagwan was clairvoyant and all-knowing, having achieved the highest human potential. When he settled in Oregon, she did whatever she could to get an invitation to move to the ranch. And then, while working a shift in Portland, she made the best margarita that Sheela had ever had. In a way, she had escaped one abusive relationship only to leap into another.

When her Moms gave her a new mission in late August 1984, Ava was more than ready to help. First, Sheela had to describe the targets, since Ava had no idea what the Wasco County judges looked like.

———————

Relations between the commune and the Wasco County government had continued to deteriorate throughout the summer. Emboldened by the recent court of appeals decision about the incorporation, the county court held a hearing in July to decide whether to strip any mention of Rajneeshpuram from the county's own comprehensive plan, as if the city didn't exist. Presiding judge Bill Hulse limited sannyasins' testimony at the hearing, interrupted them, and refused to allow some to speak, including city planner Deva Wadud. After thirty minutes, the judges voted unanimously to strike Rajneeshpuram from Wasco County's plan.

The sannyasins took it for what it was: a gratuitous slap in the face while the land-use litigation was still pending. "What I see here today is the beginning of a civil war in this county," Mayor Krishna Deva declared in the little time he was given to testify. "If that is what you want, fine."

Mere weeks later, on August 29, Wasco County judges Bill Hulse, Ray Matthew, and Virgil Ellet piled into Hulse's car and began the long trek out to Rajneeshpuram. The judges visited the commune every year after the festival to ensure that the sannyasins had dismantled all the temporary facilities the county had permitted. The visit wasn't really necessary as a matter of law, but the judges figured that their constituents would expect them to go out to the ranch every now and then to monitor what the disciples were up to.

When Ava arrived at Zorba the Buddha Rajneesh Restaurant in Antelope that morning, the judges were already sitting down, just as Sheela and Puja had predicted. They always stopped at the café for lunch before making the final forty-five-minute journey into Rajneeshpuram. As soon as Ava walked behind the counter, Hulse asked her for a glass of water. It was too easy.

With her back turned, she took out the vial that Puja had given her. The nurse hadn't said what the murky brown liquid was, although from its look and smell Ava suspected it was either salmonella, which she knew Puja was mass-producing in the Chinese Laundry, or hepatitis, with which Puja had been recently experimenting. She poured a couple of drops from the vial into a glass of water, but the brown liquid swirled about inside—too obvious. Ava poured some of the water into the sink, then added more clean water to try to dilute it.

She set the glass before Hulse. He drank from it.

Sheela had said she didn't want the county officials snooping through their affairs. Her goal was to keep their tour short and get them out as soon as possible. Puja's liquid offered the solution. Ava hadn't asked any questions. She just wanted to protect the commune and make her Moms proud.

As the Twinkie in chief, the elegant Chilean sannyasin Ma Prem Isabel was tasked with driving the county judges around the ranch during their visit. She loathed giving tours to government officials, and this one was particularly uncomfortable with all the recent hostility coming from Wasco County.

Things got dicey when they parked outside Devateerth Mall in the heart of the commune. Spotting them as she drove by in her black Mercedes sedan, Sheela stopped to chat with the lone judge she saw as a friendly voice on the court, Virgil Ellett. But she acted stunned when she saw Ellett sitting in the far back of the van, while Hulse and Matthew were closer to the front. *Isabel, what is this?* Sheela asked, loud enough for all the judges to hear. *You haven't learned anything from my training yet? How come you are sitting the snakes in the front and the friend in the back?*

Isabel stared forward with a fixed smile, hoping Sheela would just disappear.

They later hit traffic during Bhagwan's afternoon drive-by. While they waited at a corner, Sheela drove by again and flipped her middle finger at Hulse.

What a gracious lady, he said.

When the tour was over, a relieved Isabel drove the judges back to the Mirdad Welcome Center parking lot near the commune's entrance. They found that Hulse's car had a flat tire—a regular occurrence for people driving along the rutted, ill-maintained county road from Antelope to the ranch. Isabel went inside Mirdad to call the commune's garage to fix the tire while the judges waited outside beneath the hot August sun.

An unexpected character emerged from Isabel's office: Ma Anand Puja. The head of the Rajneesh Medical Corporation had no business in the welcome center, but there she was, carrying a tray with a water pitcher and three

Styrofoam cups arranged side by side. Puja chided Isabel for failing to offer the judges some water on such a hot day. She wanted to make sure they didn't get dehydrated and pass out in the parking lot. With that, she swanned out of Mirdad with her tray.

The whole scenario was strange, but Isabel found it oddest that Puja was being so kind to the commune's enemies. She supposed that Sheela felt bad about being so nakedly hostile to the judges earlier and had asked Puja to help make nice. Isabel followed her outside and watched as the nurse filled the Styrofoam cups with water and handed one to each judge.

Late that night, Judge Hulse began to experience severe stomach cramps. The next morning, at his wife's insistence, he checked himself into the hospital, where he remained for another four days. Doctors ran multiple tests but couldn't determine what was causing his illness, finally diagnosing it as general gastroenteritis. His family physician said that if he hadn't come in to the hospital, he would have died. The director of the Oregon Poison Center would later review Hulse's case and find that his condition was consistent with a person who may have ingested salmonella.

Judge Ray Matthew, seventy-two years old, also became sick two days after visiting Rajneeshpuram, although he never went to the hospital or consulted a doctor. After two days of illness he tried to resume his normal activities, but he had a relapse and was bedridden for a few more days.

Sheela's "friend," Judge Virgil Ellet, felt just fine.

Ava would later tell federal investigators that someone from the commune had intentionally punctured Bill Hulse's tire while the judges were on their tour with Isabel, to give Puja an opportunity to sicken them while they waited outside Mirdad. Krishna Deva heard a similar story when he returned to Rajneeshpuram from a business trip to Salem. It may have been an effort to get the judges off the ranch as soon as possible. It may have been pure retribution.

Whatever the reason, the Hulse and Matthew poisonings proved that the biological agents Puja was mass-producing in the Chinese Laundry could incapacitate victims. But she couldn't drive around The Dalles individually dosing thousands of people. If she wanted to sway the election, she still needed to find a mass-distribution mechanism that worked.

Puja would finally hit the jackpot in September, when she launched the largest bioterrorism attack ever perpetrated on US soil.

22 | HOW TO WIN AN ELECTION

DURING THE FIRST WEEK OF SEPTEMBER, a striking man with curly dark hair and a salt-and-pepper beard approached HARRY LOUDON outside a mission for homeless people in downtown San Diego. The dark-haired man wore a flashy red suit and a beaded necklace with an old Indian man's face staring out from the medallion. He introduced himself as Swami Jayananda.

He handed Loudon a glossy brochure featuring photographs of a brand-new hotel with a swimming pool and a gorgeous lake with mountains in the background where people were sunbathing near the blue waters. Jayananda was recruiting people to come live at this idyllic place, and he would even provide free transportation if Loudon satisfied some basic requirements. He had to be eighteen years old; he had to be a US citizen; and he had to abstain from drugs, violence, and criminal activity while living there. Loudon would receive a clean place to sleep, new clothing, three square meals and two packs of cigarettes every day, and two beers every night—all for free. He wouldn't have to work, unless he wanted to. And if he ever wanted to leave, he'd get a free bus ticket home.

It was a charity program, Jayananda said.

Loudon put his name on the list that Jayananda passed around to the guys on the street outside the mission. It sounded pretty appealing for somebody down on his luck. At forty-three years old, after five wives, five children, and multiple stints in drug and alcohol rehabilitation programs, Loudon was adrift in life. He'd only recently checked himself out of a Wyoming detox hospital and traveled to sunny San Diego. Jayananda's offer sounded too good to be true, but Loudon saw no harm in trying it out. If it turned out to be a scam, he could always take the return bus ticket and get out of there.

Voter fraud, voter fraud, voter fraud.

Even with Puja's salmonella incubating in the Chinese Laundry, Sheela had kept pressure on Krishna Deva to increase their voting population at the ranch and ensure they could win the November election. By August the situation had become desperate, fueling desperate ideas. Commune members were told to invite their American parents to stay at the ranch over the fall. Foreign sannyasins with American spouses were asked to move to the ranch, as long as their spouses came with them. College professors who had studied Rajneeshpuram were asked to stay there throughout the fall as visiting scholars. The commune called every American sannyasin living off the ranch and urged them to move to Oregon immediately.

None of these last-ditch efforts worked. The Buddhafield Experience was a bust. Sheela summoned Krishna Deva for another strategy meeting. What else could they do to increase their numbers?

Reflecting on it later, KD couldn't say whether he or Sheela had first touched on the explosive idea (Sheela says it was KD), but as soon as it emerged from one of their mouths, it became their primary strategy. There were millions of adult American citizens living on the streets and in shelters across the country. If Rajneeshpuram were to extend its hospitality to them—regular meals, a clean place to live—how could they refuse? The disciples need only persuade a few thousand homeless people to stay at Rajneeshpuram just long enough to acquire Oregon voting rights, register, and vote. Then they would get rid of them.

In late August, the Rajneesh Humanity Trust announced a radical new charitable program to house the nation's most vulnerable population. It would be called Share-a-Home, and it would commence immediately.

Harry Loudon boarded a Trailways bus in San Diego along with eighteen other homeless people en route to Rajneeshpuram. They stopped in Los Angeles to retrieve another twenty-five. The long ride to Oregon grew chaotic as people fought over the sandwiches that the recruiters doled out. Loudon finally commandeered the food and took responsibility for distributing it. An impressed disciple asked him to maintain order for the rest of the trip.

Their bus was one of many chartered Trailways buses that had started scouring the country for homeless people to come to the ranch. The first arrived in New York City the last week of August, bearing sannyasin recruiters who talked up the pampered life in Rajneeshpuram, and that bus returned to the ranch in the first week of September carrying the very first participants of the Share-a-Home program. Other buses soon arrived with hundreds of homeless people from Seattle, Portland, San Francisco, Los Angeles, San Diego, Phoenix, Denver, Kansas City, Houston, Chicago, Milwaukee, Detroit, Cleveland, Pittsburgh, Philadelphia, Boston, and Washington, DC.

When Loudon's bus finally reached the ranch after dozens of hours on the road, a representative from the Rajneesh Humanity Trust hopped aboard to welcome them and remind them that the community would not tolerate drugs or violence on its property. The new arrivals filled out paperwork, like a tedious job application, in which they had to disclose their full identities, educational and employment histories, veteran status, mental and physical health, any medications they required, and whether they received any income or government benefits, such as Social Security, disability, or retirement income. Those with any income were told they would need to pay $250 per month for the pleasure of staying as a guest at Rajneeshpuram. Everyone else—the vast majority of the Share-a-Home participants—could stay for free.

Members of Rajneesh Security next went through all their bags and patted down their bodies while Bear the German shepherd sniffed for drugs. One man grew furious when the guards confiscated his worldly belongings: his screwdrivers (potential weapons), his matchbook (fire hazard), and even his can of pork and beans (the sannyasins insisted upon a vegetarian lifestyle). Another man was forced to turn over the arsenal he had carried with him on the bus: a Hitler Youth knife from World War II, a survival knife, an ax, and his gun collection, including two Luger pistols, a nickel-plated .357 revolver, and two .44 Magnum revolvers.

At a communal shower facility, the new arrivals had to scrub with a special soap to kill lice and crabs. Their old clothes were whisked away while they bathed, supposedly to be laundered and returned to them, and they received clean clothing in sunrise colors from the ranch's collection, including leftover merchandise from previous festivals. Many program participants were sent to live in a canyon called Walt Whitman Grove, north of the airstrip and the meditation university, with A-frame cabins like those in Alan Watts Grove. Others were taken to large flat areas with weatherized tents on wooden platforms—the same accommodations used during the World Celebrations.

The day after Loudon arrived, the commune hosted an orientation meeting for all the new arrivals under a huge tent. A lanky man with a warm smile, Mayor Krishna Deva, tried to make them feel comfortable in their strange new home. But he also said there would be no deviance from the community's rules, particularly one that made some of the Share-a-Home participants squirm: new arrivals could not have sex until the Rajneesh Medical Corporation had tested and cleared them for venereal diseases. Anybody breaking any of the rules would be kicked off the ranch.

Harry Loudon wouldn't hear a thing about voting until four days later.

In September and October 1984, the sannyasins brought in nearly four thousand homeless people from across America. The problems associated with bringing in such a vulnerable, high-needs population to the insular Rajneeshpuram community became apparent almost immediately. As Puja's assistant, Ava was responsible for coordinating the medical inspection and treatment of the Share-a-Home participants. The commune's medical facilities were designed to support a modest-sized community of healthy, active individuals, mostly in their thirties and from backgrounds that had afforded them quality health care. The commune simply didn't have the space, the staff, or the resources to address the complex and intersecting medical problems that arrived with each new busload throughout September. On the first two busloads alone, Ava encountered cases of HIV, bronchitis, venereal disease, mental illness, and other serious medical conditions. Some people arrived in withdrawal from drugs or alcohol after the long bus ride. Ma Anand Sagun, one of the program coordinators, went through all the new arrivals' medical paperwork and determined that more than three-quarters of the participants reported a history of epilepsy, mental disorders, and/or being institutionalized.

Overwhelmed, Ava turned to Puja for assistance. Her boss was not interested, beyond telling the medical staff to cut costs in their treatment of the homeless people, which resulted in the doctors prescribing less expensive substitutes for more common drugs. Puja did intervene one day when a man with mental illness went rampaging near Jesus Grove, tearing phones off walls, breaking furniture, pelting Ava with rocks, and pulling people out of their vehicles. Sheela and Sagun arrived and tried to calm him, but the man punched Sagun in the stomach and started to strangle Sheela. Puja persuaded him to drink a glass of water she had spiked with something. When he was sufficiently sedated, they threw him off the ranch. Vidya and Sheela blamed the incident on Ava's poor management of his medical condition.

Among the sannyasins who had dropped everything to live at Bhagwan Shree Rajneesh's mystery school in the desert, many were horrified to find themselves suddenly elbow-to-elbow with thousands of homeless people. Most commune members were white, middle or upper-middle class, and college educated, with no experience working or living with such a volatile population. Ma Prem Hasya, doyenne of the Hollywood Group, later told a reporter, "I walked with my eyes to the ground because I felt so uncomfortable" during the Share-a-Home program. "I've never personally had contact with street people. Part of me wanted to get closer to understand what is a street person. But a greater part of me didn't know quite how. It was too strange to my being, so I just chose to ignore it."

As with everything at Rajneeshpuram, the commune members didn't get a vote when it came to the Share-a-Home program. They had to go along with it and were even encouraged to call their new neighbors "friends"—a euphemism that nauseated some disciples. The mere idea of engaging in charity work was baffling to many sannyasins, since Bhagwan had spent most of his public life ridiculing it. In India, the "Guru of the Rich" had regularly lambasted Mahatma Gandhi for "worshipping" poverty, and in America he flaunted his dozens of Rolls-Royce sedans and Rolex watches. The spiritual path, he said, was available only to those with the resources and the mental clarity to pursue it. The poor had too many worldly problems. "When a man is dying of hunger, what use is a Van Gogh painting? Or a Buddha's sermon?" he once said. "I have never seen a person who is really poor—poor in intelligence, poor in riches—ever become religious."

With the advent of the Share-a-Home program, Sheela and other spokespeople offered weak rationalizations for their sudden interest in helping the needy. Sheela called it a matter of abundance. "We don't believe in charity," she told a reporter, "and we're not into humiliating them. We want to share what's ours, our surplus." Another time she said the program was designed to "change their habits" by removing participants from the streets and immersing them in a nurturing environment.

Some sannyasins accepted these explanations and were excited to share their largesse with a vulnerable population. "Absolutely, I wanted to share my home," MA ANAND SARABI later reflected about the program, noting that she knew many other commune members who were similarly enthusiastic. For her, a young biracial woman from the American South, the Share-a-Home program was an opportunity to address the country's history of racism, genocide, and slavery by giving disadvantaged people—particularly homeless Black men—a place at the table. But others could see a cynical calculation at play. A reporter asked Krishna Deva in mid-September whether the Share-a-Home participants were there to vote.

"I never thought of it," KD said, with a cryptic smile on his face.

"Does it sound like a good idea?" the reporter asked.

"It sounds like a hell of an idea."

More than two weeks into the Share-a-Home program, Sheela held a major press event inside an open-air tent that served as a cafeteria for the program participants. The Twinkies had invited reporters from around the state to witness Rajneeshpuram's munificence. Hundreds of program participants sat at long picnic tables, wedged between the clamoring news media behind them and the commune representatives in front. With the cameras rolling, Sheela launched into a screed against state legislator Wayne Fawbush, who had recently suggested a special legislative session to tighten voter registration laws. He, like so many Oregonians, was convinced that the only purpose for bringing so many people to Rajneeshpuram was to win the Wasco County election in November, and he intended to quickly pass a law that would bar the Share-a-Home participants from voting.

Sheela told the participants that Fawbush was trying to strip them of their constitutional rights as American citizens and, in many cases, military veterans. Perched on a stool with her feet propped on another chair, she issued a series of threats. "Nobody will touch this home," she said. "You tell your governors, you tell your attorney general, and all your bigoted pigs outside that they dare touch any of our people—and I include these new friends in it, these are our people—they touch any of our people, for one of our people, I will have fifteen of their heads, and I mean business."

She deigned to address the nasty rumors that linked her charity program with the upcoming election. "I didn't even have the thought occur to me that they can vote or have anything to do with voting," she declared, jabbing a finger to the sky, her eyes boring into the men and women sitting mute at the picnic tables. "I got accused that I invited you because I wanted to take over the county and the politics. I tell you, the county is so fucking bigoted, it deserves to be taken over."

Harry Loudon, hanging on Sheela's every word, felt that the situation she described was outrageous. He asked a disciple to help him register to vote in Wasco County, and then he took it upon himself to walk around the commune and gather another fifty-seven Share-a-Home participants to register. When he approached Krishna Deva with the list of names, the mayor seemed surprised by his initiative. He said a table would be set up to register new voters—and that's exactly what happened. Three typewriters and three typists became a fixture in the mess hall. The cafeteria had a public address system over which participants were told throughout every meal that they had the right to vote and should in fact register at the nearby tables. Loudon's recruiting efforts so impressed the disciples that they invited him to take sannyas in late September. He worshipped with Rajneesh Security, helping to search people coming in and out of the commune.

The Rajneeshpuram voter registration drive was a huge success, capturing thousands of new Wasco County voters. Many were motivated by the specter of commune antagonists such as Representative Fawbush, whose names became dirty words during Sheela's evening rallies. The mere fact that politicians wanted to deny the participants' legal rights made them want to exercise them—even if they didn't particularly care about Wasco County politics or voting in general.

Throughout it all, the Wasco County official in charge of voter registration monitored the situation at Rajneeshpuram and prepared for the worst. "They're going to show us they can do as they darn well please," county clerk Sue Proffitt complained on *Nightline*. But only if Oregonians allowed them to.

23 | SOMETHING IN THE WATER

BUOYED BY THE SUCCESS OF THEIR TRIAL run on Judges Hulse and Matthew in late August, Sheela and Puja pulled Ava into a meeting in early September, one week after the Share-a-Home program had started. Puja handed Ava a half-dozen vials filled with a brown liquid that smelled horrible. She said it was salmonella. Ava's task was to spread it in as many restaurants in The Dalles as possible.

If there is a choice between one thousand unenlightened people or one enlightened master, you should always choose the enlightened master, Sheela told Ava, to try to justify the assault that was about to take place.

In Puja's bedroom, Ava changed into "blue clothes"—non-sannyasin colors—and drove to The Dalles with a man named Bodhi, who was the boyfriend of commune president Vidya. They stopped at the Recreation Cafe, a relic from the 1960s that offered a salad bar and a full bowling alley. They stopped at Arlo's. They stopped at Johnny's Cafe, an all-night favorite for blue-collar workers, wedged between shops and businesses on the main street that passed through downtown. In two restaurants, they unscrewed the lid on a coffee creamer jar at their table and poured in some brown sludge. The smell was so awful that they didn't use much, concerned that the contamination would be too obvious. At the third restaurant, Ava and Bodhi approached the salad bar and inconspicuously dumped some sludge into the blue-cheese salad dressing.

Other crews were sent to The Dalles to do the same thing in September, all armed with vials of the murky brown liquid, hitting at least ten restaurants. Puja would later brag to Ava and others that she had personally gone to The

Dalles to spread salmonella in "lots of places." Bodhi grumbled to KD that Puja had poured the salmonella with such panache that he was convinced somebody would see her.

In meetings with her top assistants, Sheela had continued to insist that they find a way to mass-contaminate voters in The Dalles before the election. She told them that the directive was no longer her own, that in fact Bhagwan had endorsed the idea of "giving people the shits" so they couldn't vote. *It's best not to hurt people,* Sheela recounted that Bhagwan had said, according to KD, *but if a few people die, don't worry about it.*

Other disciples who weren't part of the Jesus Grove inner circle would later reject the notion that Bhagwan knew anything about any of Sheela's nefarious plots, including the efforts around the Wasco County election. Krishna Deva, however, had no doubt that Bhagwan gave his explicit permission to commence with the mass poisoning, based on everything he knew about the close relationship between the guru and his secretary, as well as Bhagwan's all-consuming desire to capture political control of the county.

In the second week of September, thirty-four-year-old Geraldine Baker of Bend, Oregon, went into labor. While being admitted to the Mid-Columbia Medical Center in The Dalles, she mentioned that she had been suffering from intense gastrointestinal distress for the past day or two, ever since she ate from the salad bar at a restaurant in The Dalles.

Baker's son was born extremely dehydrated and in septic shock— a condition so dire that the obstetrician estimated he had no more than a 5 percent chance of surviving. Tests revealed that Baker was infected with S. Typhimurium, and she had passed it on to her son in utero. The infection nearly killed him.

September 9 marked the first day that anyone in The Dalles experienced the sort of severe gastrointestinal distress associated with salmonella poisoning. Over the next ten days, that number would climb to eighty-eight potentially affected people. All of them either worked at or had eaten at two restaurants in The Dalles. At one of those restaurants, everybody who got sick had eaten the same foods from the salad bar: macaroni, potato, four-bean, or pea salads. Some of those experiencing symptoms remained at home and recovered without medical intervention, but some went to the hospital, had their stools analyzed, and were diagnosed with salmonella infections.

Just as public health officials in Wasco County realized they were in the midst of a food-borne salmonella outbreak, a second, much larger wave of infections commenced on September 19 and continued through October 10, affecting at least 586 people. Most cases were traced to a group of ten restaurants in The Dalles, eight with open salad bars. As the second wave crested, state health officials urged all restaurants in The Dalles to close their salad bars while local health officials and investigators from the Centers for Disease Control in Atlanta worked to determine the outbreak's cause. As soon as the salad bars closed, the outbreak tapered to a stop.

The public health investigation was far more challenging than for a typical outbreak since the infections could not be traced to one particular food item. Salad bars seemed to be a common factor, but infected patients had not all eaten the same foods. At one restaurant the infected patients may have eaten blue-cheese dressing. At another it was lettuce. At a couple of restaurants the common source was potato salad. This suggested to investigators that the problem was not in the food itself, but in the way it was being handled by restaurant employees, who accounted for more than 10 percent of the infections. In November, Oregon health officials released a preliminary report finding that improper sanitary practices among food handlers had caused the September outbreak.

But that explanation did not satisfy some of the investigators who had been working the case for over two months. One odd quirk of The Dalles outbreak was that people who received takeout orders or used the banquet facilities of the affected restaurants weren't infected. If there were improper food handling in the kitchens, it was limited almost exclusively to the salad bars—which defied common sense. Another strange aspect of the outbreak was that all the salmonella extracted from the patients' stool samples shared some highly unusual characteristics. It seemed likely that all the salmonella infections could be traced back to one unique source that had somehow pervaded at least ten restaurants.

All told, 751 people who ate or worked at restaurants in The Dalles in September 1984 were either diagnosed with salmonella gastroenteritis or experienced consistent symptoms. They ranged in age from in utero to eighty-seven years old. At least forty-five of those affected were hospitalized for their symptoms, but no known fatalities were reported from the outbreak.

Puji, you've done a good job of making everyone sick, Sheela told her trusted nurse in the aftermath of the restaurant poisonings, as Krishna Deva later recalled it. *Too bad you didn't make more people sick.* KD saw Sheela practically flaunting the situation among her top lieutenants, while Puja bragged about how much salmonella she had personally dumped across The Dalles.

But it was just a test. Seven hundred people was a good start, but it wouldn't be enough to tilt the election in their favor. They had until early November to find a wider-scale means of distributing the bacteria.

One idea that emerged over the summer was to dump a contaminant into The Dalles's water system. At Sheela's request, a disciple acquired maps of the water system, which comprised a treatment plant in the hills west of town, six closed storage tanks around the city, and two open storage reservoirs. The system was monitored at several stations, with a central monitor in the Public Works Water Department downtown.

Puja said that rodents contained natural bacteria in their bodies. She suggested throwing a dead beaver into a water tank. Sheela tapped two sannyasins to explore the system and report whether this was feasible: Julian, the electronics whiz and coordinator of the Edison Temple, and Anugiten, boyfriend of chief accountant Savita. Upon investigation, they found metal mesh coverings that would block any large objects from being dumped into the system. Someone suggested they liquefy the beaver in a large blender. It may have been meant as a joke, but Puja seemed to think it might work. Another idea was to pour salmonella directly into the tanks—although Puja fretted that she couldn't make enough bacteria to affect the city's vast water supply.

In September, Julian and Anugiten revealed at a Jesus Grove meeting that they had twice tried to dump something into one of the six closed storage tanks in The Dalles. On the first occasion, nearby police officers had "freaked them out," so they left. The second time, they climbed a chain-link fence and mounted a hill up to the storage tank. Walking across the top of the enormous tank, they found an opening covered by a wire screen into which they had poured some substance. Nobody who has spoken about these planning meetings seems to know what went into the tank. Ava speculated that it may have been raw sewage, since she heard Puja ask a Rajneeshpuram resource manager to supply her with some around this time. Ava also noticed that a large number of rats from the Chinese Laundry cages suddenly disappeared around the time that Julian and Anugiten had gone to The Dalles. She wondered if Puja had contaminated the rodents with something before they got tossed into the water.

One year later, police officers inspecting the squat, three-million-gallon tank at Sorosis Park in The Dalles noticed old shoe prints on the tank's painted metal surface. It looked like two people had climbed the ladder and walked to the largest vent screen, which had been cut along one side and pushed open. A city employee familiar with the system would later tell investigators that it would have been virtually impossible for the disciples to have poisoned the water supply, given all the chlorine in the water, the purification system, and all the monitors that noted unusual amounts of chemicals or contaminants.

In addition to their attempts to poison restaurants and the water supply, Sheela's gang tried other ways to spread salmonella before the election. One Jesus Grove lieutenant, a young woman from Tucson named Yogini, smeared salmonella on her palms before shaking hands at a Republican political event in Central Oregon. She also may have spread it at a retirement home and a school in The Dalles, according to Ava, although Yogini has denied those allegations and no outbreak was reported at the time.

Nothing they tried had the effect required to tilt the election. Even if they could replicate in November what they had done in the restaurants—which was doubtful, given all the scrutiny the outbreak received from public health officials—the scale was simply not grand enough to make a difference. Besides, Sheela and Puja began to lose interest in the salmonella plot by the end of September. The Share-a-Home program had taken on an outsized importance in life at the commune, with thousands of homeless residents now living on the property, consuming vast amounts of resources, and requiring intense security and medical efforts to keep them under control.

September 1984 was the beginning and the end of any known wide-scale salmonella poisoning. The test remained a test—and its timing in fact threw public health officials off the scent. Even if somebody whispered that perhaps the strange cult out in the high desert was responsible, there was no way to explain it happening in September instead of November. To the extent anyone suspected the sannyasins at the time, such accusations were not made out loud.

In fact, they would not be publicly aired until six months later, when US congressman Jim Weaver would imply, while speaking on the floor of the House of Representatives in Washington, DC, that members of the Rajneeshpuram commune had instigated the bizarre salmonella contamination that ravaged The Dalles in September. His allegation prompted a furious response from commune members that would persist until later that year, when a public health official combing through the Pythagoras Medical Clinic in the commune's southern valley would find a vial containing a sample of *S.* Typhimurium, purchased from VWR Scientific in Seattle, with the classification ATCC 14028. Tests at the Centers for Disease Control would confirm that the unusual strain found at Rajneeshpuram was indistinguishable from the strain found in victims of The Dalles outbreak.

24 | DESPERATE TIMES

ON OCTOBER 10, TELEVISION NEWS crews and sannyasin videographers were waiting on the sidewalk to capture a Rajneesh Buddhafield Transport bus as it arrived outside the Wasco County courthouse. Twenty Share-a-Home participants emerged, primarily Black men, who marched up the grand staircase and into the lobby bearing their completed voter registration cards. The commune had been collecting registrations from Share-a-Home participants over the past month, and this would be the first day they would put them in the county's hands. Leading the procession was Ma Deva Jayamala, an unusually old sannyasin with long white hair, deep lines around her mouth, and steel in her eyes. She led the men to the registration table, where Wasco County clerk Sue Proffitt stood in a turquoise blouse and oatmeal blazer with a legal pad clutched in her hands. A plainspoken woman with a tight brown perm, Proffitt told the men to gather around so they could hear her prepared statement.

"Because I have reason to believe there are organized efforts to fraudulently register people in Wasco County to vote in the November general election," Proffitt read from her notepad, "I have decided to do a blanket rejection of all new voter registrations in Wasco County as of now. The rejections will constitute automatic requests for a hearing before a hearings officer."

She glanced up at the men, who were glaring at her. "This action is taken because of statements made publicly by the Rajneesh Humanity Trust . . ."

As the clerk wrapped up her prepared speech, Jayamala stepped up to the table separating Proffitt from the dozens of sannyasins and Share-a-Home participants. "All these people are American citizens. They have a right to register. Has this ever happened before?"

"Not to my knowledge," Proffitt said. "This is done on the advice of the secretary of state's office."

"I think you're being very insulting to these people who are American citizens and have just as much a right to vote as you do, and I do, and anybody else," Jayamala said.

Proffitt asked the men to hand over their completed voter registration cards so she could schedule their hearing dates. Some complained about discrimination while dropping their cards in Proffitt's hand. One man in a beret dropped a condom on the registration table and told her it was a present from a Share-a-Home coordinator.

"Next registration please," Proffitt called, her nose high in the air. "Please move on."

"We will return," one man vented at her. "We'll return with three thousand people!"

The men filed out of the courthouse singing "God Bless America," and they gave press interviews on the sidewalk about how the State of Oregon was trampling on their civil rights.

Jayamala was visibly stunned. "When we go back and tell the citizens of our city what's happened here today," she told a reporter, shaking her head, "I don't know what's going to happen, but it's not going to be good."

If anyone were poised to stop the disciples from carrying out the Share-a-Home program election strategy, it was Norma Paulus. Before she was elected secretary of state in 1976—making her the first woman elected to statewide office in Oregon—Paulus had been an attorney and a Republican state legislator. While she served on the House Elections Committee, the panel had taken up a bill to make it drastically easier for a person to register to vote in the state of Oregon. Paulus had not been convinced. She believed that county clerks should have broad discretion to determine voter eligibility, later saying that they should be allowed to reject an applicant "maybe just on a gut feeling." The committee vote on the bill came down to Norma Paulus, and she signed on only after it was amended to allow clerks significant latitude to reject applicants they felt were not qualified.

This provision came to Paulus's mind in October 1984 as she mulled over the brewing storm in Wasco County. As the state's chief elections officer, she was under intense pressure from constituents and politicians to find a way to block the thousands of Share-a-Home participants from voting. The program was receiving daily statewide and national press coverage, as were Sheela's threats to take over the county and then the state.

An anti-Rajneesh group from the Willamette Valley intended to counteract the Share-a-Home program by using Sheela's own strategy from Antelope in 1982: moving in thousands of Oregonians to Wasco County the day before the election so they could vote there. People who already lived in the state didn't need to satisfy the twenty-day residency requirement.

"They're setting themselves up for a felony conviction," Paulus had warned in a newspaper interview, trying to squelch the idea.

But the group's leader, a strident retiree from Albany named JoAnne Boies, would not be dissuaded. "If thousands of us go up there," she said, "there's no way they could arrest and process us all."

The spat escalated in early October, with Boies demanding that state officials stop the Rajneeshees from "stealing" the election; she even suggested Governor Atiyeh call a state of emergency and send in the national guard. When officials still failed to take noticeable action, she alleged that the likes of Secretary Paulus and Governor Atiyeh must have been paid off to remain silent. At a rally attended by three hundred anti-Rajneesh activists and covered on the front page of the Salem newspaper, Boies declared that Governor Atiyeh should lose his office, to roars of approval from the crowd, some of whom shouted "Recall! Recall!" In urging Oregonians to flood into The Dalles before the election, she painted a bleak picture: "If you don't get off your duffs, you're going to be wearing a picture of the Bhagwan around your neck."

Norma Paulus didn't need to be persuaded that the sannyasins were up to no good. Her skepticism went back to the Antelope disincorporation vote in 1982, which she had personally overseen. Although the disciples had acted within the bounds of the law, their tactics struck her as a flagrant abuse of a system that relied to some extent on good faith. As she saw it, the Share-a-Home program in 1984 was just a continuation of their well-established pattern: manipulating and abusing systems to get what they wanted, without any regard for the people around them. She had no doubt that the Share-a-Home program was a ploy to win the election and that the commune would dump the participants when it was over.

Amid the extraordinary pressure to act, Paulus developed a secret plan to save Wasco County. Under the provision she had insisted go into the voter registration law back in 1975, Paulus believed that Wasco County clerk Sue Proffitt had the discretion to do a blanket rejection of all new registrations based on suspected voter fraud. But the law provided that each rejected applicant would receive a hearing before an administrative judge within ten days. If Proffitt denied all of the expected Share-a-Home registrations, the state would need to hold thousands of hearings in the scant weeks leading up to the November 6 election, requiring hundreds of judges to get it done in time. Paulus had nowhere near that many administrative judges at her disposal.

While walking around Portland and chewing on this problem, Paulus happened upon an attorney, Cliff Carlsen, who was widely known as the first Oregonian to travel to the South in 1964 to offer pro bono legal services to Black Americans in support of the civil rights movement. Seeing Carlsen sparked an idea. If attorneys had flocked to Mississippi to protect people's rights, why couldn't they go to The Dalles and help the people of Wasco County? Paulus explained the situation to Carlsen and asked if he might be able to find five hundred Oregon attorneys willing to donate their time to this all-important cause. Carlsen signed on.

As the independently elected public official in charge of Oregon elections, Paulus didn't need Governor Atiyeh to approve her plan. Still, she met with him and his legal counsel the first week of October to explain what she meant to do. By that point Carlsen had found hundreds of volunteer lawyers to serve as deputized election officials, and Paulus had secured the National Guard Armory in The Dalles to host the hearings, arranged transportation for all the attorneys, and confirmed the details with the Oregon State Police and the attorney general's office. The governor gave his blessing. His guidance to state officials had always been to treat the sannyasins just like they would anybody else in Oregon—no special treatment, no discrimination. The fact that JoAnne Boies was rallying thousands of Oregonians to vote in The Dalles made Paulus's plan seem airtight. By suspending *all* voter registration in the county, Paulus could argue that she was not singling out the sannyasins, but was trying to block *any* outside interference in the county's election. (Despite her protestations of neutrality at the time, Paulus would later admit that her only concern was stopping the sannyasins from winning the county election.)

The next week, on the morning of October 10, the secretary of state's office received a report that several busloads of Share-a-Home participants were on their way to register in The Dalles—although it would turn out to be only a single bus. Paulus called Wasco County clerk Sue Proffitt and told her the time had come to spring their trap.

"The clerk of the county read a little piece of shit," Sheela told thousands of people gathered in Rajneesh Mandir that night, sitting onstage in a purple velvet tracksuit. Usually sharp and ferocious at her rallies, on this night Sheela's eyes were heavily lidded and words came slowly from her mouth, as if her tongue were too heavy. "Sue Proffitt said that she was instructed by her superior, Norma Paulus, the secretary of state. Paulus wants to become the governor. She may have gotten into the governor's pants by now, or sat on his chair, or whatever she did, I don't know. But her hopes are to become governor of the state. Well, that woman, that bitch, has made the worst mistake in her life."

Sheela invited Jayamala to recount to the crowd what had happened in The Dalles that morning. "We were just shocked and sickened at what happened when we got there," the white-haired disciple said. "We were singing on the bus, but part of my heart is in mourning."

Wrapping up the rally, Sheela declared that Rajneeshpuram would secede from the state. She commanded the attendees to dance in an empty area near the stage as the band started to play. "We will celebrate the death of the state of Oregon here. Pretend this is the body of the state of Oregon, and make sure Rajneeshpuram is not part of it. Let's celebrate and enjoy the death of the state of Oregon!" Thousands of sannyasins and their newest neighbors jumped and clapped and danced atop Oregon's corpse.

Norma Paulus scheduled a press conference in Salem on October 12 to explain her rationale for suspending voter registration in Wasco County. In the press release announcing the conference, she invited any concerned citizens in Oregon to attend—except for Ma Anand Sheela: "I have a contract with the people of this state, but that contract does not contain a clause requiring me to subject myself to shouting, screaming, or vile obscene epithets. For that reason, Sheela is not invited or welcome." In response, Sheela promised to send up to two thousand people to march in the streets of Salem during the press conference.

Paulus spent that Friday morning rehearsing with her aides, intent on remaining polite and noncombative if Sheela or another sannyasin antagonist showed up. Flanked by troopers from the Oregon State Police, Paulus gave her press conference in the capitol. The sannyasins did not appear.

Sheela later told reporters that she had called off the protest because she had learned that government agents planned to incite violence against the disciples if they came to Salem. "This was the last chance they had to destroy a thousand Rajneeshees in one go," Sheela said. "The only thing I can do is protect my people, take care of them, and see to it that these politicians don't have Rajneeshee meat for dinner, because it's too expensive. They're well-bred meat."

The statewide reaction to Paulus's plan was mixed. An editorial in her hometown newspaper, the *Statesman Journal* of Salem, claimed the secretary had "in effect declared martial election law in Wasco County" and chided her for leading a get-out-the-vote initiative in one part of the state while blocking registration in another part. Privately, the former chief judge of the Oregon Court of Appeals told Paulus that she "could have been elected queen today" because Oregonians were thrilled that a state official had finally stood up to the overbearing sannyasins.

"That means we've won," proclaimed JoAnne Boies upon hearing of the voter registration ban. While she planned to keep an eye on developments, she announced that she and the others in her group would probably no longer need to travel to Wasco County to "save" the election.

Still, as the voter registration hearings approached, Secretary Paulus worried that her plan might fall apart if non-sannyasins in Wasco County objected to the new burdens being placed on them if they tried to register. "We had to figure out how to get word out to the regular citizens that they couldn't complain about going through with it," Paulus explained years later. She contacted Laura Bentley, who led an anti-Rajneesh group in The Dalles and was known to be furious about the Share-a-Home situation. "I said here's what we're doing, you have to get it out to the regular citizens. I can't do it. You have to get it out in your telephone system that they all have to go through the same process. They have to have their rights stopped, and they have to go through a hearing."

According to Paulus, Bentley was more than happy to help if it meant foiling the sannyasins' election scheme. "So she got her little network working, as they do in smaller towns," Paulus later explained, "and started telling people what this was about, what the procedure was about, and what needed to be done legally to make it work and not be challengeable."

With the plan in motion, Paulus had done all she felt she could to impede the sannyasins' strategy. Now she could only wait to see what would happen on October 23, when the first group of prospective voters would arrive in The Dalles for their hearings.

25 | SANNYASIN HOSPITALITY

IN THE WINTER OF 1849, a large regiment of the US Army under the command of Lieutenant William Frost traveled northwest from Fort Leavenworth, Kansas, to establish posts along the Oregon Trail. Amid a brutal snowstorm in the Cascades, with the pack mules starving and exhausted from trudging through all the mud and snow, the group was forced to abandon forty-five wagons just south of Mount Hood and seek shelter downhill. The area where they dumped their goods became known informally as "government camp." A homesteader later tried to establish a town there called Pompeii, but the more utilitarian name had already become lodged in the minds of locals.

A century and a half later, Government Camp was an unincorporated town that served as the final stop along the highway to the hiking and skiing facilities at Mount Hood's southern base. At four thousand feet above sea level, the town offered a picturesque view of the snow-capped volcano. Among the handful of family-owned restaurants serving locals and tourists was Charlie's Mountain View Restaurant, a cozy, timber-lined bar and grill.

On the morning of October 18, 1984, Patrick Beckman was removing scrap metal from behind Charlie's when he noticed something underneath a large satellite dish. It looked like a mannequin placed facedown on the ground, with stiff limbs and a body so covered in filth that it blended in with the mud around it. As Beckman stepped closer, he saw that it was in fact a human body.

David Ney had been sitting in Charlie's two nights earlier when a disheveled man in his late twenties had walked in. He wore denim bib overalls with the straps undone and a long-sleeved red flannel shirt with a pink thermal shirt underneath. He looked to Ney like a transient—scruffy hair and sideburns, missing front tooth, jagged scar along his throat. The man had made a scene, staggering around the place as if totally spaced out. He waved around a bottle of prescription pills and offered to give them away. He said incoherent things about wanting to find a bowling alley and that he was looking for his mother. Ney kept an eye on him whenever he got close to an overcoat hanging near the bar. Ney was convinced the man would try to steal it, having no jacket of his own.

Finally, after he tried to walk behind the bar several times, tavern employees kicked the man out into the streets of Government Camp. When he tried to reenter, they wouldn't let him in.

A cold front had just moved in from Canada.

Judith "Sonny" Frazier, a waitress at the Huckleberry Inn, had spoken with the man when he first got off the Trailways bus that had stopped so passengers could grab a bite to eat in Government Camp. He was clearly disoriented, as if he were on drugs, and he refused the food that Frazier offered to him. The only thing he wanted was a "ticket back to the big tent."

When the bus driver called for all the passengers to reboard for Portland, the man walked out the door and started toward the bus. But then he staggered across the street toward Charlie's Mountain View instead. The driver kept calling for him to board, to no response. The bus finally lurched off to the west, leaving the passenger to fend for himself.

Frazier went outside to make sure the man hadn't fallen in the snow. He wasn't wearing a jacket, after all, and it had been snowing throughout the day. She didn't see him anywhere, so she assumed he had made it into the restaurant across the street.

The body was facedown, with legs fully extended and arms clenched under the chest. It looked as if the man had been trying to keep warm, although his flannel shirt and shoes were found far from his body under three inches of snow. His socks were torn and his feet were exposed nearly to the ankles. His toes and fingers all appeared to be scraped and frozen.

The medical examiner determined that he had died of hypothermia, abetted by a toxic amount of amitriptyline—an antidepressant mood stabilizer—found in his bloodstream. Although he couldn't say how much the drug had incapacitated the man, he was certain it had played a role in his death by hampering his ability to make sensible decisions, like seeking shelter indoors. The examiner noted that the abrasions on the man's hands, wrists, knees, and feet were common thrashing marks found on people who froze to death, and that he most likely discarded his own clothing. In the final throes of hypothermia, disoriented victims may experience a hot flash that compels them to remove their clothing. They next may engage in an autonomous, primitive urge to dig into the earth for warmth, which causes injuries to the knees, elbows, hands, and feet. It's considered a hypothermia victim's last effort to survive, since the burrowing is followed almost immediately by unconsciousness and then death.

When detectives had searched the man's body, they found a red wallet in his hip pocket. An ID card said he was William Henry Allen of Stanton, California. Buried in the snow they also found a bottle of amitriptyline tablets. The prescription label offered their first clue as to why this California man had been traveling west through the Cascade Range. It was dated October 16—just two days before his body was discovered—and it was signed by a "Doctor Krishnananda."

Krishnananda, a doctor at the Rajneesh Medical Corporation, told detectives that he had examined William Henry Allen upon his arrival at Rajneeshpuram on October 13, three days before he ended up staggering around Government Camp. Allen was among the final group of people imported to the commune as part of the Share-a-Home program, having been picked up by recruiters in California. He self-identified as a manic depressive who took amitriptyline and Thorazine, prescriptions that sannyasin physicians continued giving him at Rajneeshpuram.

Ma Mary Catherine reported on Allen's case for the *Rajneesh Times*. A source told her that soon after William Allen had arrived at Rajneeshpuram, he had been found lying motionless alongside a creek, his skin blue, with two empty prescription bottles nearby. He was taken to medical isolation and given a warm shower, which helped him come around from what appeared to be an overdose. Ma Ava from the clinic visited Allen the next day and found he was in good health but unwilling to take his medications. She wasn't surprised to learn a day or two later that he was no longer at the commune, since the medical corporation ejected anybody who seemed seriously ill.

The usual procedure when Share-a-Home participants left the ranch was to give them a three-day supply of whatever medications they had been receiving. Commune medical records stated that Allen was given six amitriptyline pills as he left. Two sannyasins dropped Allen and some other ejected participants in Madras and gave them bus tickets that would get them as far as Portland. William Henry Allen never made it beyond the Cascade Range.

––––––––––

Share-a-Home participants had been leaving in droves almost since they started arriving in September—as many as six departures for every ten brought in, by the end of the month. Some left because they felt recruiters had lied to them about the luxurious lives they would lead. Some bristled at the commune's strict rules and constant intrusions into their privacy. Some left because of the growing tension within the Share-a-Home community itself, noting racial tensions and gangs forming among ex-convicts. Some were turned off by the sannyasins' liberal approach to sexuality, particularly the "homosexual acts" they claimed to have seen at the ranch, like men hugging and kissing each other at the disco. And many left because it became clear to them that they were merely pawns in some larger game the sannyasins were playing.

Harry Loudon, who had arrived on a bus from San Diego in September, was gone by mid-October. Having taken sannyas after enthusiastically helping to register voters, he became disenchanted while standing in line at the commune's pay phones, where he overheard multiple disciples calling other sannyasins and telling them to drop everything and come to Rajneeshpuram to vote. It was the first time Loudon suspected the Share-a-Home program was nothing more than a scheme to win the local election. He spoke with a coordinator and secured transportation to Portland, where he planned to settle.

But many Share-a-Home participants didn't leave the commune by choice. Sheela and her coordinators would stalk through orientation sessions and kick out brand-new arrivals for seemingly arbitrary reasons—although many suspected that people who wouldn't work and wouldn't register to vote were the first ones gone, as well as anyone with a serious medical condition, like William Allen. The earliest program participants had been promised return tickets if they left the commune, but in late September the commune announced that it would no longer provide transportation out of Oregon for any newly arriving participants. Instead, the commune would drop them off somewhere beyond the ranch, where they would have to find their own ways home.

This new development set off alarm bells among state officials, who worried that the ex-program members would be left in small communities that weren't equipped to provide services to an indigent population. The Salvation Army asked the state for assistance in purchasing return tickets for the departing participants. The governor's office insisted that the state didn't have the funds to clean up the sannyasins' mess by purchasing bus tickets. Secretly, Governor Atiyeh called some generous Portland business owners who agreed to make donations, primarily through the Salvation Army, to cover the cost of return tickets. Atiyeh kept his involvement confidential because he didn't want the sannyasins to know they had struck a nerve.

Public reports often exaggerated the real number of participants who left the ranch without return tickets, sometimes by as much as double, but the numbers were still significant. The Oregon State Police estimated that by October 9 at least fifty people had been left stranded in Portland, and that number climbed into the hundreds over the next two weeks as every day another busload with dozens of Share-a-Home participants arrived in the city. On a particularly grim October night six days before the first voter registration hearing in The Dalles, commune vehicles dropped 140 Share-a-Home participants at locations throughout The Dalles and another thirty-nine in Madras. None of them had a bus ticket home. None of them had any way to support themselves, not even for the night.

Police and social services organizations lurched to action, arranging meals through the Salvation Army and shelter at the National Guard Armory. In the midst of those preparations, the police learned that another five buses had left the ranch to drop even more people in The Dalles, Portland, and Salem.

Although she didn't say so at the time, Sheela now admits that the mass dumping of program participants in mid-October was in direct response to

Norma Paulus's decision to suspend voter registration in Wasco County. She claims that Bhagwan was outraged by Paulus's move and that he personally ordered Sheela to leave their "guests" throughout Oregon. Shanti B, her close aide, has independently claimed something similar: that Bhagwan directed Sheela to eject the Share-a-Home participants as a way to punish the local community.

By early October, Sheela and other commune leaders realized that they would never be able to win the November election. The salmonella plot had fizzled out, and too many Share-a-Home participants had left or would be barred from voting under Paulus's plan. Sheela continued touting a bloc of seven thousand voters on Election Day—fifteen hundred commune members, fifteen hundred paying guests of the Buddhafield Experience, and four thousand Share-a-Home participants—but these numbers were a fantasy.

Still, Sheela knew better than to throw up the white flag of surrender without first trying to extract something of value out of the situation. Through federal mediator John Mathis, she conveyed to Governor Atiyeh that she would "liquidate" the Share-a-Home program by sending all the participants still in Oregon back to their original locations if the governor would intervene in and resolve all the sannyasins' major legal disputes at the state and federal level—Bhagwan's immigration status with the INS, the land-use dispute, and the attorney general's church/state litigation against the city. If the governor refused to help them, Sheela said, the conflicts brewing on and around the ranch might only get worse.

It was exactly the sort of cattle trade that Governor Atiyeh had denounced the previous year when the sannyasins offered up Antelope as a legislative bargaining chip—but now the stakes were even higher. Although he believed the sannyasins had created the problem themselves, and although he found it repulsive that they were using vulnerable people as political leverage, Atiyeh said he would investigate at least some of the requests, to keep the dialogue open. In the end, he gave them nothing.

The week after William Allen was found dead, a colonel with the Salvation Army in Portland reported a strange development to the governor's office. Officials had already provided services to more than 350 Share-a-Home participants since September, but they were noticing that something was very off about the newest arrivals in mid-October.

He described them as "space cadets." They seemed to be drugged.

In late October, a terse Puja sat for an interview with a local reporter, offering quietly simmering answers in a clipped monotone. The Oregon Board of Pharmacy had been investigating the Rajneesh Medical Corporation's orders of the drug Haldol, a powerful tranquilizing antipsychotic used to reduce aggression in patients with severe schizophrenia, and it had recently sent its investigation summary to the state Board of Medical Examiners. The Board of Pharmacy reported that over the preceding five months Rajneeshpuram had ordered an extraordinary amount of Haldol: twenty-two hundred tablets, eleven injection bottles, and forty-four liquid-concentrate bottles. Most had been ordered since the Share-a-Home program had started. The Board of Pharmacy was particularly concerned that the flavorless concentrate could be easily added to food and drinks without anyone knowing.

To the reporter, Puja refused to confirm or deny anything about Haldol. "This is privileged information. It is highly unethical to speak about it, as well as spread malicious gossip and to broadcast it all over television. Instead the focus could be on the positive things which we have done."

The reporter asked whether Haldol had uses other than as an antipsychotic.

"Perhaps it does," she responded.

The next day, Puja employed a more whimsical strategy. Flashing a crocodile smile, she told another reporter that sannyasins never abused drugs because it was against their religion. Bhagwan urged them to use their heads, not drugs. "The state Board of Pharmacy should take Haldol. We have beautiful psychiatrists here who could treat them, if they wish treatment, who could show them how to use Haldol, how to take it in effective doses."

The Share-a-Home population received their meals at a recently erected building called Hassid Cafeteria, located on the western part of the ranch near Walt Whitman Grove, where so many program participants lived in A-frame cabins.

Some sannyasins also ate at Hassid since it was closer to their worksites than the main cafeteria, Magdalena.

Soon after the Share-a-Home program started, Puja told the woman in charge of ordering food and drinks for Hassid that the kegs of beer served at the cafeteria would be segregated into two categories. One set of kegs would come directly from the Magdalena stock and would be served to commune members who ate at Hassid. The other set of kegs would go from Magdalena to Sheela's home compound, Jesus Grove, before going to Hassid, and those kegs would be served exclusively to the Share-a-Home population. Puja didn't say why the beer was being segregated or what was being done to it at Jesus Grove, but the worker assumed it was somehow doctored to address the program participants' many medical conditions.

A year later, Ma Ava and Krishna Deva would tell criminal investigators that Sheela and Puja had decided to pour Haldol in the beer of Share-a-Home participants to try to maintain order over the chaotic and sometimes violent people they had just welcomed to their commune. Puja chose Haldol because it was clear, it had no taste, and she considered it to be a mild enough sedative that its wide-scale administration would not be obvious. She kept a large supply of it in her bedroom at Jesus Grove, where she would open the top of a keg and inject one to one-and-a-half bottles of Haldol directly into the beer before sending it on its way to Hassid. Ava dosed the beer with Haldol a couple of times, but it was usually Puja who did it.

Puja told some Share-a-Home coordinators that many program participants had been taking Haldol before they came to the ranch and she was simply continuing their treatment. She even gave some of the program workers jugs of doctored water or bottles of Haldol to keep on hand in case anybody got violent. Her scant explanation was enough to pass muster for some workers, given all the epileptic and mental health conditions that so many of the Share-a-Home participants had reported in their arrival forms.

According to Ava, when the Board of Pharmacy began investigating the Haldol orders in late October, Puja created false medical records to try to justify all the purchases. Ava herself fabricated records documenting that a commune physician had prescribed Haldol to various Share-a-Home participants, even though no such diagnosis or prescription had been made. During the investigation, Puja relinquished several bottles of Haldol to the state Board of Medical Examiners, but Krishna Deva later told criminal investigators it was just a ruse to cover up the true amount of the drug she had already administered, since the bottles she offered had apparently come from another source.

Still, Puja's documentation and explanations were enough to dodge any further scrutiny, for the time being.

———————

The commune never faced any criminal consequences for the death of William Henry Allen, who was sent on a bus to Portland with a bottle of amitriptyline, even after his apparent overdose at the ranch, and no jacket, despite the cold weather.

In the weeks after his death, a group of protestors marched outside the Hotel Rajneesh in Portland, carrying a flag-draped coffin that was meant to represent Allen's death. "Clearly he is an example of what is being done to the homeless and how they're being used and abused by the Rajneesh," said the protest's leader.

The hotel manager, Ma Prem Arup—Sheela's old rival from the Pune ashram—told a reporter that the protest was nothing more than a cheap publicity stunt by anti-Rajneesh radicals.

"Nobody was taking care of the homeless until the Rajneeshees."

26 | THE ELECTION OF 1984

NO, NO, NO, WE'VE GOT to get rid of that! Norma Paulus cried, pointing at the enormous ammunition shell that propped open the front door of the National Guard Armory. A bus from Rajneeshpuram was approaching The Dalles, and the last thing she wanted was a bunch of instruments of violence at hand. Volunteers hurried to move all the military relics out of view before the bus arrived. Paulus wanted the place to be "all American flags and honors students" on this first day of voter registration hearings, October 23. Forty-seven volunteer officers sat at tables in the armory's main hall, waiting to process the three hundred registrants scheduled to show up throughout the day.

It would serve as a test run for what was to come the following week. Only nineteen Share-a-Home participants had interviews scheduled. The vast majority of people from Rajneeshpuram—about three thousand applicants—would come the next week. Still, Paulus was extremely agitated because she had no idea how the Rajneeshpuram contingent would react if the hearings officers rejected any of their registrations. She also didn't know whether the people of Wasco County would mount any sort of opposition. Everyone seemed to be holding their breath.

Much like the Antelope disincorporation election in 1982, the Wasco County election attracted broad media attention. When the silver, white, and red Rajneesh Buddhafield Transport bus pulled up outside the armory, local and national press clustered around the door to capture each person stepping out. Sixteen Share-a-Home participants had arrived for their appointments—three were no-shows—along with a dozen commune attorneys and advisers, led by Swami Prem Niren, widely considered to be the "senior partner" of Rajneesh Legal Services.

Cliff Carlsen, the attorney who had helped Paulus muster all the volunteer hearings officers, prowled about in a stiff black suit as their supervisor. After one Share-a-Home participant got rejected based on his marriage in another state, Niren marched up to Carlsen and demanded that he reexamine the decision. Reporters and cameras mobbed them to capture the exchange, which grew louder.

"We are following the policy of the state of Oregon—" Carlsen started.

"A policy that was made up when, over breakfast this morning?" Niren said. "When was it made up?"

He insisted that Carlsen ask the hearings officer why he rejected the man.

"I don't need to ask him, because I'm not going to overrule it."

"Oh, you don't need to know the facts?" Niren said, cheating out for the cameras. "So your statement is that you don't need to know the facts."

They tangled again after a second man from Rajneeshpuram got rejected. "Why are you allowing this travesty to continue?" Niren asked.

"You are the travesty," Carlsen shot back.

By the end of the day, all but two of the 207 people interviewed were declared eligible to vote in the Wasco County election. The two rejected voters were Share-a-Home participants. Niren got in Norma Paulus's face and insisted on being present when Wasco County clerk Sue Proffitt and the hearings officers conferred about these rejections. Paulus, a short but powerful fifty-one-year-old with artfully tousled blonde hair, placed a hand on Niren's arm to guide him away from Proffitt's table.

"You just put your hand on me!" the lawyer could be heard shouting all the way in the lobby. "I don't want to be touched!" An assistant hurried from the room, calling for a deputy sheriff.

Sue Proffitt declined to speak with Niren or anybody from Rajneeshpuram that day. She announced to the press that she agreed with the hearings officers and would reject the registration of the two Share-a-Home participants. Proffitt then escaped from the armory through a back door.

Six days later, sitting on a stool before a wall covered in photographs of Bhagwan, Sheela adjusted a gold microphone and smiled out at the reporters crowded into the Mirdad Welcome Center to hear her announcement. She was dressed conservatively in a turtleneck sweater beneath a red suede jacket, with her hair perfectly coiffed and her huge eyes bright and vivid. The press conference would be among the strangest of Sheela's colorful career, but perhaps the oddest aspect was the paper she held in her hand and from which she read. Sheela was an off-the-cuff speaker, almost never using a script or even notes. Krishna Deva stood alongside the cameras with his hands clasped before him, watching as Sheela began an extraordinarily subdued performance. He knew the words before she said them, because he had helped write them—he and a higher power.

"I have been misunderstood on a few points, which I'd like to make clear," Sheela said. "First, I have no interest in politics, although I have been dragged into politics in every possible way. I pray to the politicians to please leave me alone.

"I have no interest in any elections, and I'm not interested in the county either. But unfortunately, you don't understand my sense of humor." She paused and grinned up at the cameras, as if waiting for it to sink in that she had been playing a massive joke for the past two months. "I have no interest in anything smaller than the universe, and that, too, spiritually, not politically."

Sheela went on to claim she had no personal grudge against Governor Atiyeh, that the State of Oregon had been "very protective," and that the courts had been "fair." As for the rumors that the Share-a-Home program was all about voting: "My master teaches me never to miss any opportunity for a joke."

A reporter asked if this was the beginning of a new Sheela.

"You never know!" she laughed. "Sheela is extremely spontaneous. She moves with the moods, moves with the wind, moves with the time of the day. Personally, people can't figure me out. I'm not the same person you think I am."

As the Share-a-Home program had crumbled and the numbers were no longer in their favor, KD contemplated the embarrassment they would suffer if they mounted such a huge campaign, brought everyone out to vote, and *still* lost. When Norma Paulus had suspended voter registration, he felt relief. It gave them an out. They could withdraw from the election altogether and blame it on the bigotry of officials like Paulus and Proffitt.

But still they had to wind down the Share-a-Home program without making it obvious that everyone's suspicions had been correct about its real purpose. To get ahead of the story, KD drafted a press release that attempted to frame events in a positive way for the commune. Sheela mentioned it to Bhagwan during one of her meetings with the guru, and he insisted on dictating the message himself. He invited KD to join him and Sheela while he read the draft and then dictated his own version of the press release, which KD says is the version that Sheela read out loud, word for word, in her unusually restrained press conference on October 29.

The next night, in Rajneesh Mandir, Krishna Deva told a crowd of more than six thousand people that he believed they should boycott the election altogether, given the conspiracy led by Norma Paulus to disenfranchise their guests. He claimed that transporting everybody to The Dalles for registration hearings would cost $35,000 to $40,000 and would shut down all the food, cleaning, and governmental facilities at Rajneeshpuram during those days.

This carefully orchestrated event was met with raucous applause from the people in the hall. But it was nothing compared to the response when commune president Ma Yoga Vidya closed out the night by taking the microphone and making an announcement that shocked the crowd: the community was in for a sea change.

———————

Two days after KD's speech urging the boycott, not a single person from Rajneeshpuram showed up at the National Guard Armory for their voter registration hearing. By midafternoon, Paulus sent home dozens of volunteer attorneys because there was nothing for them to do.

———————

Hey, hey, what do you say? Norma took your vote away!

The main event at Rajneeshpuram on Election Day, November 6, 1984, was a protest in front of Socrates, the city's polling place.

While the sannyasins boycotted the election, nearly 80 percent of registered Wasco County voters showed up to vote, a record turnout. President Ronald Reagan won reelection in a landslide, taking forty-nine of fifty states and receiving the highest number of electoral votes in American history. Attorney General Dave Frohnmayer won reelection with 66 percent of the vote. Incumbent Wasco County judge Ray Matthew won reelection, and liquor store owner Jim Comini took the seat that had been held by Sheela's "friend," Virgil Ellet.

All of the sannyasins' schemes to capture the county had failed—the Buddhafield Experience, the Share-a-Home program, poisoning the water system in The Dalles, the salmonella outbreaks. What Bhagwan and Sheela had tried to fend off since the beginning of the year would now come to pass. In January, three anti-Rajneesh judges would preside over Wasco County—and the fate of Rajneeshpuram.

At the height of the Share-a-Home program, Sheela told a reporter that the participants could stay at Rajneeshpuram "for eternity," as long as they melded with the community and didn't fall into their old negative habits.

By November 14, the commune reported that more than half of the Share-a-Home participants who had arrived in September and October had left or been ejected. To encourage additional departures, the commune ceased the cigarette ration and decreased food service. By early 1985, only one hundred of the estimated four thousand Share-a-Home participants remained at Rajneeshpuram. Nearly everyone who remained had taken sannyas and become integrated with the community.

A reporter asked Sheela if the mass departures indicated that the program was a failure.

"The seed has been planted in anyone who comes here," she said. The program was "one-hundred percent successful" for people who spent even one hour at Rajneeshpuram. They had been forever transformed by simply dipping their toe into the Buddhafield.

Indeed, the Share-a-Home program was so successful that the commune was already looking forward to its next humanitarian venture. After helping so many homeless people, Sheela said that in the summer she would bring in prostitutes.

27 | THE LOST DISCOURSE

SWAMI DEVAGEET STEPPED to the front of the austere little room in Lao Tzu and gently uncovered the oatmeal-gray winged easy chair. The room had no other furnishings, just gleaming wood floors, walls, and doors, all meticulously swept and polished. Two dozen disciples sat around the empty chair, stockinged feet crossed before them, freshly scrubbed and fragrance free and beaming with excitement. If they happened to catch each other's eyes while the silent moments ticked by, they smiled and chuckled, as if they couldn't believe this absurd secret they were all in on.

The door swung open and Bhagwan's sprightly caretaker, Ma Yoga Vivek, breezed into the room. Bhagwan himself walked behind her with a namaste greeting at his lips, locking eyes with the disciples he had chosen for this special event: some people who lived and worked in his household, some members of the Hollywood Group, and a few other longtime sannyasins.

Settling into the easy chair, Bhagwan crossed one leg over the other, a gesture so familiar to those who had seen him do it thousands of times back in Pune in a much grander space before a much larger crowd. Sheela clipped a bejeweled microphone to his robe, near his majestic white beard. Then she sat down at the front of the group and read a question from a piece of paper.

"Bhagwan, why do you call your religion the first and the last religion?"

A long pause.

"It is a little difficult for me to speak again," he said. "After one thousand, three hundred and fifteen days of silence, it feels as if I am coming to you from a totally different world. In fact it is so."

On that same night, October 30, 1984, Krishna Deva had urged six thousand people in Rajneesh Mandir to boycott the Wasco County election. He had then ceded the microphone to commune president Ma Yoga Vidya.

"So I have a very, very special announcement to make to everybody in Rajneesh Mandir tonight," Vidya said, with a glassy smile. "Bhagwan is beginning to talk about his religion."

As soon as the news sunk in, the crowd leaped to their feet, clapping over their heads, embracing each other, tears flowing down cheeks, hands clutched over hearts, shocked and elated by the news. They had been given no reason to think that Bhagwan would ever speak again. Now he was about to pick up his abandoned practice of offering his wisdom directly to his disciples.

"The picture I have been painting all my life needs a few touches here and there to complete it," Bhagwan told the intimate crowd at Lao Tzu that night, "because on that one day when I became silent everything was left incomplete." He said he would complete that picture before departing his physical body.

The only public glimpses of Bhagwan in Oregon had been his flamboyant afternoon drive-bys and his silent appearances on celebration days. Beyond that, he spent his days alone at Lao Tzu with a handful of disciples, who attended to his personal needs, and he met privately with Sheela for hours each day.

On two occasions, he had been compelled to break his silence to provide testimony: once for his INS examination with George Hunter in 1982 and again at a deposition in a defamation case in August 1984. The portrait Bhagwan painted of himself on those two occasions was that of an aloof master living in complete seclusion, oblivious to the most basic facts about his commune or the way it was being run. He maintained that he never spoke with Sheela about temporal matters. "I am no more concerned with the commune, its day-to-day work, its ideals, its economics, its finance," he testified at the deposition. "I am not concerned, at all, with any mundane, worldly affairs. Now, my disciples are prepared enough to take care of the commune. I am just an outsider. They can ask only their spiritual questions to me, nothing else." Underscoring his cluelessness about modern events, Bhagwan testified that he had never seen Sheela's appearances on television and didn't even know that Krishna Deva had been mayor of Rajneeshpuram for the past two years.

By seizing the megaphone from Sheela's hands, the guru was about to reveal who exactly was calling the shots.

———————

Swami Toby, whose lilting flute music had accompanied Bhagwan's triumphant arrival at the INS offices in 1982, worshipped in the Edison Temple under electronics guru Swami Julian. When Bhagwan began speaking again, an Edison team was assigned to record each Lao Tzu discourse and then play the video for commune members the following evening, allowing everybody an opportunity to drink in their master's words. As a videographer, Toby was thus one of the few sannyasins who got to sit in his master's presence every night. In a place where physical proximity to the master was the point, being in such a small room with Bhagwan every night was the apex experience.

Toby had a musician's ear, and as he sat there night after night behind the video camera, he noticed the rhythm of Bhagwan's words and the techniques he used to capture his listeners' interest for ninety minutes. His soothing, barely audible voice, his trailing sibilant *S* sounds, his deliberate tempo—it all seemed to pull the listener down deeper and deeper and deeper until they were mesmerized. Bhagwan would keep his audience in that trance until he was ready to bring them up again, at which point his tone would shift and it became clear to old hands like Toby that he was winding up for the night.

He had often told his disciples to listen not to his words but to the silence in between, but on a cold winter night in mid-December 1984, Bhagwan kicked off his discourse with a question that made Toby sit up and pay close attention to exactly what the guru was saying. *Isn't organization a necessity for a religion to survive?*

Ever since he had started speaking two months earlier, Bhagwan had focused his lectures on religion. Commune members felt it was a "juicy" time, because he was so freely offering up his thoughts on God, the true story of Jesus Christ, great philosophers and spiritual figures throughout history, cults, communism, and even some colorful stories from his childhood. He also picked up a familiar theme from his days in India. "Politicians are dangerous people," Bhagwan said within his first week of speaking. "They want this city to be demolished because of their land-use laws. And none of those idiots has come to see how we are using the land. If this is against land-use laws, then your land-use laws are bogus and should be burned."

Toby perked up at the question about the necessity of the organization surrounding a religion, because it conjured up the specter of all the officious women who ran Bhagwan's own organization. Commune members had been privately grumbling about Sheela's outsized control over their day-to-day lives—a control that many believed was a product of her own domineering nature, not anything having to do with Bhagwan. Toby was excited to hear the guru address this conflict himself.

After criticizing other religious movements throughout history, where abuses of power and political ambitions in the organization had led to the strangling of any true religion, Bhagwan explained that Rajneeshism was different because he had created decentralized organizations in his lifetime that would not concentrate power in the hands of any one person when he was gone. In meticulous detail, he laid out the structure that would continue his religion after his death: the Rajneesh Foundation International would look after his words and religious matters; the Academy of Rajneeshism would express Bhagwan's spiritual power; the communes around the world would all be autonomously operated and governed. "Sannyasins can have a totally different organization," he said. "That promise you can always remember: I will not leave you in a state of chaos."

He gave this speech while sitting mere inches from Ma Anand Sheela, the Pope of Rajneeshism, the president of the Rajneesh Foundation International, and the de facto ruler of Rajneeshpuram and every Rajneesh Meditation Center around the world. Some of the disciples in the room that night believed that Bhagwan's warning about the concentration of power in one person was a direct stab at his secretary and her inflated ego.

But that wasn't all he said.

———————

Swami Toby packed up his equipment after the discourse and raced down to Magdalena for a quick bite before going to the editing bay in Zarathustra, where he would prepare the video for the next night's presentation to the entire commune. While eating, he grabbed some close friends.

You'll never fucking believe what he said tonight.

Toby described the part of Bhagwan's discourse that had left his jaw on the floor. It wasn't the talk about the decentralized organization he was creating that would separate him from other failed religions. It wasn't the possible digs at Sheela. For roughly twenty minutes in the middle of his lecture, Bhagwan tried to demonstrate that he was in control by going on at length about his personal involvement in controlling their community. He had stated unequivocally that he knew everything that was taking place at Rajneeshpuram, that he was responsible for it all, and that Sheela was doing his bidding. And he didn't just say it as a general claim—Bhagwan walked through particular legal and political issues facing the commune, like the attorney general's litigation against the city, the land-use disputes, and more. In each case, he explained what he had directed Sheela to do.

Toby was taken aback by Bhagwan's discourse because so many commune members were convinced that Sheela was on a power trip, having twisted the Buddhafield into her own totalitarian state. Many believed that Bhagwan lived in pure oblivion up at Lao Tzu, driving each day through a Potemkin village of smiling, celebrating sannyasins without any idea how hard they worked, how restricted their lives had become, or how much Sheela and her team of coordinators dominated their every moment. Toby couldn't believe that the mystic on the hill would admit that he was knowledgeable about everything going on at the commune, and that he was in fact orchestrating it all himself. He expected this part of Bhagwan's discourse to go off like dynamite when the commune watched the video the next evening.

At the same time, Toby wondered if Bhagwan had said too much. The commune's official position was that Bhagwan took no part in anything having to do with the commune except spiritual matters. What he had just confessed on video- and audiotape, destined to be published in a printed collection of his lectures, would reveal that to be false.

Upon reaching the Zarathustra building in the ranch's southern valley later that night, Toby and the other members of the Edison team climbed to their second-floor offices and unpacked their tapes. Sheela and Vidya suddenly appeared with a cardboard box. Sheela told them to put everything from that night's discourse into the box—the videotapes, the audiotapes, everything. She ordered them not to leak a single word of what Bhagwan had said that night. If anyone asked, they were to say that a mechanical failure had caused the tapes to be destroyed.

It was an absurd idea, since it was common knowledge that Bhagwan's precious words were picked up by multiple recording devices, including backups. Nobody would believe they all failed at the same time. Toby offered Sheela another idea: perhaps they could just edit out whatever parts of the discourse Sheela did not want shared publicly. She remained firm. All evidence of the discourse vanished from Zarathustra. The next day, Toby tracked down his friends and swore them to secrecy. If word got out that he had revealed what Bhagwan had said, he knew the consequences would be severe.

As Toby had suspected, gossip began percolating as soon as commune members found out about the "technical difficulty" that meant they would miss a night of Bhagwan's lectures. It didn't help that anybody who had been in the room at Lao Tzu that night dodged questions about what Bhagwan had said, including Toby. The prevailing rumor was that Sheela was suppressing negative comments Bhagwan made about her. It became so pervasive that Sheela called a commune-wide meeting to berate disciples who would make such a suggestion.

A week later, the *Rajneesh Times* printed a version of the discourse that had been "reconstructed with the help of Bhagwan Shree Rajneesh." It contained much of the discourse that Toby recalled, particularly the part where Bhagwan explained the complex hierarchy that would continue running his religion after he was gone. Missing were the parts where he claimed awareness and control over everything happening at the commune.

Around the same time as the "lost discourse," attorneys at Rajneesh Legal Services got an intimate glimpse of Bhagwan's full involvement in his affairs when he convened them all in his home to resolve a dispute among the lawyers.

Attorney General Frohnmayer's church/state litigation was in full swing. The state argued that the entangled nature of the City of Rajneeshpuram and the various Rajneesh corporations violated the Establishment Clause. To help develop his argument, the attorney general had brought in a big gun: eminent Harvard professor and constitutional scholar Laurence Tribe. Tribe had recently argued and won a major Supreme Court case on the Establishment Clause, *Larkin v. Grendel's Den*, which invalidated a state law that gave churches the power to veto liquor license applications for establishments within five hundred feet of the church. Seizing on this opinion, Tribe argued that if a church could have no role in a city's power to grant liquor licenses, then a state granting full municipal powers to a church would certainly be unconstitutional.

The trouble within Rajneesh Legal Services was that some sannyasin attorneys agreed with Professor Tribe. The department's resident strategy guru, SWAMI DEVA BHAKTI, dug through the commune's law library, pored over case law, and consulted with other attorneys, but no matter how he looked at it, he found that Tribe was right. The only way they might be able to win the case would be if the Church of Rajneeshism—the Rajneesh Foundation International—divested the corporations that linked it to the city. Doing so would leave the Church as a standalone entity, while the now-secular corporations would operate the commune and own the property on which the city sat.

Bhakti's arguments went nowhere. Sheela blocked any efforts to restructure the corporations. Swami Prem Niren, the lead attorney in Rajneesh Legal Services, advocated a middle-of-the-road approach: rather than change anything about their corporations preemptively, they should ask the judge to give them an opportunity to fix things according to the court's guidance. This unresolved dispute bubbled all the way up to Bhagwan, who called everybody from legal services to Lao Tzu for a meeting: lawyers, paralegals, and Moms who coordinated the department. Bhakti's only personal experiences with his master until that point had been spiritual: at the Pune ashram in discourse and darshan, in Rajneeshpuram witnessing his drive-bys every afternoon, and, recently, watching the videotaped discourses along with thousands of others. But now he sat at Bhagwan's feet with a group of his colleagues talking legal strategy.

Without hesitation, Bhagwan sided with Sheela. They would not change anything about themselves or their commune to appease the state. But he also agreed with Bhakti that the attorney general's argument was correct. There was no separation between church and state at his commune. That didn't mean they should change. Bhagwan wanted Bhakti to defend the city while admitting that the underlying basis of Frohnmayer's argument was true.

Bhakti later compared this guidance to a koan, an unanswerable question that a Zen master employs to teach a student to drop the mind. Bhagwan was smart enough to understand that they could never win the case if they conceded that Rajneeshpuram was indeed a theocracy. Bhakti also saw Bhagwan's position as one of his Gurdjieffian devices. Whether or not they won the case didn't matter, it seemed, as long as the situation was uncomfortable enough, desperate enough, unsolvable enough to trigger personal growth among the attorneys arguing it.

Throughout his work on the Frohnmayer case and others, Bhakti continued to encounter situations where the best legal arguments were swatted aside and replaced with absurd, unintelligent, or legally indefensible positions. Sometimes the guidance came directly from Bhagwan, and other times it came from Sheela or the many coordinators responsible for extending his vision into every aspect of life at the commune. It became such a common occurrence by 1985 that Bhakti no longer felt that Bhagwan was ambivalent about the future of his Buddhafield.

He became convinced that the guru in fact wanted to lose.

PART V
OREGON, 1985

Sheela at Rajneeshpuram's casino, with Swami Dipo at her side. *Photo courtesy of The Oregonian*

28 | DESPERATE MEASURES

ARE YOU UP FOR AN ADVENTURE? Sheela asked Ava in early January 1985.

A couple of nights later, Ava sped west along Interstate 84 bearing two passengers in her car who reeked of lighter fluid. Yogini and Anugiten had both proved themselves to be loyal Jesus Grove foot soldiers in recent months, with Anugiten pouring something into The Dalles' water system and Yogini smearing salmonella on her palms before shaking hands at a political meeting. Now they had proved themselves once again. As Ava drove them from The Dalles to Portland late that night, the duo removed all their clothes and tossed them out the window, along with a screwdriver and a lighter. Yogini complained that she had injured her leg climbing through a window. Upon reaching their secret flop house in Portland, they called a line at Rajneeshpuram and hung up after one ring to signal they were safe.

A few weeks earlier, while walking through the commune's legal department, Sheela's lieutenant Shanti B had made a blithe comment to the workers at their desks about the Wasco County planning director who had been causing the commune so much grief in recent months.

As I drove past The Dalles, I thought of Dan Durow's office, said the soft-spoken Australian, *and I thought how much I would like to have it burn down.*

Seeing her again weeks later, a paralegal had said, *Jesus, Shanti B, we had no idea you were that powerful.*

Everyone laughed. There was no way, of course, that anybody from the commune would have set Durow's office on fire. It was probably just an electrical problem.

You better watch out, Shanti B had said, laughing along with them.

The electric wall clock inside the county planner's office stopped at 1:39 AM on January 14. One hour later, a passing motorist saw a fire within the small blue building with stone skirting. Firefighters arrived and put out the flames before they could cause much damage to the structure. Investigators later found that an exterior window to the building had been pried open and that Durow's files had been pulled from filing cabinets, scattered on the middle of the floor, and doused in lighter fluid. The arsonists had taken little care to conceal their crime, leaving all the filing cabinet drawers open and documents, books, and manila folders strewn about all the desks and floors. They even left four cans of Wizard Charcoal Lighter Fluid at the scene. No effort had been made to try to make it look like an accident.

The investigation tapered down and was soon suspended. No charges, no arrest, and no real suspects.

Tensions between the sannyasins and the Wasco County government were boiling over by the start of 1985. Sue Proffitt had collaborated with Norma Paulus to stave them off at the polls, and the sannyasins would be squaring off against three anti-sannyasin county commissioners throughout the coming year. County officials had persisted in blocking any new development at the ranch, led by planner Dan Durow—the "prime asshole" in Wasco County, as Ava described him.

In 1982, Durow had taken over the planning office from his boss, who over the previous year had granted sannyasins dozens of residential permits for their farmland. Commune leaders had worked to develop a personal relationship with Durow's predecessor, taking her out to dinner, hanging out at her home to watch television, and giving her small gifts. When Durow took over, his relations with the commune were friendly enough at first, although KD described him as a "little old lady" who was painfully slow and methodical in considering their requests. After Rajneeshpuram's incorporation, the county retained control over development on the enormous portion of the ranch beyond the city's boundaries. As county officials caught wise to the commune leaders' often duplicitous methods to get what they wanted, Durow began rejecting their development projects on county land.

His influence exploded in the summer and fall of 1983, after the Land Conservation and Development Commission issued its temporary rule that threw Rajneeshpuram's incorporation into legal limbo. Wasco County joined 1000 Friends of Oregon in seeking the injunction that granted the county full land-use authority over the Big Muddy Ranch. From the county's perspective, there was no longer any such thing as the "City of Rajneeshpuram"— just unincorporated farmland with a bunch of illegal buildings and too many residents. Tensions with Durow increased when Sheela, Puja, and planning director Deva Wadud pushed him to approve a hospital at the ranch and he steadfastly refused.

Around the summer of 1984, Sheela began to suggest to her inner circle various ways they might impede Durow's work. While surveilling Wasco County government buildings in a car, Sheela wondered out loud whether blowing up a nearby gas tank would set fire to Durow's office. As they drove back to the ranch later that day, Krishna Deva heard Sheela tell Anugiten to find a way to "destroy the records" in the office. They prepared a diagram of the office layout and discussed possible ways to burn it down—an idea that Anugiten continued exploring throughout the fall and into the winter.

While these discussions were taking place, Durow made a series of ill-fated inspection visits to the commune. In September, he tried to visit Walt Whitman Grove, where the Share-a-Home program participants were living, but KD threatened to cite him for criminal trespass and ordered him off the ranch. Undaunted, Durow conducted a flyover of the ranch and saw 640 weatherized tents across the property; he later discovered they had electricity and gas heat connections, windows, doors, and wall-to-wall carpeting. He demanded the tents be torn down within fifteen days because they violated both the injunction against new buildings and the Wasco County building code.

Receiving no response, Durow again drove out to Rajneeshpuram to inspect the tents, armed with a court order and accompanied by two Wasco County sheriff's deputies. Before they could reach the commune, they found the winding, narrow county highway entirely obstructed by a commune-owned semi truck whose engine had mysteriously quit that morning. "They've done an excellent job of blocking the road," one of the deputies told a reporter who happened to be on the scene. "Couldn't have done it any better." After waiting for an hour and a half for a truck part that never materialized, Durow finally returned to The Dalles.

He came back a week later with a sheriff's deputy and was able to conduct some of his inspection, with KD following him everywhere. After driving to the far eastern part of the ranch to inspect the farm, Durow found that the only road back to Rajneeshpuram—and out of the ranch—was blocked by a farm trailer that had inexplicably tipped over. A mechanic arrived within minutes and determined he needed a front-end loader to move the trailer, but the operator with the key was out to lunch and couldn't be found. Durow and the deputy sat there for three hours, trapped. By the time the front-end loader finally arrived to clear the trailer, it was too dark to complete the inspection.

Ma Anand Sagun, KD's girlfriend and a Share-a-Home coordinator, would later confess that they had blocked Durow's progress that day because they didn't want him to see an unlawful makeshift cafeteria they had erected in the southern valley for the Share-a-Home participants. Puja had given Sagun two vials of clear liquid and a pair of rubber gloves and told her to go to the place where Durow was stuck and give him some coffee laced with the liquid. Since Durow had wisely brought his own thermos, Sagun never had the chance to poison him.

At a congressional subcommittee hearing in Portland six days later, Wasco County judge Bill Hulse testified about Durow's great difficulties accessing the property for his inspection visits. In the midst of his testimony, Hulse mentioned becoming "violently ill" after drinking a glass of water while touring the ranch in August, as had judge Ray Matthew, and said that he would have died without medical treatment. He claimed he was "just stating what happened," not accusing the sannyasins of intentionally poisoning him. It was the first time that Hulse had spoken publicly about his suspicious illness immediately after visiting the ranch, and newspapers across the state carried his comments the next day.

Reached for comment, Ma Prem Isabel said it had been a friendly gesture for Puja to give Hulse water on such a hot day. "We don't engage in poisoning people," she said. "This is a clear example of no matter what we do, they are going to find some kind of negative connotation."

Bhagwan had a more pointed response. "It is proof enough if you are alive after six months that we have not given poison to you," he said during a Lao

Tzu discourse. "Otherwise, you would not be alive. We never do anything halfheartedly."

———————

A new battlefront with Wasco County had emerged at the very end of 1984, when the county court considered whether to grant a mass gathering permit for the Fourth Annual World Celebration. The commune leaders hadn't expected any difficulty securing the permit, but at a small, sparsely attended hearing right after Christmas, the court, the county planners, and the district attorney voiced concerns about all the weatherized tents from the previous festival, which Dan Durow said were permanent structures. When the court voted to delay approving the permit and to instead hold another hearing the following week, disciples in the court had an "explosive response," according to Durow.

Only five sannyasins showed up to make their case at the next hearing on January 2, unaware that it would be a circus that, for once, they had not orchestrated. Laura Bentley, the local citizen who had so efficiently facilitated Norma Paulus's voter registration plans, had once again worked her phone tree to urge locals to show up and voice their disapproval. More than 150 anti-Rajneesh citizens showed up—so many that the judges moved the hearing to the largest courtroom in the building. Bentley and other Rajneeshpuram opponents received an opportunity to air all their grievances, including the negligent operation of the Share-a-Home program, the sannyasins' overt desire to take over the county government, Sheela's menacing statements in the press, and the ranch's arsenal. Some urged the court to delay the decision on the festival permit for a couple of weeks until Jim Comini was seated on the court and Sheela's "friend" Virgil Ellett was out.

Representing the Rajneesh Foundation International as its treasurer, Sheela's aide Shanti B stomped to the microphone with a red jacket draped over her narrow shoulders, fired up and ready to launch a broadside. The quiet but fierce Australian woman had climbed the ranks within Jesus Grove to become one of Sheela's top confidants and a central figure running the commune. Some disciples thought of Shanti B as Sheela's clone, since she dressed like Sheela, wore her hair in a similar style, and swaggered around the ranch projecting Sheela's bravado.

As soon as she opened her mouth at the hearing, there could be no question that she was there as Sheela's alter ego. "All I hear this afternoon is a bunch of codswallop about weaponry. There is a woman sitting here in the second row—" Shanti B spun around and pointed to the audience. "That woman sitting there is knitting. She said to her friends, 'You remember the French Revolution, when the women sat around knitting by the guillotine? Well that's what I feel like.' And these people are asking why do we have weaponry at Rajneeshpuram!"

Her voice rose into a rapid-fire shout. "They're not the least bit interested in our festival. They don't know how to celebrate. They don't know what celebration is! They've never been able to celebrate in their lives! They're dried up old prunes." Indignant sounds swelled from the crowd behind her. Judge Hulse gestured for a sheriff's deputy to stand near the witness table.

"The festival speaks for itself," Shanti B continued. "It's happened three years in a row. It's a joyous event without any violence, without any incidents whatsoever. For this court to allow itself to be degraded in this way is disgusting. The state of Oregon is dead." With her ferocious glare locked on the commissioners, Shanti B rose from the table and stalked back to her seat in the gallery. When a county attorney suggested that the court continue the proceedings to another day to allow even *more* testimony, the sannyasins marched out of the room, to cheers from the crowd.

Two days later the court offered forty-five minutes to each side of the festival permit debate. Weapons, secretive underground construction, the booming population, the potential for violence—it all came out again from Rajneeshpuram's opponents. The sannyasins were ready to fight back this time. While offering his rebuttal, sannyasin attorney Prartho Subhan handed each county judge a letter asserting a claim for more than $5 million against the commissioners if they refused to grant the petition for the festival. And in light of all the testimony about weapons, Shanti B launched into a screed about their need for guns "so that should the day ever come when fifteen heads have to be taken for one, I for one am ready to do it."

Shouting over the angry crowd behind her, Shanti B laid bare the plot between the Wasco County judges and concerned citizens like Laura Bentley to drag out the proceedings and ensure they did not get their festival permit. She paraphrased a comment from the congressional hearing in November: "Congressman Bob Smith said to you, Judge Hulse, that if you want to fuck the Rajneeshees, you mess with their festival. And that's exactly what you've tried to do.

"It started with you." She pointed a finger at Hulse and then jabbed it toward the planning commission's attorney. "Then it went to Will Carey, who has to talk to this bitch back here." She gestured at Laura Bentley in the gallery. "Then we have Dan Durow, who needs a good fuck and takes his aggressions out on Rajneeshees."

The judges approved a motion to close the hearing to public testimony, but Shanti B was not having it. "I demand that you sign the festival permit today!" she shouted, beating her fist on the table.

During a recess, Shanti B walked to a pay phone outside the courthouse and called Sheela, who was delighted to learn that her aide had so caustically and so publicly put the Wasco County officials in their places. No matter what it took, Shanti B was to return to Rajneeshpuram with the festival permit in hand.

At the conclusion of the hearing, the judges voted to grant the permit for the Fourth Annual World Celebration, provided the sannyasins agreed not to use the 640 weatherized tents that Durow had deemed unlawful permanent structures.

Ten days later, Durow's office went up in flames.

29 | DOWNWARD SPIRAL

ON A CLEAR DAY IN JANUARY, three dozen members of the Rajneesh Security force knelt on a snow-dusted field at the commune, bowing in the direction of Bhagwan's home and chanting the gachhamis. In addition to their tan jumpsuits, pink hooded sweatshirts, and red stocking caps, they wore protective headphones. When the prayer was done, they each retrieved an Uzi from a nearby table and took a position across from a line of human-shaped targets hundreds of yards away.

"Check that your weapon is clear," called out Prabhat, the former Israeli soldier who served as the commune's weapons instructor. "When we move from the hundred-yard mark up to fifty yards, it's all going to be body shots. After that you're going to fire to the head."

With a whistle blast, the sannyasins hustled forward a dozen feet, dropped to their stomachs, and fired. They ran forward again, dropped to a knee, and fired. They kept moving under Prabhat's orders until they were finally close enough to the bullet-shredded paper to assess how deadly they'd been. Throughout the exercise, Shanti B paced among the lingering security force members and monitored the shooters with a sharp eye.

When the exercise was done, the gaggle of reporters Sheela had called to the ranch surrounded a commune representative. "Why are we here today?" one asked.

"We're here hopefully so that Wasco County can relax a bit," the representative said. The county's district attorney, Bernie Smith, had recently aired public concerns about all the weapons at Rajneeshpuram and suggested that the disciples weren't properly trained in how to use them. The demonstration was a direct response. Around the same time, a news crew caught Sheela and Krishna Deva sitting amid the chaotic Rajneesh Legal Services offices, where they offered only cryptic answers about their weaponry. "You think I'm crazy enough to give you numbers so it can be broadcast to all the bigots who want to do harm to these people?" KD asked the reporter. "We're well prepared, we're equipped, we'll wipe out anybody who does harm to this community."

Another disciple confirmed what Sheela had been saying all along: "We are not going to turn a cheek. We're not willing to say, 'Gee, weapons don't make sense in the world, wouldn't it be nice if they didn't exist?' They exist. If they're coming in here shooting, we're going to shoot back."

An atmosphere of paranoia that started wrenching the commune in the last part of 1984 became fully evident to outsiders by the start of 1985. Sheela had long suspected that government agents were hunting for any reason to raid the compound and arrest her and the other leaders. Her fears were confirmed in September, when federal mediator John Mathis told KD on a wiretapped phone conversation that an intergovernmental conspiracy, which he said went "all the way up," was working to bring down Sheela. Mathis, who represented the US Department of Justice, was supposed to be an impartial mediator working to resolve tensions in Central Oregon—but he later admitted that he grew too close to KD and shared confidential government information with him. KD had carefully curated his relationship with Mathis, at Sheela's instruction, for exactly this purpose. Throughout 1985, KD would continue trying to manipulate Mathis to gain information about any government actions coming their way.

In particular, Sheela and other leaders were concerned that the INS might take a sweeping action against hundreds of sannyasins who had entered sham marriages. In July 1984, the agency had revealed that it was investigating suspected violations of immigration laws by disciples and various sannyasin corporations, and that it had already turned over an extensive report to the chief federal law enforcement officer for Oregon, US Attorney Charles Turner. The following month, the *San Francisco Chronicle* published a confidential memo from the Portland INS office claiming that 95 percent of sannyasin marriages were "phony" and suggesting that applying pressure to the immigration situation "may cause them to pick up stakes and leave the US." Ma Prem Isabel, whose marriage to attorney Swami Prem Niren was among those under investigation, called it "a witch hunt if I ever saw one."

As it turns out, Sheela had good reason to be paranoid about the possibility of government action against the commune in early 1985. In January of that year, US Attorney Charles Turner opened a federal grand jury investigation into sham marriages at Rajneeshpuram. The proceedings were kept strictly confidential, even within the government, and the targets were not made aware they were being investigated. Turner's office was looking at individual marriages as well as the possibility of charging commune leaders with a criminal conspiracy to violate federal immigration laws—a conspiracy that Turner believed went all the way up to Bhagwan Shree Rajneesh.

Although Sheela didn't know about the grand jury, she had the sense that it was only a matter of time before agents swooped in with arrest and search warrants. She gathered her top lieutenants in her bedroom almost every evening to talk about how they could preserve the commune. A regular topic of conversation was who would be the most likely witnesses called to give grand jury testimony and who would be their worst witnesses—meaning the worst liars—and what to do about it.

This spiraling paranoia and these constant concerns about invasions, arrests, and attacks offer perhaps the best way to make sense of the senseless events that would take place in 1985 and that would mark the darkest period in the commune's short existence.

30 | THE TURNING POINT

ON THE NIGHT OF FRIDAY, MAY 24, 1985, Helen Byron and her daughter, Barbara, sat in a federal courtroom in Portland, about to learn whether they had eked out a victory against the all-powerful Rajneesh Foundation International. The jury had heard complex and conflicting testimony over the previous week about the Byrons' entanglement with Bhagwan Shree Rajneesh's organization going back to the 1970s. The widow of a successful miner from Colorado, Helen's considerable wealth had brought her to the attention of Ma Anand Sheela, who had persuaded her to part with $300,000 to purchase a piece of property in India (which was never bought). She also convinced Helen to transfer $80,000 into the ashram's bank for safekeeping, since Indian banks couldn't be trusted.

At Rajneeshpuram, Helen and Barbara grew disenchanted with the way Sheela was running Bhagwan's community. Life there was far too restrictive, turning something as simple as a drive to the Madras grocery store into an absurd luxury. After repeated conflicts with commune leaders, they dropped sannyas and left Rajneeshpuram. The real problems started when Helen demanded her money back from Sheela. She wanted all of the nearly $390,000 that she had given over the years, which she said had been a loan. Sheela denied the request, saying that Helen had given only nonrefundable donations. Sheela's lieutenant Shanti B understood that Helen's demand letter had gone all the way to Bhagwan, who took personal offense at the request and instructed Sheela that the money would not be returned under any circumstances.

Helen sued in Oregon federal court in 1984 for all her money plus punitive damages. The trial in late May 1985 became a small media circus, with reporters hanging on to every salacious allegation that Helen, Barbara, and others made about life at Rajneeshpuram. On the witness stand, Sheela denied everything the Byrons said about her. Shanti B, as the treasurer for the Rajneesh Foundation International, took the stand to certify that the foundation's bookkeeping records—which logged the amounts as donations—were true and accurate. In reality, Shanti B could tell from just glancing at the records that somebody had doctored them before trial to reflect the story the commune wanted the jury to believe. Still, she played the loyal foot soldier, perjury be damned.

At 5:00 PM on Friday, after mere hours of deliberation, the jury came back with a landslide victory for Helen Byron: $1.65 million. Cameras captured the ebullient plaintiff as she left the federal courthouse in Portland, her white hair cropped just above her eyes, wearing a simple turtleneck and clutching her purse. She was flanked by her daughter, her attorney, and her friends, some of whom had served as witnesses over the past three days. They made straight for the Library Lounge in the lobby of their hotel, the downtown Marriott, where they pulled some tables together and spent the next couple of hours drinking and celebrating.

An *Oregonian* reporter made an appearance to congratulate Helen on her victory. Having spent a lot of time at Rajneeshpuram covering the sannyasins over the past years, he silently noted three commune members sitting one table away from the Byron group. They were dressed in regular street clothes, without the sunrise colors and the malas, as if trying to disguise themselves.

The disguises worked on Helen and Barbara, who did not recognize them.

The Byrons' revelry continued into the night: barhopping, eating dinner in the back room of a Chinese restaurant (on Helen's dime, of course), dancing with abandon at a disco, and reconvening in a hotel room to watch reporters trumpeting the verdict on the 11:00 PM news.

Helen had spent the whole night surrounded by her friends and supporters. There was never a moment when anybody could have even gotten close to her.

The situation doesn't feel right, Ava had told commune president Vidya over the telephone, sitting in her room at the Marriott in the midst of the Byron trial. *There's too much security. This whole situation isn't fun.*

Ava had been searching for her opportunity throughout the week. All three of them had: Ava, Yogini, and Anugiten. Yogini had tried to get a job in the hotel's kitchen so she might be able to find Helen's room. Anugiten tried to find it by wandering the corridors, but he was trailed by security. Ava, wearing a disguise, had stood next to Helen in the hotel's elevator and complimented her shoes. They sat close to the Byrons and their friends in the hotel's bar, trying to eavesdrop on what they might be saying about the trial, about Sheela, about their former lives as sannyasins. There was never an opportunity to use the little travel kit that Puja had given them at the beginning of the mission, with its syringes, pills, and eye-dropper bottles filled with Haldol.

Ava would later tell criminal investigators that Sheela had sent them to the Marriott that week to follow Helen Byron and find an opportunity to "do her in." The request had startled Ava. They had engaged in plenty of dirty tricks, like Yogini and Anugiten setting fire to Dan Durow's office and Ava contaminating salad bars with salmonella and sickening a county judge. But this was the first time Sheela had asked them to kill somebody. She figured Bhagwan's secretary knew best what was necessary to protect the commune and their beloved master. Ava was willing to do it. So were Yogini and Anugiten.

Executing the plan proved to be much more complicated than they expected. Security was intense. The hotel wouldn't tell them where Helen's room was. After continually striking out, the trio grew paranoid. Ava managed to calm them all down and check them out of the Marriott on Friday night. They returned to the Hotel Rajneesh in Portland, where Sheela had been staying throughout the trial.

They found her completely despondent. The verdict had just come in. She told them she was depressed about the enormous judgment and angry at the way the presiding judge had spoken harshly to the sannyasin attorney, Prartho Subhan, throughout the trial. Her mood darkened further even as she spoke to them. The sannyasins would never get a fair trial in Oregon, she said. A war was brewing. To survive, they would need to take the law into their own hands. Yogini would later recall how much Sheela's words resonated with her.

The Byron verdict felt like a collective loss for all sannyasins. Losing that much money, she said, "led to fury. Just led to fury."

Moved by Sheela's anger, the trio went straight back to the Marriott to finish the job. They brought the travel kit. Puja had explained to them in meticulous detail how each drug should be administered and what it would do to Helen's body. As Ava put it, their goal was to "bump her off" that night.

They found her in the lounge with her friends, ostentatious in their celebration. From a nearby table, the trio watched. They waited. They saw the *Oregonian* reporter stop by to congratulate Helen on her victory. They saw him leave. Helen was always surrounded. They couldn't get close enough to inject her without somebody noticing. They couldn't dose her food or her drinks without getting caught.

The next day, Sheela would berate them for failing to take care of Helen Byron. *I'm sick and tired of things going wrong and things not getting done,* Yogini would later recall that Sheela had yelled at them. *I'm sick and tired of your incompetence. Are you cowards, or are you sannyasins of Bhagwan Shree Rajneesh?*

According to all of Sheela's confidants who have spoken about it, the Helen Byron verdict in late May 1985 sparked a drastic change among Sheela's inner circle.

The day after she returned to the ranch from Portland, Sheela paged a select group of aides to her bedroom. All the people who ran the commune were there: Mayor Krishna Deva, chief accountant Savita, commune president Vidya, president of the investment corporation Su, medical director Puja. Sheela's husband Jayananda was in attendance, as was Vidya's boyfriend Bodhi. Other trusted henchmen had been paged as well, including Yogini, Anugiten, Ava, and Shanti B.

As they entered the bedroom, Sheela said that anyone who had morality would need to either leave it at the door or leave the room altogether. It set the tone for what was to come. Although Sheela could be playful with her intimates, with a sense of gallows humor in discussing the latest calamity to befall the commune or the latest outrageous request from Lao Tzu, at this meeting she was dead serious. Sitting on the only chair in the room and looking down at the disciples in a circle on the floor, she ticked off the external forces massing against them. US Attorney Charles Turner might be launching a grand jury against them for immigration violations. Attorney General Frohnmayer's litigation threatened to wipe their city off the map. Helen Byron received her obscene verdict against the Rajneesh Foundation. Wasco County officials wouldn't let them build. If left unchecked, these forces would crush the flower that they were nurturing in the desert.

They had spent the past four years trying to play within the system. Now it was abundantly clear that the system was rotten to the core, filled with close-minded bigots who would never treat them fairly. Their only option at this point, Sheela said, would be to take the law into their own hands. She wanted to assassinate their enemies.

Before proceeding any further, Sheela asked who was in and who was out. She promised that she wouldn't force anyone to participate against their will. Su, Vidya, Ava, Yogini, and Anugiten all said they supported murdering their enemies. In fact, Sheela had told Ava, Yogini, and Anugiten back in Portland that they *had* to support her at this meeting, to help persuade anyone with doubts to go with the crowd. Patipada, who was responsible for ensuring all Rajneesh Meditation Centers were in conformance, said she could never kill a person. Padma, who handled accommodations at the commune, made a strong case against any plans involving murder. Bodhi, Jayananda, and KD all said it was a bad idea.

Sheela urged the naysayers to consider how valuable Bhagwan's life was in comparison to anyone else's. *If there is a choice between one thousand unenlightened people or one enlightened master, you should always choose the enlightened master*, she reminded them, according to Ava. Shanti B recalled Sheela playing her a tape recording from the Lao Tzu bug in which Bhagwan uttered words to this same effect, after Sheela had asked him the lengths to which his disciples should go to protect him. *If ten thousand people have to die in order to protect the enlightened master, then so be it*, he had said. KD also remembered Sheela repeating a similar idea as they sketched out their darkest plots. *Life is meaningless unless one is enlightened. A master's life is worth a million other lives. If a million died to save one enlightened master, it is OK.*

With a critical mass among the inner circle persuaded that murder was necessary to protect Bhagwan, the planning hurtled forward throughout the rest of June. Sheela would eject reticent Bodhi and Jayananda from the room while they plotted, but KD, as one of Sheela's top lieutenants, remained involved.

He would later claim that he saw his role as trying to talk them out of their deadly schemes.

The conspirators' first order of business was to decide whom to kill. Sheela named her desired targets:

- Attorney general Dave Frohnmayer
- Wasco County planning director Dan Durow
- State representative Wayne Fawbush
- Helen Byron and her daughter, Barbara
- Les Zaitz, a reporter for the *Oregonian* who was about to unleash a twenty-part exposé on Rajneeshpuram

KD threw out his own suggestion: *Why not include Charles Turner on the list while you're at it?* He meant it as a joke, he later said, to point out how absurd the whole exercise was. But Sheela added US Attorney Charles Turner to the list. A consensus grew in the room that Turner in fact posed the biggest existential threat to the commune—and particularly to Bhagwan, given the potentially catastrophic consequences of a grand jury indictment. Additional targets would be added to the list over the coming days.

Next, Sheela appointed a "hit team": Ava, Shanti B, Yogini, Anugiten, and Su. They were to drop their other responsibilities and devote themselves full-time to preparing for the assassinations. Sheela said she would take care of them in whatever they needed, including airline tickets out of the country and money.

With their targets identified and assassins tapped, the Jesus Grove conspirators began brainstorming how they could go about killing their enemies. Since they couldn't use weapons that could be traced back to the commune, Anugiten suggested ways to buy untraceable weapons in other states. KD later recalled that chief accountant Savita offered to find money to buy them, and that Shanti B—Sheela's "clone" who had disrupted the festival permit meetings with her foul insults—volunteered to shoot Charles Turner, since she was regarded as a skilled marksman. Yogini offered to kill Helen Byron and her daughter Barbara in New Mexico.

The Turner assassination team began surveilling his home and office and making steps to purchase murder weapons. Krishna Deva realized with alarm that the sannyasins might actually kill him. What had seemed like a silly idea mere days ago was now a plot in rapid motion, developing granularity and probability every day. When he tried to deter the group, it went nowhere. Sheela would remind them all that the lives of these regular people were meaningless compared to the precious being they were trying to protect.

———————

Within days of the first meeting in Jesus Grove where the murder list was created, three sannyasins in disguise walked into The Dalles Liquor Store. They cased out the interior. They checked out the exterior. They got back into their car and drove off.

Back at Rajneeshpuram, Ava, Yogini, and Anugiten—three members of the hit squad—reported to Sheela that they didn't think it would be feasible to plant a bomb in Wasco County judge Jim Comini's liquor store. An even better opportunity landed in their laps almost immediately, when they learned that Comini was about to enter the hospital for an ear surgery.

On June 6, Puja, Ava, and Yogini drove to St. Vincent Hospital in Portland. Ava and Yogini waited outside while Puja went inside with a syringe. Ava didn't know what was in it, but she later told investigators that Puja had been experimenting with high-potency potassium and adrenaline, which in high doses could cause death while being difficult to detect as a poison.

Puja returned, dejected. Not only was it difficult to access Comini's hospital room, but he wasn't receiving an intravenous drip. She had planned to surreptitiously inject whatever was in her syringe directly into the IV and make her escape. They had to abandon their plan. Jim Comini was discharged the next morning, still alive.

———————

In late June, a pair of women knocked on the front door of the Santa Fe residence that Helen Byron shared with her daughter, Barbara. The Byrons recognized one woman on their doorstep, Samadhi, from Rajneeshpuram, but they didn't know the other. The women said they were passing through New Mexico on their way to California, and Samadhi thought she would stop by to say hello to an old friend from the ranch.

Barbara invited them in for coffee, although she found their story incredibly suspicious. Neither woman was wearing sunrise colors, although they were both sannyasins. While they chatted, Barbara never took her eyes off their guests, and she certainly never allowed them to wander around the house alone. After a couple cups of coffee, they left.

When the Jesus Grove conspirators had discussed various ways to take out the Byrons, among the ideas thrown out were to poison the sugar in their home or sabotage their car in some way. Whatever the plan, it didn't work. Helen Byron lived to collect her judgment.

As the murder plots were getting underway, Sheela, KD, and Patipada boarded a plane for India. The trip was a product of Sheela's increasing certainty that US Attorney Charles Turner may soon arrest them on immigration charges. According to KD, Sheela had discussed her concerns with Bhagwan, who had told her to travel to India, find his old secretary Laxmi, and have her locate a place in the Himalayas where he could move on short notice if needed.

Sheela was not pleased. She hated India and didn't want Bhagwan to move back there—and she certainly didn't want Laxmi to reclaim her throne. Bhagwan's former secretary had come to America with Isabel in the summer of 1981, at his request, and she spent some months at Rajneeshpuram, where she fell into a depressed state with nothing to do, nothing to manage, and no real access to Bhagwan. Satya Bharti, who had known Laxmi for a decade by that point, would visit the older woman in her small trailer for late-night chats, and Laxmi would grumble about power-hungry Sheela clawing her way to the top. Soon Sheela prohibited anybody from visiting Laxmi and commanded disciples to treat her like an ordinary person so she could focus on her own enlightenment. She evicted Laxmi from the ranch upon learning that she was trying to lure Bhagwan to open a new commune elsewhere. After some time floundering around the United States and sparring with immigration officials, Laxmi returned to India.

And now Bhagwan wanted Sheela to ask Laxmi to create a fall-back ashram in case he had to leave America suddenly. For reasons KD claims he didn't understand, before the trip Puja had urged him to take some poison in his luggage. He accepted a vial of clear liquid that he thought might have contained hepatitis, but he refused to bring cyanide. *That's OK*, Puja said, *Sheela has some.*

While in India, Sheela made only the lamest efforts to contact Laxmi or try to find a place where Bhagwan could live. They returned after just a few days. It's not clear why they brought the poison or whether they used it. On the flight home, KD became suddenly, violently ill with diarrhea. Sheela downplayed it as nothing more than "Indian sun poisoning." Back at the ranch, he wound up confined to bed at Jesus Grove, with Puja as his nurse. She was about to administer an intravenous solution when KD stopped her. *Just like Devaraj?* he said, referring to Bhagwan's doctor who had received a contaminated IV drip the previous summer.

KD didn't know if he had been poisoned on the trip back from India or if Puja meant to kill him. He'd been negative about all the murder plotting over the past month, and Sheela had previously suggested that she might have to kill sannyasins who didn't fall into line. KD recalled that she entered a very dark mood during this period. She was extremely negative about her life as the Queen of Rajneeshpuram and her unrelenting work to keep everything afloat. Her daily meetings with Bhagwan became more of a chore than a privilege. It seemed to KD that Sheela's drug abuse increased: Valium, other tranquilizers, and some sort of IV that Puja administered. She was spiraling.

———————

The assassination of Charles Turner remained the subject of nearly daily meetings in Sheela's bedroom throughout the rest of June 1985, whether she was there or not. Members of her inner circle developed plans and shared information they were gathering about Turner. They decided that Shanti B, known to be the best shot at the ranch, would kill him with a handgun. She and a disciple who managed the commune's restaurant, Rikta, procured five revolvers under a phony ID in New Mexico. Shanti B carried the guns by bus all the way back to Oregon and showed them to the Jesus Grove conspirators. They nicknamed the guns "five easy pieces" after the Jack Nicholson movie, and Anugiten stored them in his clandestine workshop in an Alan Watts Grove cabin. He was to manufacture some sort of silencer to attach to the barrels, but he reported back that the guns could not be silenced. Undaunted, Sheela suggested they buy guns during an upcoming trip to New York in mid-June.

But after visiting just one shop on Forty-Second Street, Shanti B realized the state's strict laws would make it impossible for them to buy a gun or a silencer.

In the meantime, Samadhi, Ava, and Yogini had moved to Portland to plot Turner's assassination. By the middle of June they had found his home in a rural suburb, identified his car and license plate number, and located the parking spot he used in the garage near his office at the federal courthouse. After surveilling his house on multiple occasions, they came up with a potential plan: they would feign car trouble on the country road while Turner drove to work, and when he pulled over to help them, Shanti B would shoot him dead. Yogini also walked around the downtown parking garage to consider various angles and escape routes. She decided it would be a suitable place to ambush and murder him.

While in Portland for a press conference, commune president Vidya traveled to Turner's house and talked through the potential plans with the hit team. Shanti B, the gunwoman, also traveled to Portland to weigh in. The plan needed a little more fine-tuning, and they still needed the right weapon for the job. As soon as the pieces fell into place, Shanti B would attack.

31 | INTERNAL AFFAIRS

MA YOGA VIVEK WAS RARELY AWAY from Bhagwan, but on a summer day in 1985 she drove out of the ranch alone on some urgent business. As the guru's caretaker for the past ten years, the gentle, pale-skinned beauty from England was responsible for all his personal needs—food, clothing, medications, the comfort of his home—which required her to be at his side nearly round the clock. For her to be away from Bhagwan at all was unusual, and for her to be driving alone from the ranch was an extraordinary event.

Passing down the rough, winding county road, Vivek reached the steep incline with the sharp curve where everybody had to slow down. That's when the road grader smashed into the side of her car. She died the moment she hit the bottom of the steep embankment.

At least, that's how the Jesus Grove plotters dreamed it would happen. Another idea was to simply ambush her car as it was leaving the commune and have Shanti B shoot her dead.

But finding a way to get Vivek away from Lao Tzu and alone proved to be nearly impossible. She had been glued to Bhagwan ever since she was a twenty-one-year-old waif wandering the streets of Mumbai, uncertain of what had pulled her away from her family in Europe and inspired her to travel to India. She wound up at a parade ground filled with thousands of Indians listening to a white-robed man lecturing in Hindi. His sheer magnetism drew her forward through the crowd until she sat in the front row, utterly transfixed by Acharya Rajneesh. At a meditation camp, Bhagwan spotted in the crowd the blue-eyed girl with long, straight auburn hair, and he summoned her to his room, where he gently explained to her in English how his meditation worked and what it was supposed to accomplish. He told her that she was the reincarnation of his former lover. She took sannyas and became Vivek, which means "awareness."

She moved into Bhagwan's Mumbai apartment and shared the crawlspace under the living room floor with Satya Bharti, although she would often slip away at night to be with her master. By the time he moved to Pune, Vivek had edged out his previous caretaker, a cousin, and become the woman responsible for tending to all his personal needs. In Oregon she remained a distant figure, rarely mingling with other commune members.

And in mid-June 1985 she had become an urgent problem that needed solving, at least as Sheela saw it. They talked about car accidents, they talked about ambushes, they talked about piping lethal gas into Vivek's trailer. But it was all just talk. Late one night, sitting on her bed and surrounded by her coconspirators, Sheela insisted that the time for talk was over. They would take care of Vivek that night.

With its armed guards, electrified fence, and watchtower, Bhagwan's personal compound was the most secure spot on the ranch. Commune president Vidya reshuffled Lao Tzu's overnight guard shift at the last minute, ensuring that only members of Sheela's inner circle would be on duty at 11:00 PM when Ava, Julian, and Su drove up to the security gate. The trio parked and quietly walked the dark grounds until they neared the porch outside Vivek's bedroom. Beneath the shadows of a nearby grove, Su poured an anesthetic fluid—perhaps ether or ketamine—over a rag. Ava held a syringe that Puja had given her. They moved toward the door.

Since the Helen Byron verdict two weeks earlier, the nightly chats in Sheela's bedroom had turned from the assassination of public officials to killing the people closest to Bhagwan. At the top of Sheela's list were two of her oldest enemies from back in India: Bhagwan's personal physician Devaraj, and his caretaker and companion Vivek. He trusted them with his physical health and safety, but, Sheela had told her inner circle, they had become catastrophically negligent in their duties.

The antipathy between Sheela and Vivek went back more than a decade, to when they first met in Bhagwan's Mumbai apartment. The American writer and early disciple Satya Bharti witnessed the beginning of their relationship and saw it as a personality clash from day one. Vivek was a quiet, serene presence who wanted nothing to do with Sheela's aggressive, disruptive energy. (Bhagwan and Laxmi had taken to calling Sheela "the atom bomb.") At the Pune ashram, Sheela came to view the people closest to Bhagwan as self-righteous snobs. "They thought of themselves as spiritually advanced souls," Sheela later wrote about Vivek and the other people who lived in Bhagwan's home. "Their feet never touched the ground. It was difficult for me to get along with these people. I often thought that if serious, sour faces and apathy towards others are the outcomes of spirituality and enlightenment, then I am happy to be far from it all."

Many people who witnessed the relationship described Sheela's attitude as one of unmistakable envy. Vivek was physically close to Bhagwan and exercised complete control over his household, a position Sheela wanted for herself. The jealousy became so blatant that Bhagwan had asked Italian Deeksha in New Jersey to try to protect Vivek from Sheela. But after Deeksha dropped sannyas and left the commune, the women's relationship deteriorated so publicly that Bhagwan brokered a truce by which Sheela and Vivek had to stand in front of a mass gathering of commune members and pledge their support for each other. If they didn't make peace, Bhagwan had told them, he would "leave his body."

Sheela found new kindling for her burning hatred of Vivek in the wake of the calamitous Byron verdict, when those around Sheela felt she had already reached an emotional rock bottom. She came across a letter to Bhagwan from the commune pharmacist expressing concerns about all the drugs Devaraj was prescribing for people who lived and worked in Lao Tzu and who did not appear to have any medical problems. The drugs included strong barbiturates, tranquilizers, and painkillers. The letter confirmed what Sheela had been telling her confidants for the past year: Devaraj was experimenting with Bhagwan's body by pumping him full of dangerous drugs, and Vivek—the guru's so-called caretaker—was allowing it to happen.

Sheela told her Jesus Grove intimates that Devaraj and Vivek were playing games with Bhagwan's health. What's more, she seethed about the risk for the commune if the state and federal law enforcement circling Rajneeshpuram found out about the rampant drug use in Bhagwan's inner sanctum. It became an obsession for Sheela, something she talked about at all hours of the day and night, always chewing over the same question: How could they stop Devaraj and Vivek from harming—or even killing—their beloved master?

———————

Armed with their soaked rag and lethal syringe, Ava, Su, and Julian stepped onto Vivek's porch. Su had retrieved the Lao Tzu master key. She pushed it into the lock.

Meanwhile, Sheela and Krishna Deva were arguing back in Jesus Grove. KD had tried to talk the group out of killing Vivek, since he thought their method wouldn't work or—worse—they would get caught. Sheela told KD he was a coward who only tried to sabotage their ideas. A couple of others had expressed similar concerns, including Vidya's boyfriend, Bodhi, and Sheela's husband, Jayananda, but the larger group had vetoed them and agreed upon a plan that came from Puja's dark imagination. A small team would sneak into Vivek's bedroom while she slept, place an anesthetized rag over her mouth to knock her unconscious, and inject her with a mixture of potassium and adrenaline to stop her heart. Vivek would be discovered the next morning, dead from an apparent heart attack.

Su turned the key in Vivek's bedroom's door. It didn't move.

If Bhagwan is killed, it will be your fault! Sheela vented at the would-be assassins when they returned to her bedroom late that night. Su and Ava were both suffering from horrible headaches and nausea after accidentally inhaling fumes from the soaked rag, but Sheela didn't care. The Vivek debacle was yet another example of the incompetence surrounding her. They hadn't been able to kill Helen Byron, they hadn't been able to kill Wasco County judge Jim Comini, and now they couldn't do something as simple as find the right key for Vivek's bedroom door.

———————

Days later, Krishna Deva lay in bed, eyes closed, as commune president Vidya approached him with a pillow. Before she could seal it over his face, KD leaped to action and fended her off.

He lay down again as Anugiten approached with the pillow. Again, KD fought him off.

Now it was Anubhavo. Again KD defended himself.

He turned to the twenty people watching from the floor of Sheela's bedroom. It was proof, he declared, that their plan to kill Devaraj would not work.

Devaraj had recently been called to Jesus Grove for a meeting. While sitting on the back porch with Savita, Sheela's second-in-command, a disciple had brought him a cup of coffee. The next day, he was admitted to the Koran Grove clinic with symptoms similar to what had landed him there the previous year: dizziness, weakness, and severe diarrhea.

Sheela told her gang they needed to keep Devaraj in Koran Grove as long as possible to protect Bhagwan. Or, better yet, make sure he never left. They decided to seize the opportunity by sneaking into his room, covering his face with a pillow to muffle his screams, and jabbing him with a lethal injection. But, as KD demonstrated to the plotters, Devaraj might be able to fight them off or cry for help, and then it was all over.

KD was still feeling ill after his trip to India, but he was even more queasy with doubts. It was one thing to speak abstractly about killing a far-off US Attorney. It was another thing altogether to murder commune members within their care and control, people they had known for years going back to India, people whom Bhagwan trusted so much that he selected them to live in his home. While these plots were unfolding in June 1985, KD became so despondent that his girlfriend, Sagun, threatened to leave him and the commune unless he told her what was going on.

KD's efforts to talk them out of killing Devaraj failed. The plotters decided to use an anesthetic-laced rag instead of a pillow. Sheela selected the assassination team that night. Puja assured them that Devaraj would be sleeping, since she had given him a Benadryl capsule that she had emptied and refilled with a strong sedative. The small team crept through Koran Grove, carrying a rag and a syringe. Julian found Devaraj's door and opened it.

Devaraj was awake and looking at him.

Their plan depended on the element of surprise, so the assassins retreated.

Back at Jesus Grove, Sheela again told her crew that if Bhagwan died, it would be their fault. She insisted they had to take out Devaraj while he was a sitting duck. Days later, Sheela cornered Krishna Deva, the persistent naysayer, and asked if he was ready to do something about Devaraj before it was too late. She was testing his loyalty, it seemed, to both her and their number-one mission of protecting Bhagwan.

KD said he was ready.

The assassins parked near a darkened warehouse and walked along the creek toward the clinic that night. Shanti B and Ava walked in, hypodermic needles concealed in their palms. KD followed. His job was to hold a pillow over Devaraj's face.

Inside the clinic, KD opened the door to the wrong room. The patient sat up and looked at him. Back in the hallway, KD opened another wrong door and made a loud noise. The assassins decided he had drawn too much attention and they should abort the mission. They hadn't even found Devaraj's room yet. KD hadn't meant to raise such a ruckus, but he later wondered whether his subconscious had done it to protect both himself and Devaraj.

Reporting the events back in Sheela's bedroom, the assassination squad broke out in laughter as they described KD's clumsy antics. The mood turned sour when Sheela stopped laughing. She again told KD that he was a coward who was sabotaging their efforts.

Days later, KD became so ill with cramps and diarrhea that he had to be admitted to Koran Grove. Before he went to the clinic, Puja again tried to give him an IV drip that KD refused, fearing what she might put in it. Another patient was placed in the room next to KD's: Yogini, the nutritionist who had smeared salmonella on her palms before shaking hands with politicians in The Dalles and who had volunteered to murder Helen Byron.

Based on his run-ins with the intense woman over the years, KD had come to consider Yogini to be a little bit deranged and perhaps the most dangerous of all the people in Sheela's inner circle. He realized that he might become victim to the exact same plot they had just tried to spring on Devaraj—Puja intentionally sickening him with poison so he had to go to the clinic and then killing him in his sleep. He stayed up all night, convinced that Yogini would sneak into his room and murder him.

When KD was released, he confronted Sheela and accused her of plotting to kill him. She simply waved her hand, as if disgusted that he would even suggest such a thing.

Throughout the rest of June, before the Fourth Annual World Celebration, Sheela continued beating the drum among her inner circle that Vivek and Devaraj must die to protect Bhagwan. But as their efforts continued to fail, as more time plodded by, some members of the Jesus Grove group began to question, both privately and in their meetings, whether Bhagwan would actually want them to kill two of his closest staff. And if he did want them dead, shouldn't that order come directly from him?

Sheela told her intimates one night that she had taken the question to Bhagwan for his guidance but had framed it in a broader way: What should be done with people who got in the way of his vision? The bug in Bhagwan's personal quarters recorded their subsequent conversation, Sheela said, and she had Julian set up a tape player so her gang could hear the master's words for themselves. The recording quality was poor, but KD—who often listened to the Lao Tzu bugs—could make out what was being said.

Bhagwan talked for more than ten minutes about Adolf Hitler. He spoke glowingly of the Nazi leader, claiming that he was a misunderstood genius, a visionary creating his own form of the New Man. Bhagwan approved of Hitler's use of Jews as a scapegoat to unify the Aryan people and gain political power, since the führer knew that fulfilling an extraordinary vision could require extreme measures. Comparing it to their own situation, Bhagwan said that eliminating people was acceptable if it were necessary to preserve the vision. In fact, killing people wasn't such a bad thing. Sheela should do whatever was necessary, as long as it didn't create problems for her or the commune.

When the tape ended, Sheela told her inner circle that she interpreted Bhagwan's words to be a blanket authority to kill their enemies. Since Devaraj and Vivek threatened his life and his work, they were both fair game.

This recorded message, which became known as the "Hitler Tape," echoed the message that Italian Deeksha had been horrified to hear at Kip's Castle four years earlier, when in his private study Bhagwan had called Hitler a genius and had instructed Sheela and Deeksha to study Joseph Goebbels, the Nazi propaganda master who was so skillful at manipulating people. Bhagwan had told Deeksha he would succeed where Hitler had failed. He had prodded Sheela to declare that she would kill for him. Four years after that message repulsed Deeksha right out of the sannyasin movement, nearly twenty members of

Sheela's inner circle were discovering their master's darkest thoughts. But they weren't repulsed. They were *relieved*. The Hitler Tape helped persuade them that Sheela was right and that Bhagwan would want them to kill their enemies.

Still, some of them just weren't cut out for murder. Within days of the unsuccessful attempts to kill Devaraj in his Koran Grove bed, Sheela's husband, Jayananda, and Vidya's boyfriend, Bodhi, were put on planes to Europe. They had constantly objected to any murder plans, and Sheela also worried they would crumble under grand jury scrutiny if it came to that. And thus Jayananda, the man who had helped usher Sheela, Bhagwan, and the international neo-sannyas movement into America, found himself exiled in Germany.

Krishna Deva was not sent away. He was too important to the commune, as its mayor and very public face. He also suspected that Sheela kept roping him in to the murder plotting because it would be too dangerous for her to exclude him. It was far safer to keep him in the fold, where his hands would get just as dirty as everyone else's.

Sheela didn't forget about her other domestic enemies while they plotted to kill Vivek and Devaraj. The list of potential murder targets expanded to include Devaraj's wife, Hasya, and rich physician Dhyan John, both members of the much-loathed Hollywood Group.

Swami Michel received an order from Julian that summer to bug the trailer where Hasya and Dhyan John had recently moved, far in the southern valley near the Pythagoras Clinic. Until that point, Michel's spying work had focused on external enemies. He felt very uncomfortable invading the privacy of fellow commune members, but he knew the Jesus Grove cohort would kick him out if he refused, and he had no intention of leaving Rajneeshpuram. While the Hollywood Group was away on a three-day vacation, Michel installed sixteen microphones in the trailer's air vents. He ran a telephone cable from beneath the trailer to his clandestine office in Zarathustra and eventually extended the connection all the way to Jesus Grove so Sheela and her staff could listen directly to what Hasya and Dhyan John were saying.

After Michel installed the microphones, Julian gave him another project that made him uneasy. Michel had been experimenting with a device that emitted a high-frequency, inaudible pitch that, when pointed at a person, could make them immediately nauseous. Julian had originally requested the device so he could use it on a member of law enforcement who was seen repeatedly attending Bhagwan's daily drive-bys and monitoring the crowd, as if he were looking for particular people. Julian thought the sound device would make the man so sick that he would have to leave the ranch.

Michel never learned whether his boss used it on the officer, but in the summer of 1985 Julian asked him to install a similar device within the wall of Dhyan John's bedroom. Michel understood that Dhyan John had been heard saying negative things about Sheela and the people running the commune and that the device was meant to punish him. Michel had no intention of installing a device that would harm another commune member, but, again, he didn't want to be evicted from the ranch for disobedience. He managed to talk Julian out of the idea only when he said that the device's amplifier would make crackling noises that Dhyan John would be able to hear through the wall.

Hasya received special attention as well, according to Ava. In mid-June, when Hasya flew on a commune airplane from Rajneeshpuram to Portland, one of her fellow passengers was Yogini. Hasya continued on to Los Angeles, oblivious to Sheela's henchwoman who had been watching her every movement throughout the flight, unsuccessfully searching for a way to administer the poison she carried.

Just before the Fourth Annual World Celebration kicked off in June, Vivek accepted Sheela's invitation to join her for lunch at Jesus Grove. Arriving that day, she found a large contingent of Sheela's loyal foot soldiers around the table. Vivek accepted a cup of tea.

Within fifteen minutes, she was sweating, had a headache, felt dizzy and nauseous, and her heart was beating extraordinarily fast. She struggled to her feet and told the others that she wasn't feeling well, and then she collapsed into a bathroom on her way to the exit. As Vivek tottered toward her car, Sheela ran out after her.

You're too sick to drive! she cried. *Let me drive you!*

By the time Sheela dropped her outside Lao Tzu, Vivek was soaked in perspiration. Inside, Devaraj took her pulse and found it was twice the normal rate, but her blood pressure was lower than normal. Dr. Shunyo arrived and gave her a drug to slow her rapid heartbeat. After four hours, Vivek finally had a normal pulse, although she continued to feel ill. Shunyo later speculated that she may have been administered an oral adrenaline, since Puja had been asking the pharmacist about such drugs.

A couple of nights later, Vivek drove to downtown Rajneeshpuram to get a drink at the bar. She perhaps didn't even notice two bartenders who swooped in as soon as she arrived: Ava and Yogini. They were eager to offer her another drink, but she left after just one round.

The Jesus Grove plotters had known Vivek would be at the bar because KD had heard her talking about it over the Lao Tzu bugs. He and others had been told to pay attention to her movements and to look for opportunities to poison her. Puja had distributed vials containing various poisons that they were to use if they could. The same direction extended to other enemies of Jesus Grove: Devaraj, Hasya, and Dhyan John.

Through a stroke of luck, Vivek had only one drink and didn't give them the opportunity to contaminate another. After she escaped the bar unpoisoned, the Jesus Grove crew would never again try to kill her.

Devaraj was not so lucky.

32 | THE GARDEN OF EPICURUS

WHILE SANNYASINS JOURNEYED into the heart of the valley for the Fourth Annual World Celebration in early July, Swami Anand Megha boarded a van that took him west out of downtown Rajneeshpuram, past the meditation university and the welcome center, past the commune's spire-topped crematorium, past Krishnamurti Lake, where people lounged in the balmy summer evening. He traveled miles beyond any settled part of the ranch before turning onto a small gravel road that dipped over a hill, erasing from view any sign of the commune. The van finally came to a stop at a flat spot near a creek where two trailer homes had been sited thirty feet apart. The area was called Desiderata Canyon.

The driver, in a surgical mask, gown, and rubber gloves, waved goodbye and departed. Megha joined the small group of men who had arrived earlier that day and were waiting with their luggage outside the trailers. After saying hello, Megha asked each man to step forward so he could conduct a brief physical exam and assess their condition.

It broke his heart to segregate them in such a callous way. Thirty-seven years old with hints of gray already showing in his curly black hair, Megha was a general practitioner from Holland who'd served as a doctor at both the Pune ashram and the Oregon commune. He knew some of the men personally, but now all that mattered was their health. He assigned all the symptomatic men to live in one trailer, while he and the other asymptomatic residents would go together in the other. He felt especially horrible when he had to put a good friend in the symptomatic trailer.

Reflecting on it later, Megha regretted that he, a gay, Jewish, European man, had assumed the role of a "Nazi camp guard," as he called it, separating the healthy from the sick, simply because Ma Anand Puja had snapped her fingers and told him to do it.

———————

Days earlier, the Fourth World Festival kicked off with a whimper. After Shanti B and others had fought so aggressively to get the festival permit from Wasco County, the commune had received only seven thousand registrations by late June—less than half the registrations from two years earlier. Local law enforcement reported that buses coming into the ranch seemed far emptier than in previous years. Registrations did receive a bump after the commune announced that Bhagwan would be giving public discourses on the big stage in Rajneesh Mandir. Until that point, he had been speaking only to small groups of invited disciples at his home, with the recordings rebroadcasted to the commune the following evening. The festival offered the first opportunity since India for most disciples to hear his voice live.

Megha was a commune member, having married an American woman to secure a green card, but he'd spent the previous six months at a meditation center in Cologne, West Germany, with his boyfriend, a disciple named Mandir. He'd returned to Rajneeshpuram for the festival with Mandir in tow, excited to be back with his fellow commune members and to hear Bhagwan's voice. But then Puja had derailed everything. He'd known her since she was one of many unassuming nurses at the ashram clinic in India, before she got swept into Sheela's inner circle and elevated to such a high position. In Oregon, Puja had asked Megha to work as a general practitioner at the commune's main clinic, Pythagoras, where he had to keep his practice off the books since he wasn't licensed in the United States. She seemed to like him, probably because he was a hard worker who never questioned her orders or expressed negativity. And for his part, Megha felt drawn to Puja and the other brazen Moms who ran the commune. He would sometimes hang out in Jesus Grove, just to be close to their extravagant power.

When he ran into Puja just as the summer festival was starting, she got right to business. *Do you have my Haldol?*

While Megha was in Cologne, he'd received a message from the ranch. He was to buy a large amount of Haldol in its liquid form and bring it back to Rajneeshpuram. Megha didn't know why they needed so much of such a powerful antipsychotic drug, but his place was not to question. Still, after buying the drug from pharmacies all over Cologne, he lost his nerve and dumped the bottles down a sink drain.

He told Puja that he did not have the drugs. At the time, she didn't seem bothered by it.

Once the festival was underway a few days later, Puja called Megha to the office she kept in the Hotel Rajneesh near Jesus Grove. They chatted about nothing—how things were in Europe, whether he had any plans to move back there permanently. Strangely, she asked if he knew of a Swiss man who might be interested in marrying her. He did not.

Puja suddenly leaned forward. *Megha, I have something to tell you.* She reminded him of a blood test he had given at her request before leaving Rajneeshpuram for Cologne. Megha hadn't known what it was for and had forgotten all about it over the past six months.

It later struck him how bizarre Puja's demeanor was while she delivered the news that he had tested positive for HIV antibodies. He was her old friend and colleague, and yet she seemed delighted to be telling him.

He walked out of her office in a daze. The virus had no known treatment. He considered the diagnosis to be a death sentence, allowing him, at most, six months to live. After sharing the devastating news with his boyfriend, Megha numbly gathered his belongings and prepared to move to his final home.

Bhagwan had taken an unusual interest in the emerging HIV/AIDS crisis from the time the virus was first identified and described in the United States in the early 1980s. According to Sheela, he saw the AIDS epidemic as a device he could employ to teach his disciples awareness of their bodies and their sexuality. (Bhagwan used "AIDS" as an umbrella term, and he rarely if ever spoke about HIV, the virus that causes the syndrome.) In March 1984, he issued a startling prediction: AIDS would kill two-thirds of the world's population unless humanity chose to adopt celibacy, monogamy, or thorough protective measures. He selected the latter approach for his own commune, which was known to be a sexually open place where people often had multiple partners.

After Bhagwan's prediction, Puja as the head of the medical corporation was tasked with implementing stringent regulations intended to prevent the spread of HIV within the sannyasin community. Since little was known then about how the virus was communicated, the commune's measures included using condoms and latex or rubber gloves during intercourse; avoiding oral sex, anal sex, and kissing; and washing "scrupulously" before and after any sexual encounter. Free condoms and other protective gear were made available across the commune and were given to every festivalgoer in a small cardboard box placed on their beds.

Some disciples grumbled privately about this intrusion into their bedrooms, while others ignored the restrictions altogether, to their own peril. The commune's cleaning staff was said to monitor the trash in disciples' bedrooms and report noncompliance to Jesus Grove, and some couples were ejected from the commune for having unprotected sex. To avoid detection, American writer Satya Bharti and her partner tossed unused condoms and gloves into the trash bin every night. Many other commune members went along with the new restrictions as part of their surrender, with some even treating the protective measures as a device that allowed them to participate consciously in sex.

The commune's restrictions became more invasive over time. Rubbing alcohol appeared in every bathroom, and sannyasins were told to scrub their hands with it, as well as the faucets, toilet seats, and doorknobs. They could no longer share food, drinks, or cigarettes. They had to shower before swimming in the lake. ("Before you *svim*, you *vipe!*" a German woman would bark while handing out sanitary wipes at the changing-room door.) Disciples could no longer lick envelopes or even their fingers to turn the pages of a book. Reminders and warnings appeared in the weekly *Rajneesh Times* newspaper:

> Friends and lovers, restrain the urge to let your mucous membranes merge! Though tempting—succulent and slippery—can you be certain they are AIDS-free?

> Oral and anal sex are through, but don't let the changes make you blue, just find new depths of intimacy in nose and earlobe harmony!

To make sex less clinical, Puja suggested in an interview that participants "place a beautiful bowl on a tray by the side of the bed. Fill the bowl with warm water and in it float a plastic container of contraceptive jelly," she said. "Each partner puts on gloves, and by this time the jelly is warm to the touch rather than cold and intrusive."

Throughout his discourses in 1984 and '85, Bhagwan often said that the only way to truly eradicate AIDS was to end the practice of male homosexuality. Even before AIDS, and despite his famously liberal approach to sexuality, Bhagwan had often encouraged the gay men among his disciples to stop having sex with men, since he believed that heterosexuality was the only path to true fulfillment. Still, he retained many openly gay male disciples and, under Sheela's leadership, the commune became an outwardly gay-friendly place while the master was in silence. In 1983 the Rajneeshpuram City Council passed a gay-rights ordinance, believed to be the first of its kind in Oregon, which prohibited discrimination based on sexual preference or orientation in public accommodations, housing, or education. An advertisement in the *Rajneesh Times* addressed to "Gays of America" suggested Rajneeshpuram as "the ideal city for your conventions, conferences, and other functions." During the 1983 summer festival, Sheela hosted gay disciples in Rajneesh Mandir, where she declared that "the religion of Bhagwan Shree Rajneesh supports individual freedom and sexual preference" and promised that the commune would set aside a special park for gay people called the Garden of Epicurus.

But after Bhagwan reclaimed his microphone in October 1984, he made clear that his dim view of homosexuality had not changed. Responding to a disciple's question on whether he felt that gays were second-class citizens, he said, "As a homosexual, you are not even a human being, what to say about a second-class citizen? You have fallen from dignity. I have great love for you, but that does not mean that I will support your perversion." He told a reporter that gay sannyasins either needed to take a "deprogramming" course to drop their "degradation," or else they would have to leave the commune. The HIV/ AIDS epidemic provided Bhagwan with a new reason to condemn male homosexuality. "We don't want homosexuals here because they are potentials for AIDS. Either they have to change or they have to leave. The choice is theirs."

Indeed, his commune would save the world from AIDS, he claimed, because he was waging war against the thing that caused it: homosexuality. At Rajneeshpuram he was "trying to destroy all kinds of perversions and bringing people back to nature, to their natural being, respecting their bodies, loving their bodies. And trying to understand that sex is natural only with the opposite pole." All of his communes would become "like oases where people will be back to the garden of Eden from where that idiot God pushed them out."

In January 1985, when Puja drew Megha's blood before he boarded a plane for Cologne, there was no test on the market for HIV, so it's not entirely clear why she wanted the sample. But while he was living in Europe, the US Food and Drug Administration approved the first tests to screen donated blood for HIV. The tests were very sensitive and had a high rate of false positives, and thus they were not intended to make individual diagnoses. That didn't stop Puja from telling certain disciples over the summer, including Megha, that the commune's laboratory had run tests and diagnosed them as HIV positive.

To protect the health of the other commune members, Puja told anybody diagnosed with HIV who wanted to stay at Rajneeshpuram that they would need to live in Desiderata Canyon in near-total isolation. The canyon complex was supposed to represent a new model of caring for people living with HIV, one that Bhagwan, Sheela, and Puja would soon tout to the world. Rather than reject patients altogether, the commune would provide them with a beautiful home and delicious vegetarian meals, offer top-notch medical care, and treat them with love and compassion.

Megha was among the first arrivals at Desiderata Canyon when he moved there on July 2, 1985, three days into the Fourth Annual World Celebration. Within weeks, the two trailers hosted ten other people living with HIV who were to be his roommates and companions for the rest of his abbreviated life. About half the residents were commune members and half were sannyasins visiting from elsewhere. Some, like Megha, had received their diagnosis from a test administered by the Rajneesh Medical Corporation, while others—including all those visiting from Europe—had been diagnosed elsewhere. There were ten men, including Megha—all gay, he believed—and a single American woman, Ma Anand Zeno. The residents formed their own little commune-within-a-commune. Swami Anand Lazarus planted a Japanese garden. An Italian sannyasin created a humble little path near the trailers they jokingly called the Via Appia. They received fresh meals from Magdalena delivered right to their doorstep three times a day. The trailers were modern and comfortable, and each resident had a private bedroom—a rare luxury at Rajneeshpuram.

But the isolation soon became oppressive. Canyon residents weren't allowed to go anywhere else on the ranch—not even to the county road. They couldn't have visitors. They had a telephone, but only Megha was authorized to use it, and only for medical emergencies. If the residents wanted to send a note beyond the canyon, the paper would first need to sit beneath an ultraviolet light for twelve hours to disinfect it. Accustomed to "worshipping" for fourteen hours a day, the residents begged for work, but week after week the medical staff who checked in on them said no. To fill their time, they would read from a small library that had been arranged for them. They would take walks along the stream. They would clean their trailers three times a day, out of a desire to feel industrious.

Their one saving grace came each morning, when a clinic worker in full protective gear would drive all the residents to the Rajneesh Mandir assembly hall for the daily discourses that Bhagwan was now giving from his dais. While thousands of sannyasins hugged and danced and sang arm-in-arm before their master, the eleven Desiderata residents had to sit in the rear corner, physically and emotionally separated from the celebration. One day, a good friend approached Zeno and gave her a spontaneous hug. Puja spotted it and told Zeno that she would be banned from discourse if it ever happened again.

At first, nobody knew about Desiderata Canyon or the people living there. But then Bhagwan mentioned it one day during discourse. Heads swiveled to stare at the small group cordoned off in the back. As a doctor in India, Megha had treated people with contagious diseases and had imagined what it would feel like to be a pariah. Now, as he wilted beneath all those pitying looks, he was astonished to find that he was living it himself.

For Zeno, it felt like a miserable way to spend her remaining days, surrounded by men—some of whom were strangers—with no hope of ever being part of the larger community again. She contemplated suicide throughout her time at Desiderata Canyon. She considered leaving the commune altogether. But then she would see smiling, beautiful Bhagwan on his dais and realize that she could never leave.

When she first offered Megha's diagnosis, Puja had left the door slightly ajar. *We're going to test you again, because maybe this test wasn't right.* A month passed before she finally arrived with a technician who drew blood from all eleven residents. Megha knew the results should take only twenty-four hours, but Puja didn't return until nearly a week later, when she cryptically told them that all the tests were positive, but that some were "more positive" than others. Ten days later she took additional samples for a Western blot test, which required the blood to be sent to a laboratory in Portland. Days went by. Weeks. The results never arrived, no matter how forcefully the residents demanded them from the medical staff.

During a lecture in August, Bhagwan encouraged all the Desiderata Canyon residents to have sex with each other. "As I see it, if people having AIDS start making love to each other, perhaps their AIDS will disappear. If these people live longer than two years, we have proved the point. And perhaps we will be the people to give the cure to the world. No medicine is needed, just put two AIDS victims together." Puja went to the canyon to warn the residents to ignore what Bhagwan had said. She didn't want them to risk having sex with each other in case one of them happened to be negative.

One month later, when Megha finally learned the truth about Desiderata Canyon, he would reflect on Puja's warning and wonder whether it offered a very rare glimpse at whatever conscience she had left.

33 | MASTER'S DAY 1985

WHEN THE BIG MOMENT came on the morning of Master's Day, Bhagwan Shree Rajneesh was at the edge of his dais in Rajneesh Mandir, dressed like an Arabian prince in a white robe with gleaming, opalescent sleeves and a bejeweled satin cape, making vigorous arm gestures to drive his disciples' energy higher and higher and higher. Even at the back of the enormous hall, close to the stage for the live band, disciples were cheering and clapping and praying with their fingertips at their mouths and wiping tears from their cheeks. Many flung up their arms as if trying to grasp their master's energy in an invisible embrace.

The band gave it all they could. Saxophones wailed up and down complicated scales, snare drums marked an unsteady rhythm, guitars plucked atonal tunes in their deepest registers. Above it all was Swami Toby's flute, trilling and dancing. Bhagwan gave one final namaste to the crowd as he walked to the exit. The music crested into a loud, discordant wail.

Nobody could hear Devaraj scream.

A couple of days earlier, while the festival was already underway, a panicked Sheela had convened some of her closest intimates, including Krishna Deva, Julian, and Puja, in her Jesus Grove bedroom. She told them that Devaraj was about to kill Bhagwan.

To prove it, she played a tape from the Lao Tzu bug in which Bhagwan told his doctor that when it came time for him to die, he wanted to go gracefully and without pain. Devaraj suggested a sequence of injections that would accomplish this task: muscle relaxants, tranquilizers, potassium. Bhagwan told him to procure enough of the drugs to kill three people and to bury them in the garden until they were needed.

With a grave expression, Sheela told her inner circle that the medical center already had the drugs on hand that Devaraj would need. Bhagwan had declared the previous year that he would die on July 6 sometime over the next twenty years. Sheela said she was now convinced that he planned to kill himself on *this* Master's Day, mere days away.

Over the next couple of days, a group of nearly two dozen trusted Jesus Grove intimates learned of the "suicide tape" by either hearing it or reading a transcript. They came to agree with Sheela that Devaraj was about to kill Bhagwan. On the night before Master's Day, looking tired and pale, Sheela said it was now or never. They would either kill Devaraj or allow him to kill their master. She asked who would be willing to do the deed.

Shanti B would later say that her response spontaneously leaped from her mouth. Upon repeating it, she found that her resolve was already hardening. It was the right thing to do, if it meant saving Bhagwan.

I will do it.

———————

The music swelled, the drums pounded, the instruments sawed and blared. Bhagwan shuffled about his dais, shaking his palms to the sky, propelling his disciples' energy into the stratosphere.

On the other side of the hall, Swami Devaraj sat in his red robe just off the left corner of the band's platform—an unusual position for him on an extraordinary day. For many years, he had read excerpts from Bhagwan's discourses during the satsang ceremonies, typically while sitting on the band stage opposite his master's dais. Next to Devaraj would be Taru, an older Indian woman who had been with Bhagwan since she used to dye his hair black in Mumbai and who sang Hindi chants during satsang. But on this morning—Master's Day, July 6, 1985—Devaraj and Taru had been shunted from their usual position on the band's stage and forced to sit on the floor with everybody else. Two of

Sheela's minions had said they needed extra space on stage so the musicians could jump and dance.

Devaraj still conducted his readings throughout the hour-long service. "Sannyas is renouncing your dreams, renouncing your sleep," he read to the silent crowd scattered across Rajneesh Mandir's two-acre linoleum floor. "But this is possible only if you love the man, if you love the master, so much that you say, 'Okay, if he is going to hell, we are going with him. Hell will be heaven with him. Without him, we are not going to heaven.' Only then can you be awakened."

When it happened, Bhagwan was prowling on his dais to the chaotic music. Devaraj sat on the ground, clapping and swaying. A hand wrapped around his left shoulder. A mouth came close to his ear. A woman mumbled something about Devaraj making an announcement at the end of satsang. He turned and saw it was Shanti B.

It wasn't so much a prick as a sudden pressure in his left buttock. Devaraj knew it was an injection. He grabbed Shanti B's wrist. She yanked it away. An uncomfortable pressure crawled up his right side and into his temple. Devaraj climbed to his feet. Shanti B was with Yogini, both watching him with strange expressions that told Devaraj they were complicit in whatever was happening to him.

He shouted, but nobody could hear him over the music and the cheering crowd. He staggered about, swinging his arms wildly.

What's wrong with you? Shanti B asked. *What's the problem?*

Devaraj moved past them and practically collapsed on top of old Taru in her chair.

Shanti B has poisoned me, he said into her ear.

As he struggled to get upright, Devaraj saw a white handkerchief on the ground near where he had been sitting, with something that looked like a pen wrapped inside. A hand grabbed it, and it vanished.

With Taru's help, Devaraj staggered through a rear entrance and out to a grassy area behind Rajneesh Mandir, where he collapsed onto the ground. Celebrants began filtering out of the hall and gawking at Bhagwan's doctor vomiting and rolling on the grass in agony. When he spotted his colleague Dr. Shunyo, Devaraj got up and pulled him across the road. With some privacy, Devaraj lifted his robe and pulled down his underpants, revealing a small black-and-blue mark on his left buttock.

I've been injected by Shanti B, Devaraj said. *In case I die, I want you to see this.*

Shunyo tried to comfort his friend while they waited for an ambulance to arrive, concerned about the unbelievable garbage coming out of his mouth.

———————

Shanti B fell in with the crowd bounding out of Rajneesh Mandir into the beautiful summer morning. She gradually detached herself to walk back to Jesus Grove alone. Wending her way through festival tents arranged in rows with military precision, she contemplated what she had just done. Jab, plunge, retract—

Devaraj had grabbed her wrist as she tried to withdraw the syringe from his butt. She had to struggle with him a bit before she could break free. As planned, she had dropped the syringe to the linoleum floor behind her, and KD's girlfriend Sagun was there to scoop it up and drop it into a plastic bag. She presumably had passed it off to Julian, who was to destroy and bury it in a remote part of the ranch.

After volunteering to kill Devaraj the previous night, Shanti B had accepted the tiny syringe from Puja filled with adrenaline—sufficient, the nurse believed, to kill him in a medically undetectable way and small enough for Shanti B to conceal between her fingers. Puja had served as a human pin cushion so Shanti B could practice her technique. Jab, plunge, retract, escape. Vidya and Su had arranged the security schedule so that only members of the Jesus Grove set would be standing guard in Rajneesh Mandir that morning.

Shanti B felt invincible. She felt shattered. Bhagwan had said that one should always choose the life of an enlightened being over the lives of any number of unenlightened people. But even if she knew it had been the right thing to do, taking another man's life was a step too far down a dark path. She couldn't continue on at Rajneeshpuram as if nothing had happened. By the time she reached Jesus Grove, Shanti B resolved to leave Bhagwan's community forever.

They welcomed her back as a hero. Sheela was mama-bear protective of her little assassin. She promised that she had money available to take care of people who did "special things" for her. She told Su to get the commune's crematorium ready for Devaraj's body. But in the midst of all the crowing about what they had pulled off, Ava phoned with an update from Pythagoras Clinic.

Sheela seemed bewildered when she heard about Devaraj's condition. *Oh shit*, she asked her crew, *what if he lives?*

The medics, with help from Krishna Deva, had loaded Devaraj onto the ambulance outside Rajneesh Mandir and transported him to Pythagoras, at the far southern end of the commune. His blood pressure was dangerously low, he had fluid in his lungs, and he was coughing up blood. Shunyo worried that Devaraj would die within the hour unless they could stabilize him.

Shunyo administered an intravenous drip and other treatments: high-level oxygen, drugs to increase his blood pressure, steroids, hydrocortisone, antibiotics. In the midst of it all, Puja suddenly waltzed into the room and offered to help. Shunyo knew from experience that she would try to commandeer Devaraj's medical treatment. Indeed, she told Shunyo to remove an IV drip he had administered so she could apply her own solution. In a rare show of defiance, Shunyo refused. She still walked around holding a syringe that she said contained antibiotics, eager to jab them into Devaraj. Both Shunyo and a nurse would later recall that all the medications and preparations they had laid on a nearby counter disappeared as soon as Puja arrived on the scene.

When he was stable enough to speak clearly, Devaraj insisted that everybody leave the room except Shunyo. He told Shunyo not to let Puja give him any injections. He again spoke of Shanti B injecting him with poison. Shunyo comforted him, but he still didn't believe a word of it.

After more than two hours of lifesaving treatments, Devaraj was finally stable enough for an air transport to St. Charles Medical Center in Bend. As Devaraj was loaded into the ambulance outside Pythagoras, Puja told the driver to drive very slowly. She had them stop at the pharmacy in Devateerth Mall so somebody could collect some medication that she wanted on the plane to Bend. After they arrived at the airstrip and loaded in Devaraj, the plane didn't move. Puja wouldn't let them leave, for some unknown reason.

They finally took off. Devaraj vomited, but then he immediately started to feel better as they ascended high above the desert. He spent the entire flight with his eyes locked on Sheela's henchwoman Ava and the other medical staff who were accompanying him. He worried that if he drifted off, they might throw him out of the plane.

_____

Later that day, Sheela told Shanti B and Krishna Deva that Bhagwan had called her to his room to ask her what had happened. Word had reached him that Devaraj had accused Shanti B of poisoning him. Unconvinced by Sheela's denials, Bhagwan directed her to do whatever was necessary to get the truth out of Shanti B, even if it meant drugging or beating her. Sheela said she had played it straight and promised to investigate Devaraj's claim.

As the day wore on, Ava provided updates from the hospital in Bend. It looked like Devaraj was recovering and would live. KD witnessed a "general freak out" among the conspirators at Jesus Grove. They may have saved Bhagwan's life that day, but Devaraj could bring them all down if he persisted in naming Shanti B as his attempted murderer. Without a pause, Sheela told her crew that they would need to try again. She selected two women to finish the job. They were to travel to Devaraj's bedside in Bend and see if they could inject something into his IV drip. The women made it to the hospital, but they weren't able to do anything because there was always somebody with him.

Another way to cover their tracks virtually landed in their lap. Someone from Jesus Grove had retrieved Devaraj's robe and washed it thoroughly to destroy any possible traces of adrenaline or blood. In so doing, they came across a safety pin in the robe's pocket. It provided a perfect scapegoat. Devaraj had merely sat on an open pin while Shanti B happened to be nearby.

The safety pin explanation became generally accepted among the small group of people who heard about the Shanti B allegations. Even Bhagwan adopted it. When Shunyo told the guru that he was investigating possible poisons that might have caused Devaraj's condition, Bhagwan told him to drop it. And he passed a message to Devaraj at the hospital: forget about the possibility that he'd been poisoned.

_____

Two weeks after being admitted to the hospital, Devaraj was released. His discharge diagnosis included malnutrition, low blood pressure, and a possible toxic exposure. When he walked into Lao Tzu house, his friends greeted him with a huge welcome-home card. He broke into an irrepressible grin, and then he collapsed into his bed, where he would recover for the coming weeks.

Monitoring the wiretaps and bugs, the Jesus Grove set determined that only two people at the commune believed Devaraj's story that Shanti B had injected him with poison: Devaraj himself and his wife, Hasya.

34 | CATHARSIS

"CATHARSIS CAN BE NEGATIVE, it can be positive. If catharsis is negative, there is no end to it," Bhagwan told disciples while in Pune. "If positive catharsis is learned, then there is an end to the negative catharsis, because the same energy starts moving into positive channels. Hate becomes love. Anger becomes compassion. Aggression becomes softness. Otherwise the negative path is endless and creates much hell."

In the weeks after Devaraj's murder attempt, a powerful catharsis from a senior leader at Rajneeshpuram triggered a sequence of events that would forever alter Bhagwan's community. Ma Yoga Vidya had been running the commune's personnel department since the beginning, one of the three most powerful women in Bhagwan's orbit. If Sheela and Savita were away, Vidya would meet with him at night to discuss the commune's business and receive direction. As one of Sheela's closest allies and enforcers, she was also involved in nearly all of the darkest plots that had emerged from Sheela's bedroom: the internal and external murder plots, the wiretapping and bugging of the ranch, the use of Haldol on Share-a-Home participants, the salmonella poisoning before the 1984 election, the plans to contaminate the water supply in The Dalles, the burning of Dan Durow's office. According to Krishna Deva, Vidya was at least aware of them all, and in many cases she had helped to plan or facilitate the efforts.

Members of Sheela's inner circle chart Vidya's deterioration from the moment that Sheela sent her longtime lover Bodhi to Europe in June, after he and Jayananda spoke out against killing Devaraj and Vivek. Sheela had said she would have to kill Jayananda some day—a statement that, according to Ava, made the Jesus Grove crew realize that Sheela might kill *anyone* who opposed her. For Vidya, that meant her beloved Bodhi was a potential target as well. Rather than refute the idea that she might harm Bodhi, Sheela told Vidya to forget about him and move on.

Her mental state only worsened after the Master's Day attempt on Devaraj's life. Vidya would later say that she "short-circuited" after realizing that she was powerless to stop people at the commune from being harmed. With a gang of yes-men now sitting around Sheela's bed every night and going along with whatever she suggested, a dangerous groupthink had emerged where any naysayers—Jayananda, Bodhi, Krishna Deva—were belittled and ostracized. Even if she tried to stop the train from leaving the station, Vidya felt that the thing would just mow her over.

She got mowed over nonetheless. One Jesus Grove resident recalled seeing a confrontation between Vidya and Sheela around this time where Vidya cried out, *Oh Sheela, you're not going to kill Bodhi, are you?* She suffered what she later described as a "nervous breakdown" and was hospitalized for three weeks under Puja's care in a private room in Koran Grove, where she says she was involuntarily confined and drugged on Sheela's orders. By the time she emerged, she felt like a shell of the strident woman who had led the commune for the past four years. Sheela stripped Vidya of her corporate positions and instead set her to work in the private kitchen preparing food for the Jesus Grove residents—a humiliating demotion.

While Vidya had been in isolation, the conspirators had continued to talk of murder. The Devaraj debacle stripped them of their appetite to go after other commune members, but they had not yet given up their plans to kill US Attorney Charles Turner. On August 1, Krishna Deva traveled to a law conference to photograph Turner with a tiny camera, since the would-be assassins didn't know what their quarry looked like.

When Vidya was brought back into the plotting, she snapped. Her catharsis came while lying on the floor of Sheela's bedroom, surrounded by her coconspirators. *I can't do this!* she cried. *I can't kill anybody!* Weeping uncontrollably, she insisted that they stop talking about any more murders.

Sheela summoned Shanti B and asked her—ever the loyal foot soldier—to talk some sense into Vidya. But Shanti B didn't try to rope her back into their plots. She didn't try to justify the murder attempts. Instead, she told Vidya not to worry. Nobody was going to get hurt anymore. Nobody was going to get killed. It was over. Shanti B, too, had reached her limit.

Everything had changed after Devaraj. The mood, the sense of urgency, their brash confidence. All the murders they had been discussing for the past month—Helen Byron, Vivek, Devaraj, Charles Turner—had been plotted and rehearsed and joked about and, in some cases, even attempted. But once Shanti B jabbed a needle into Devaraj, the abstraction that had sustained them for the past weeks evaporated and they were confronted with the reality that they had tried to murder a fellow disciple, surrounded by thousands of people, within view of their master. And they had failed.

That Shanti B, the most ferocious of them all, was throwing in the towel served as a wake-up call. Others in the room took her lead and declared that they, too, wanted no more part in the murder plots. *I can't do this either,* Anugiten later recalled saying to the group. *It's too crazy. We can't go through with this.*

More and more people piled on. They were done talking about murder.

They looked to Sheela on her bed to see how she would respond to their mutiny.

OK, she said. *That's fine.*

It was time for Plan B.

35 | PLAN B

FRANCES FITZGERALD, THE PULITZER PRIZE-WINNING journalist, had visited the ranch on several occasions over the years to chat with sannyasins and gather information for a *New Yorker* story. When she arrived for another visit in August 1985, the place looked to her like it was shutting down. The buzz of excitement and frenetic activity had fallen to a soft whisper. Trees that had been planted just months earlier for the festival were being left to die. Horses that had been available for recreation had vanished. It was as if the people running it had already given up.

FitzGerald's hunch was correct. After Vidya's catharsis in early August, Sheela's interest in running Bhagwan's utopia had faded. She had been detaching since at least May, when the Helen Byron verdict demonstrated to her that the entire world was conspiring against them and the sannyasins would never prevail. Upon returning from her trip to India, KD felt, Sheela's mood had reached an all-time low, and he also thought her drug use had drastically increased. She was miserable in her job and no longer willing to go to jail to protect Bhagwan. The discord among her top lieutenants seemed to be the final straw.

For a long time, Sheela and her aides had been tossing about the notion of one day leaving the commune together. At first the idea was to build a successful business enterprise, use the profits to pay off the commune's debts, and invite Bhagwan to join them. By the summer of 1985, though, the old man was dropped from the equation and their discussions centered on how Sheela and her crew could support themselves if they abandoned him altogether.

They called this idea of striking out on their own "Plan B." After Vidya's breakdown, Plan B became *the* plan among Sheela's inner circle.

Sheela had been working on her own private Plan B for some time. Right after Bhagwan started lecturing again at the end of 1984, she had married a Swiss disciple, Swami Dipo, during a quick trip to Mexico City. With thinning blond hair, a limp mustache, and a vacant stare, Dipo was an unremarkable member of the Jesus Grove clique, perhaps most notable for being an openly gay man. After their wedding, the newlyweds had gone straight to the Swiss embassy to register their marriage, and soon thereafter Sheela applied for a Swiss passport. Sheela hadn't divorced American Jayananda, which meant she was unlawfully married to two men at the same time. She never mentioned Dipo in public statements during this time, like when she testified under oath in a February 1985 deposition that Jayananda was her (only) husband.

She received her Swiss passport that spring and quietly tucked it away for whenever she might need it. After the botched attempt on Devaraj's life in the summer of 1985, Sheela went back to Mexico City, this time to try to get a backdated divorce from Jayananda so that it would look like she had been single when she married Dipo. Unable to find a judge corrupt enough to fabricate her divorce, she returned empty-handed.

In the meantime, she asked Krishna Deva to research places in the world where people of different nationalities could live together without visa problems. She didn't want a repeat of the never-ending INS investigation in some other country. KD returned with a matrix of possible locations, including Bermuda, the Cayman Islands, the Bahamas, some South Pacific islands, and Singapore—his top recommendation since it had the best commercial opportunities.

At the end of August, Sheela traveled to Thailand, Nepal, and Singapore. The trip came together so quickly that the August 30 edition of the *Rajneesh Times* didn't have time to revise its advertisement for an August 31 event for visiting parents: "An evening with Ma Anand Sheela." While in Singapore, Sheela called KD and gave him the impression that she was seriously considering it as the new home for her Jesus Grove circle. She later told him that she had also visited Nepal and finally obtained a backdated divorce by using a man pretending to be Jayananda.

While in Bangkok, Sheela mailed a postcard to Rajneeshpuram city hall: "Beloved KD, this is your new career under Plan B. Love, Sheela." The reverse side featured a photograph of a boy riding a water buffalo through a rice paddy. By the time it arrived at the Rajneeshpuram post office, Sheela, KD, and her entire crew were long gone.

———————

On the night of September 12, Sheela and a few intimates huddled in the Jesus Grove bedroom where they could listen to the Lao Tzu bug concealed in Bhagwan's easy chair. They heard Savita, Sheela's second-in-command, walk into the room and greet their master. Sheela had just returned from Asia with a cold and claimed she couldn't be in Bhagwan's presence for fear of making him sick, so she sent Savita, who handed Bhagwan a letter. In it, Sheela wrote that she struggled with the responsibility for all of the many issues facing Rajneeshpuram and could no longer find joy or pleasure in her work. She suggested that she might need to leave the commune or change her worship to another job. She closed by requesting his guidance. The eavesdroppers in Jesus Grove held their breath to hear how Bhagwan would respond to the news that Sheela was unhappy and wanted to leave.

To their astonishment, he launched into a deeply personal attack against Sheela, saying that she was jealous of him speaking publicly and just wanted him to shut up, which he would not do. If Sheela wanted to leave, he told Savita, she could go to the European communes and raise money for him there. But she would have to resign from all of her many corporate positions, including president of the Rajneesh Foundation International. He also said that Sheela was not to divert any money from the ranch or any meditation center for her own personal use. Whatever she wanted to do, she would have to do on her own dime. Finally, he told Savita that she would take over as his new secretary when Sheela left. His underlying message was clear: life would certainly go on at Rajneeshpuram without Ma Anand Sheela.

A disciple in the Jesus Grove listening post recalled that Sheela yelled and threw things upon hearing Bhagwan's cool indifference. To KD, it seemed that she was most aggrieved by the implication that she would steal money from the ranch for her own use.

The next night, Savita handed Bhagwan another letter.

"Beloved Bhagwan, I want to thank you for offering me one of the most gracious and absolutely educational opportunities in my life. With this letter, I wish to resign as your personal secretary with the same love and respect. In love, Sheela."

Ma Mary Catherine received a tip the following afternoon that something big was happening at Jesus Grove. The *Rajneesh Times* reporter found a flurry of activity in Sheela's home: people packing, making travel arrangements, shredding documents, ordering drugs from the pharmacy. At the center of it all, Sheela seemed unusually disheveled, with dark circles under her eyes. Some other commune leaders seemed catatonic. Nobody would give Mary Catherine a straight answer to her questions about why they were leaving so abruptly.

Even today, the picture of why Sheela left when she did is cloudy at best. Sheela, KD, Ava, and Shanti B would later say that Sheela had become overwhelmed by Bhagwan's unreasonable demands. While Sheela had been in Asia in early September, Savita had begged her to come back because she was exhausted from trying to conjure the money to fuel Bhagwan's relentless appetite for luxury items. Upon returning to Oregon, Sheela says it hit her that she, too, was burned out. She no longer even wanted to see him. The magnetism that had kept her with the master was gone, and she knew then it was time for her to go.

But this explanation—that it was an impulsive decision borne of exhaustion and frustration—doesn't address the long-term groundwork that Sheela had laid over the previous year, such as her marriage to Dipo in late 1984, her acquisition of a Swiss passport in early 1985, and her Plan B plotting in the months before September.

Sheela's assistant, Ma Prem Geeta, believed that she left because she was slipping in Bhagwan's estimation and feared that he would soon fire her for failing to meet his demands. Others have similarly speculated that Sheela heard via the Lao Tzu bug that Bhagwan was planning to replace her with members of the Hollywood Group, and she got out before that could happen. Federal mediator John Mathis felt that Sheela left when her power had become so diminished that she could barely control events at Rajneeshpuram anymore.

US Attorney Charles Turner would later claim that Sheela had more pressing concerns. A federal court was about to lift the stay on the immigration investigation, and everybody knew that indictments might soon be issued against the commune leaders. Around this time, Sheela had also been questioned in an Internal Revenue Service investigation regarding suspicious transfers of money from the Chidvilas Rajneesh Meditation Center to Sheela's brother in the late 1970s and early '80s. Turner believed that she wanted to get out before federal charges trapped her in the United States.

A few dozen people were waiting at the Rajneeshpuram Airport at 4:45 PM on September 14, 1985, to see off Sheela, Vidya, Su, Puja, and some others. Well-wishers danced alongside the tarmac, but the celebration was strained. While airport staff loaded in about twenty pieces of luggage and boxes, Sheela waved around two bottles of vodka and offered to share them with the crowd.

What about AIDS? somebody called out.

Fuck AIDS, she said.

Before boarding the plane, Sheela gave a short speech. *Remember to take care of this place, and yourself.* As an afterthought, she added, *And take care of our master.*

While they rose above the Big Muddy Ranch for the last time, Vidya turned to her fellow Jesus Grove matrons. *Well, at least we left like queens.*

36 | COLLAPSE

LATER THAT NIGHT, after Sheela left Oregon, a small group of her remaining confidants stood around a pile of audio equipment in a Jesus Grove bedroom. They had just used it to listen to Bhagwan's private conversations one last time before dismantling the Lao Tzu surveillance operation. Savita had gone uphill to tell Bhagwan that she, too, would be leaving Rajneeshpuram within days, once she felt certain that the commune's financial matters were squared away. From the Jesus Grove listening post, KD heard Bhagwan accept Savita's resignation and approve most of her recommendations to fill vacant corporate positions, with a few exceptions. Savita had suggested Dutch Arup—Sheela's old nemesis from Pune—to be his new secretary, but Bhagwan said he wanted Hasya instead. He chose a new commune president to replace Vidya, and he selected Hollywood Group physician Dhyan John to head up the Rajneesh Investment Corporation.

Before Sheela left, Julian had begged her for more time to take down the sprawling surveillance operations across the ranch, but she told him to get it done immediately. Although he couldn't access Lao Tzu to remove the concealed equipment there, removing the listening post at Jesus Grove at least made it more difficult to detect that Bhagwan's home was crawling with microphones.

Around midnight, KD and Anugiten drove up to Alan Watts Grove to remove equipment from the A-frame cabin that had become Puja's secret laboratory after she had moved from the Chinese Laundry earlier in the year. Among the items they loaded into their van was a toolbox containing the "five easy pieces" that Shanti B had purchased in New Mexico to kill US Attorney Charles Turner. They also removed a few small refrigerators, jars of acid, canisters full of a metallic powder, and a piece of equipment with hoses and a motor that Anugiten called "Puja's salmonella maker." They tossed the powder into an outhouse near the commune's firing range. They left the "salmonella maker"—most likely an incubator—and the jars of acid in a commune warehouse, hoping they would blend in with other equipment from Rajneesh Medical Corporation.

The next morning, KD went to Rajneesh Legal Services to submit letters of resignation for his various posts in the city and Rajneesh corporations. As he walked out of the Zarathustra building, sannyasins were starting to fan across the commune after Bhagwan's morning discourse. KD was surprised at all the cold, distrustful eyes on him as he moved about the ranch. He soon learned why. The guru had used his first post-Sheela lecture to savage his former secretary and her lieutenants, while also trying to instill confidence among the remaining disciples that he would choose smarter, better people to run the commune. Bhagwan had specifically mentioned KD, saying that, as a part-time member of Rajneesh Security, KD at any moment could have turned his gun on the enlightened being he was supposed to be protecting.

Even after everything that KD had done over the past four years, even with his growing sense of disillusionment, Bhagwan's words obliterated him. As KD saw it, he had gone to extreme—even criminal—lengths to *protect* Bhagwan. He wasn't aware of anybody in Jesus Grove who would want to kill their master. But nobody would understand that, especially with the guru on his dais portraying Sheela's crew as a gang of dangerous, self-serving turncoats.

KD knew that he had to get off the ranch as soon as possible.

Later that morning, Savita pulled together everybody remaining from Sheela's inner circle and told them to finish packing. Frenetic activity was already underway across the compound to destroy anything that might be considered evidence of the schemes they had hatched over the previous four years. Ava tore up any papers she could get her hands on that might link them to crimes, including surveillance transcripts, catalogs for gun silencers, and notes that Rikta made about obtaining false IDs to purchase the "five easy pieces."

She flushed a bunch of pills down the toilet. Others were similarly sweeping through Jesus Grove and their workplaces to locate and destroy anything that might be incriminating. Sheela's houseboy Anubhavo grabbed a pile of tapes and transcripts from the surveillance operation and drove them up to a quiet spot near Alan Watts Grove, where he burned the paper and demagnetized the tapes.

It was all a rush job. Unmethodical, disorganized, and—as they would soon find out—woefully inadequate.

Early that evening, Savita, KD, Ava, Shanti B, and the other remaining members of Sheela's inner circle convened in Mirdad Welcome Center. While waiting for the last of their group to join them, they swapped stories about their wild efforts over the past twenty-four hours to wipe the slate as clean as they could. Anugiten said he had rowed to the middle of a remote lake overnight and tossed the "five easy pieces" overboard. Others talked about their mad dash to yank out wiretapping equipment from across the ranch.

The more they shared stories about failed plots and frenzied destruction of evidence, the more they began to laugh, hysterically, about the situation they were in. It seemed, for the briefest of moments, that they might escape the commune, join Sheela, and get away with it all.

But then Swami Julian joined them, and his story put a damper on everything.

37 | GLAD NEWS

MA PREM GEETA WAS PROBABLY the first one to fold. The thirty-seven-year-old from Pennsylvania had been in Sheela's close orbit for many years, serving as her assistant and the corporate secretary for the Rajneesh Foundation International and the Rajneesh Investment Corporation. Like most people who worked in Jesus Grove, Geeta had been drawn into at least some of the clandestine schemes that unfolded there. She served as a monitor at the wiretapping operation behind the Socrates building, listening to and recording conversations that her fellow commune members had with people outside the ranch. In 1984, she had helped to steam open and read all the personal mail at the ranch, reporting anything dangerous—and any juicy gossip—to Sheela. Although she claimed to be ignorant about the plots to murder Vivek and Devaraj, Geeta did overhear Sheela referring to them as "scum" and questioning how to "get rid of them." She had also become aware of the bugs at Lao Tzu and the listening post in one of the Jesus Grove bedrooms.

The day that KD and the others prepared to leave the commune, Geeta made an appointment to see Bhagwan's caretaker Vivek to confess what she knew. Vivek was disgusted to learn that her home had been under constant surveillance, but she was hardly surprised. While standing out on her back porch late at night, she had often seen the elusive Brit Swami Julian skulking about the Lao Tzu grounds for no obvious purpose. He'd stay for a couple of minutes and then vanish. If Vivek ever asked him what he was doing, he would say it had something to do with the security lights.

263

After Geeta recounted what she knew, Vivek called a maintenance worker, Deva Allen, and asked him to look for microphones. Allen had seen Julian fiddling with an outdoor telephone box and a locked cabinet in a bathroom near the guard tower behind Bhagwan's residence, so he went straight to those spots, opened the locks with a bolt cutter, and found what appeared to be tapped phone lines, batteries, and chargers. He did what he could to remove the equipment, but then he learned that Vivek had called Julian himself and demanded that he come up to Lao Tzu.

Surprisingly, Julian agreed. When he arrived, Vivek, Allen, and a couple of other Lao Tzu staff confronted him about Geeta's allegations. He admitted it was true—he had bugged Bhagwan's home. But when Vivek told him to remove it all, he refused. The bugs had been installed at Bhagwan's command, Julian said, and he would remove them only if the master commanded it himself.

Vivek repeated three times that Bhagwan wanted the equipment taken out before Julian finally cooperated. He gamely pointed out the various devices he used to monitor everything that happened at Lao Tzu: the outside telephone box from which he had tapped all the Lao Tzu phones, the bathroom cabinet where he had installed an amplifier, the telephones with their built-in microphones that picked up any nearby conversations, the microphone under Vivek's bed, and the microphone concealed in the buzzer attached to Bhagwan's chair in his living quarters.

When Julian met up with the other Jesus Grove members at Mirdad that night, he told them that Vivek was now aware of the Lao Tzu listening operation. They all immediately departed the ranch.

Although Julian's surveillance operation had come to an end, Vivek's role as intelligence gatherer was just getting started. Another disciple with tangential dealings with Jesus Grove contacted her that same afternoon and told her about some far more sinister plots that had emerged from Sheela's bedroom. Vivek went to Bhagwan with what she had learned.

During a public interview that night with the *Journal of Humanistic Psychology*, Bhagwan offered a new take on Sheela. His discourse that morning had characterized Sheela and her gang as untrustworthy people who betrayed him and his community. In his evening interview, Bhagwan explained that Sheela had far exceeded her authority and done many things without his knowledge. He offered up a prime example: Sheela had bugged his private room. He characterized it as an expression of her paranoia that somebody might talk to him without her knowing about it. It was the first time Bhagwan spoke publicly of any surveillance at Rajneeshpuram.

Later, deep into the interview, Bhagwan made another allegation that shocked sannyasins like Ma Prem Isabel, who was watching the interview from the floor of the Jesus Grove press room: "Just today I have come to know that Sheela and her group tried even to poison my physician. They wanted to poison other persons who were close to me, for the simple reason that nobody should be close to me, except Sheela."

Isabel tuned out the rest of the interview as the magnitude of what her master had said began to sink in. Sheela had bugged Bhagwan's home and tried to kill the people who took care of him. It was unconscionable. Isabel thought back to all the inflammatory allegations that people had made against the commune since they arrived in Oregon and that she, as the press relations coordinator, had denied and decried on a near-daily basis. Things like Representative Jim Weaver accusing them of poisoning people in The Dalles with salmonella, and Wasco County judge Bill Hulse implying that Puja had poisoned him. If what Bhagwan said were true, Isabel wondered, then what about all those other allegations?

"I spent three years defending this community against allegations that were crazy or insane," she would say the next day, "but now it seems to me that the people I worked with all this time are insane."

By the next morning, word had spread around the commune about Bhagwan's explosive allegations. Rajneesh Mandir was packed with sannyasins eager to hear it from his own lips at discourse. From his dais, Bhagwan calmly laid out the information that he said had been coming to him from knowledgeable sannyasins. Sheela's crew had plotted to murder Devaraj and Vivek. They had bugged his home and Hasya's, and tapped every external phone line at the commune. They had burned down Dan Durow's office. Bhagwan reported a rumor that Sheela's gang might have tried to poison the water system in The

Dalles. And he said it was possible that Sheela and Savita embezzled more than $50 million from the commune.

Disciples emerged from the hall, many arm in arm and consoling each other, struggling to come to terms with Bhagwan's claims and how oblivious they had been to it all. "My mind is in shock and my heart is hurting," one sannyasin told a reporter, "and that's it."

At Bhagwan's command, the public relations staff worked the phones to invite all their contacts to a major press conference that night. As the event approached, thousands of sannyasins stood in a single-file line outside Rajneesh Mandir beneath an oppressive gray sky, waiting for their turn in the tents where they would check their shoes and bags before entering the hall. Joining them for this extraordinary event were members of the local, national, and international press who were able to scramble to the ranch on such short notice, including reporters from the *Oregonian*, the *San Francisco Examiner*, the *Los Angeles Times*, and the Associated Press.

The crowd cheered as Bhagwan walked on stage in a multitoned blue robe with a hem that floated just millimeters above the floor and a matching stocking cap. He kicked off the press conference by distancing himself from the news he was about to announce: "I have been silent for three and a half years. The people who were in power took advantage of my silence. Because I was not in contact with the sannyasins, I was not aware what is being done to them."

He repeated the same allegations he had made at the morning discourse, but he added some new claims, such as Sheela's dual marriages to Jayananda and Dipo and her efforts to poison Devaraj and Vivek. After laying out what he had learned, Bhagwan struck an uncharacteristically conciliatory tone. He implored the people of Oregon to give them another chance and allow the sannyasins to become an intrinsic part of their community. Although he had just weeks earlier said that his people would never coexist peacefully with the people of Oregon, Bhagwan now pinned the regional hostility entirely on Sheela, who had transformed his meditation commune into a totalitarian state without his knowledge. "I have called you media people here especially to inform you of glad news, that this commune is free from a fascist regime. Adolf Hitler has died again."

Exposing the allegations so publicly was a massive gambit. Bhagwan was inviting scrutiny from outside law enforcement, which now had no choice but to intrude into the secretive compound to investigate what had happened.

Among their chief questions was how the man at the top, who met with Sheela for hours every day and who had once insisted that he knew every single thing that happened within his community, could possibly have been oblivious to the vast criminal conspiracy that he now laid at their feet.

PART VI
FLIGHT, 1985

Bhagwan addresses the press and his disciples in Rajneesh Mandir, September 1985. *Photo courtesy of The Oregonian*

38 | CRACKS IN THE DAM

JUST AFTER NOON ON OCTOBER 2, a beige recreational vehicle with dark brown stripes pulled into the parking lot near the original white farmhouse where ranch foreman Bob Harvey's family had once lived. The lot was packed with vehicles belonging to state and federal investigators who had been working at the ranch since Bhagwan had made his explosive allegations three weeks earlier. The farmhouse had become home base for a joint task force investigating criminal activities at the ranch. After coming to a stop and killing the engine, the RV remained still. The blinds on its small windows stayed shut. Nobody emerged from within.

Inside the farmhouse, Lieutenant Dean Renfrow kicked off the task force's daily 1:00 PM internal briefing. The typical contingent was in attendance that day: plainclothes officers from the Oregon State Police, investigators from the attorney general's office, FBI agents, Rajneeshpuram Peace Force officers, and five private attorneys hired to represent various sannyasin corporations and individuals. The usual people sat in their usual places talking about the usual things, with the members of outside law enforcement giving no hint about the dynamite that Lieutenant Renfrow was about to unleash on the disciples.

After Sheela left and Bhagwan revealed all her criminal activities from his dais, the new commune leadership said that they welcomed an investigation and would cooperate with outside law enforcement. In the first couple of

271

weeks, they helped to arrange interviews with sannyasin witnesses, offered working space for investigators, and provided Peace Force officers to escort them around the ranch. But by the end of September, the cooperation had become spotty and unreliable. Law enforcement questioned whether the sannyasins were steering them toward evidence that they wanted investigators to uncover while concealing other information.

A major confrontation erupted when Governor Vic Atiyeh announced that he was transferring investigation and prosecution authority from the local district attorneys to Attorney General Dave Frohnmayer. Given his aggressive litigation against the City of Rajneeshpuram, the attorney general had been portrayed around the commune for the past two years as "Herr General Frohnmayer," a fascist bigot intent on smothering their peaceful religious settlement. "Damn near mass hysteria" broke out at the commune when the governor's move became known, according to a state police officer. On stage that night at a large press conference, Bhagwan had declared, "It is finished. Cooperation is finished!" He laid out his theory that Frohnmayer had in fact commandeered the criminal investigation to fulfill his longtime goal of destroying their commune.

The sannyasins did continue to cooperate in dribbles and spurts after that. By early October, the task force had interviewed dozens of witnesses and collected evidence of a staggering array of crimes, including the attempted or plotted murders of Devaraj, Vivek, Helen Byron, and Charles Turner; the poisoning of Wasco County judges Bill Hulse and Ray Matthew; the salmonella poisoning in The Dalles; the Haldol drugging of Share-a-Home participants; wiretapping and bugging throughout the ranch; and the arson of the Wasco County planning office. Still, they decided that a more formal, compulsory process would be required to bring the investigation to the point where they could issue indictments. Law enforcement began quietly drafting subpoenas for more than one hundred witnesses to appear before a criminal grand jury and search warrants to seize evidence from around the commune. Serving the papers required intense preparation, since it would mark the first moment that outside law enforcement would force the sannyasins to play according to their rules rather than depend on their cooperation. Officials at all levels of state and federal government entertained the possibility that the heavily armed, highly secretive sannyasins might respond to any intrusion into their privacy with violence—particularly if they imagined that their master was in danger.

Governor Atiyeh had been raising red flags among his cabinet members about the potential for an all-out battle in Central Oregon ever since Bhagwan unleashed his allegations against Sheela. In late September the governor met with Attorney General Frohnmayer and representatives from the Oregon Military Department (OMD) to discuss a strategy for responding to violence in the region. One major concern was the ranch's accessibility. The long, winding, rutted county road from Antelope was the only feasible way to enter the ranch by land, and, as Wasco County planner Dan Durow was well aware, the sannyasins were known to bar access to their property when it suited them. If violence erupted at the ranch and the county road were blocked, the potential for human casualties would be high.

The week before the task force planned to serve the subpoenas and search warrants, the OMD briefed Governor Atiyeh on the plans it had developed to protect law enforcement. Within days military personnel and equipment— including helicopters, personnel carriers, a bulldozer, a "tank retriever" that could move any road blockages, and a communications van—would move into the towns around Rajneeshpuram. If a gunfight broke out at the ranch, the National Guard would use helicopters to drop armed soldiers along the ridgeline surrounding the ranch and drive fifteen armored personnel carriers across the John Day River and straight to city hall at the center of the commune. To be prepared to set this in motion, the governor's staff drafted an unsigned executive order declaring martial law that Atiyeh would carry on his body at all times. The FBI also brought in a ten-person SWAT team to remain on standby.

The OMD moved in equipment and personnel over the next few days, quietly, so as not to draw alarm from the ranch. But the press caught wind of the operation, and by the end of the week Rajneeshpuram's new mayor—Swami Prem Niren, Bhagwan's attorney—was on the phone with the governor's office demanding to know whether Atiyeh intended to declare martial law. Reporters asked state officials the same question, requiring them to dodge or downplay the potential use of military force at the ranch.

Over the last weekend in September, members of the task force—minus the sannyasin representatives—met at the Jefferson County courthouse to finalize their plans to serve the papers over the coming week. They split into teams that would tackle the seven locations named in the warrants: four medical facilities and offices, the hotel, the welcome center, and the Zarathustra building, which housed Julian's electronics laboratory. Commune leaders knew that witness subpoenas were in the offing, but the search warrants would be sprung on them, to minimize the chance that disciples might conceal or destroy the targeted evidence.

As the October 2 joint task force meeting wound to a close, the moment arrived. Lieutenant Renfrow pulled out the search warrants. The sannyasin attorneys exploded in outrage, as had been expected. Following the plan, each of the seven task force team leaders walked out of city hall, spaced three minutes apart, and approached the beige RV sitting in the parking lot, from which a uniformed officer emerged to accompany the leader to his targeted site. The vehicle had been preloaded with state police officers, lawyers from the attorney general's office, and a stockpile of weapons. If there were any conflicts, all the task force members had been trained to secure themselves at their locations, return gunfire if necessary, and wait for assistance. More than one hundred state troopers had been placed on alert, and three helicopters were hidden in a nearby hangar in case emergency evacuation were required.

To the relief of everyone involved, there were no violent confrontations that day. But the task force was dismayed to find that their element of surprise had not worked as anticipated. Furniture in several locations had obviously been moved, and records that officers had seen just days earlier were gone, with some even disappearing in the middle of the search. Major Robert Moine of the Oregon State Police would later tell a reporter that the disciples had previously offered to voluntarily turn over documents if the investigators would just provide a list of what they wanted. After the task force provided a list, Moine suspected, the sannyasins had used it as a shopping list to identify records to conceal.

Some disciples later reported to law enforcement that the commune's leaders and attorneys were indeed obstructing the investigation into crimes at Rajneeshpuram. One disciple saw boxes stacked six feet high in the office of the commune's lead criminal counsel; the attorney said the boxes contained records subject to the search warrants and that he was hiding them from investigators under the guise of attorney-client privilege. Others reported that the commune's lawyers were meddling with the information witnesses were providing to law enforcement, in an effort to protect disciples who remained at Rajneeshpuram and keep blame focused squarely on Sheela's crew. Before speaking to investigators, commune members with knowledge of potential criminal activities were asked to first share what they knew with sannyasin attorneys and paralegals—a process that some felt was designed to shape their testimony and filter out information that might implicate people still at the ranch.

The head of the joint task force came to believe that investigators were being spoon-fed only the information that commune attorneys wanted them to hear, and Attorney General Frohnmayer's office reached a similar conclusion, noting in a memo, "It is the feeling of the staff that the sannyasins are working on their own agenda which consists primarily of providing information only about Sheela and her gang and nothing about those who remain on the ranch or about the interrelationship between the key Rajneesh players and the Rajneesh corporations."

Despite the setbacks, within the first three weeks of the investigation, the task force managed to gather more than twenty-three thousand documents and twenty-five hundred tape recordings, and officers interviewed 104 witnesses. On top of that, two key sources of information were about to fall into their laps: disciples who would unlock nearly every criminal case under investigation.

Sheela's abrupt departure had sparked a celebratory, confusing, fraught period among the roughly two to three thousand commune members who remained at the ranch. The vast majority of disciples had never set foot in Jesus Grove or Lao Tzu, had few personal interactions with Sheela or her top lieutenants, and knew nothing about the boggling array of crimes and misdeeds they planned and perpetrated. The allegations Bhagwan kept dropping on them day after day at his discourses left some feeling disillusioned. "I'm doubting a lot more than I was before," a visibly distraught sannyasin told a reporter outside Devateerth Mall. "I'm not as willing to believe just anything I hear. I want to know the facts."

As Bhagwan told his disciples, he was the last person anyone should blame. "Whatever happened in these three and a half years while I was silent—almost absent—you cannot make me responsible for it. You are responsible. You behaved like idiots." He offered a solution to anybody who was angry with him: "Simply pack your luggage and go to hell."

Mayor Niren tried to calm the waters and rally the community around the things that were important to them. "I'm here to be with Bhagwan. I'm here to be with you," he said at a commune meeting in late September, in a strained voice and with tears running down his cheeks. "And what hurts me is that we have been hurting each other. We are doing more to hurt each other than Sheela could have ever done." He urged anybody who didn't want to support Bhagwan and the community to leave, and for the others to stay and continue doing their worship and continue loving each other.

Bhagwan kept using his morning discourses to distance himself from everything Sheela had done over the past four years, setting her up as the Machiavellian villain who had defrauded them all while he meditated in Lao Tzu. With her gone, he explained, and with a new team at the helm, things would get better. In late September, he told disciples they no longer needed to wear their malas or sunrise colors, since Sheela had used those devices to exploit them. The next day he said that Sheela had created the Rajneesh Bible, *Rajneeshism: An Introduction to Bhagwan Shree Rajneesh and His Religion*, by herself in 1983, without his input or knowledge. Three days later, a cheering mob of disciples gathered at the commune's crematorium to celebrate the death of Bhagwan's religion. Four thousand copies of *Rajneeshism* were carried to the pyre on flower-laden pallets. Presiding over the celebration, Bhagwan's new secretary, Hasya from the Hollywood Group, held up Sheela's embroidered "pope robes," at which the crowd laughed and jeered, before she draped them on top of the books, as if Sheela were lying there herself. Hasya accepted an Olympic-size torch and set the whole thing ablaze.

Krishna Deva had left the ranch in September with the final stragglers among Sheela's crew, but while they continued on from Portland to Europe to join Sheela, he instead traveled to Palm Springs to see his parents. While he was there, Bhagwan held his first major press conference to make his allegations against Sheela. KD was stunned to see the guru laying bare so many crimes that, as far as he knew, Bhagwan had orchestrated or approved himself. Realizing that he would be implicated in the investigation, KD scrambled to find an attorney in Portland who could contact the task force and try to strike an immunity deal in exchange for his full cooperation.

Somebody had already beaten him to it. Twenty-five-year-old Ava, Puja's former assistant and expert margarita maker, had also split off from the departing members of Sheela's group as soon as they left Rajneeshpuram. While spending the night with them at the Flamingo Hotel in Portland, Ava felt like she was having a nervous breakdown. The tipping point for her came when Sheela called the group from Europe and said she wanted to buy a disco in West Germany for them all to run. Ava hated that Sheela was still trying to call the shots, and she thought opening a disco seemed like a horrible idea.

Rather than go home to California, Ava called Geeta at Rajneeshpuram and received permission to return to the ranch. There, she spilled everything she knew to the new commune leaders and their attorneys. She found a particularly sympathetic ear in Hasya, who treated her like a victim of Sheela's manipulations and who buffered her from disciples angry at her role in the Jesus Grove misdeeds. Hasya made sure the commune secured legal representation for her, perhaps in an effort to keep her in the fold. By the first week of October, Ava's lawyer had arranged a deal in which she would receive complete immunity from prosecution if she agreed to tell investigators everything she had seen and done and to testify at any criminal proceeding.

Ava spent most of October in Portland providing prosecutors with an unprecedented glimpse into the darkest plots that had emerged from Sheela's Jesus Grove bedroom. She confessed her own involvement in multiple crimes, including the arson at Dan Durow's office; poisoning restaurants in The Dalles; poisoning Judge Hulse during his visit to Rajneeshpuram; serving Haldol-laced beer to Share-a-Home participants; attempting to murder Helen Byron, Vivek, and Devaraj; and plotting to murder US Attorney Charles Turner and other public officials. Like most immunity agreements, the deal hinged on Ava's candidness and truthfulness. If prosecutors learned at any point that she had not been, they could charge her with perjury or making a false statement and could also use anything she had told them—including self-incriminating admissions—to prosecute her for the underlying crimes.

The stiff penalties for lying may explain why Ava became so aggravated upon receiving a message from Hasya in the midst of her weeks-long interview with investigators. According to Ava's lover at the time, Deva Ananya, who was with her in Portland, Hasya said Bhagwan was concerned that Ava's version of events might not line up with the version he had been laying out publicly. As Ananya understood it, Bhagwan wanted Ava to make clear that he had known nothing about Sheela's criminal activities—something Ava felt was not true because, among other things, she had heard a tape recording of Bhagwan praising Hitler and saying that some people might have to die for them to stay in Oregon. Ava grew upset as she mulled over this directive from the man she still considered her spiritual master, who presided over the community of which she still wanted to be a part. It's not clear whether this apparent attempt to manipulate Ava's testimony had the desired effect, although reports from her interview are notably silent about Bhagwan's awareness of the crimes. A decade later, after she had dropped sannyas, she would provide sworn testimony at a criminal trial that directly implicated the guru.

Much of what Ava told investigators received ample corroboration after Krishna Deva managed to ink his own deal and became a government informant. Both US Attorney Charles Turner and Attorney General Dave Frohnmayer had their own reasons for wanting to sink their hooks into KD. Turner believed that his cooperation would be essential if the federal government had any hope of prosecuting Bhagwan himself. And Frohnmayer wanted to tap into KD's insider knowledge about the City of Rajneeshpuram and its many interconnections with the Church of Rajneeshism in support of the ongoing church/state litigation.

Still, the prosecutors refused to offer KD immunity because he had been a top leader at Jesus Grove and because they had already received substantial assistance from other sources—particularly Ava. Instead they offered a deal by which KD would plead guilty to a subset of all the crimes they could charge him with and prosecutors would urge the court to sentence him to probation instead of jail time. KD accepted.

Starting in late October, KD spent eight days with state and federal investigators sharing what he knew. The prosecutors got what they had wished for. KD signed a fifteen-page affidavit admitting that Bhagwan Shree Rajneesh and his "church," the Rajneesh Foundation International, controlled everything about the City of Rajneeshpuram, including KD's own election as mayor. And KD told them that everything Sheela said came from Bhagwan. He believed that Bhagwan was aware of everything that occurred at Rajneeshpuram, with the only possible exceptions being the conspiracy to kill his doctor, Devaraj, and the fact that his personal room at Lao Tzu was bugged.

After entering his guilty pleas in November, KD went into the federal witness protection program under a new identity and moved to an undisclosed location. He requested this protection because, as he later wrote, "a great deal of danger existed because of my cooperation. Both Rajneesh and Sheela had an investment in my continued silence."

Despite the hardship of being separated from his friends and family, he saw a glimmer of hope for his post-Rajneesh life. "Notwithstanding a mountain of legal debts, the isolation of being a protected witness, and the uncertainty of my professional future because of legal clouds," he wrote in a 1986 statement to the court, "I feel optimistic and hopeful. I feel I have learned a lot, albeit much of it through mistakes. Thankfully, I am confident that these are mistakes I will never make twice."

39 | A REVELATION

DURING A SMALL PRESS CONFERENCE in mid-September in the Jesus Grove press room, Bhagwan's new secretary, Hasya, crawled across the carpeted floor toward her master to read from a piece of paper she had just received.

"Dr. Shunyo has sent in a message that Swami Lazarus died within the last hour," she told Bhagwan while news cameras clicked and recorded. "We consider he has AIDS. He probably died of lymphoma cancer."

"A beautiful ceremony should be arranged," Bhagwan replied.

"Because of the AIDS questions, he is being retested. Because of the criminal inquiries, we are in touch with the state medical examiner. Normally we wouldn't."

"No. In fact, tell them that the AIDS virus dies immediately as the person dies. So if the person is dead, you cannot find anything related to AIDS in his body. So it is just a waste of time. But if they want to do it, they can do it."

Swami Lazarus was among the first sannyasins known to have HIV at Rajneeshpuram. Even before Puja created the Desiderata Canyon ward, Lazarus lived in isolation with another man with HIV, Swami Svadesh. Lazarus and Svadesh had moved to Desiderata Canyon when it opened during the 1985 summer festival. They were joined by Swami Megha, Ma Anand Zeno, and seven other men who had been diagnosed with HIV. When Megha, the Dutch physician, had divided symptomatic and asymptomatic patients between the two trailers in July 1985, he had no doubts that Lazarus belonged in the symptomatic trailer. At first Lazarus was healthy enough to go for walks to the nearby creek with the other residents and to join them for their "family meals" brought in from the cafeteria, but his condition worsened throughout the summer.

In August, Megha examined Lazarus and found that his liver was hugely enlarged. Puja reluctantly agreed to send him to the hospital in Bend for a full examination. His fellow Desiderata Canyon residents could hardly contain their excitement that one of their number would be allowed to leave isolation and go into town, even if for a medical exam, and they prepared a shopping list for while he was there.

At his exam, doctors found that forty-three-year-old Lazarus had an inoperable lymphoma. There was little they could do, given the advanced stage of his illness. He responded, in his soft Texas drawl, *Thank you. Can I go shopping now?*

As his health deteriorated for the remaining weeks of his life into mid-September, the other residents received an unvarnished view of the fate in store for them all, thanks to the cruel new virus that had invaded their bodies. Megha was with Lazarus when he finally left his body, and the physician described it as a beautiful, gentle death. Lazarus had said before dying that he had made his peace and was happy to die in his master's Buddhafield.

At Bhagwan's command, a huge celebration of life took place that night at the commune's on-site crematorium. Hundreds of sannyasins chanted, sang along to a live band, and made speeches around Lazarus's body, which lay on a pile of firewood, draped in a heavy blanket of pine boughs and a rainbow of carnations and mums. The ten remaining Desiderata Canyon residents were allowed to leave their isolation to attend. Huddled close together beneath the spire-shaped crematorium's chimney, Megha, Zeno, and the others clapped and sang with tight smiles on their faces as they watched the bonfire consume Lazarus's frail body.

While most of the Desiderata Canyon residents were Europeans who had been diagnosed with HIV off-site, Megha and Zeno had both received their diagnoses directly from Ma Anand Puja. She had repeatedly told them that additional testing was needed to confirm their diagnoses, but she had never provided them with the results from their most recent tests in August. As they reflected on the chain of events that led to their isolation in the canyon, and as they learned about Puja's various misdeeds at the commune, they both grew suspicious about whether they were actually HIV-positive.

When criminal investigators began to swarm the ranch in September, Megha asked a Rajneesh Medical Corporation worker to find the most recent test results among Puja's files. She responded that Puja's records were a mess and the best option would be to retest them all. The next day, the Desiderata Canyon residents provided new blood samples that were sent off to an independent laboratory in Portland.

Three days later, on September 19, 1985, Swami Devaraj—the newly appointed vice president of the Rajneesh Medical Corporation—called Zeno and Megha to Jesus Grove. Both had tested negative for HIV.

Before the stunning news could even sink in, Devaraj told them to return to Desiderata Canyon while medical staff ran some confirmatory tests.

I'm never going back! Megha exploded. He told Devaraj to study up on testing sensitivity and specificity. If the independent test said he and Zeno were negative, they were negative. After some argument, Devaraj relented.

Once he was out, Megha asked one of Puja's lab technicians if he could see the results from the prior blood tests that Puja had performed. The assistant seemed baffled by the question. She had never tested Megha's blood. Puja had told her that Megha had already been diagnosed in Europe before coming to Rajneeshpuram, so he didn't need to be tested anymore.

Puja's reason for intentionally misdiagnosing Zeno and Megha and sending them to Desiderata Canyon remains a mystery. They may have been selected to live in isolation because they had run afoul of Puja or Sheela. Zeno was said to have been a challenging presence at the Edison Temple, where she butted heads with Julian and had long been considered antagonistic toward Sheela. Megha had refused Sheela's requests to serve as her personal physician, and he says he failed to bring Puja the Haldol she requested from Germany. He also considered the possibility that Puja wanted a trained physician to live among the HIV-positive sannyasins and found it most convenient to send in Megha under the false pretense that he, too, had the virus.

Whatever the reason, Megha and Zeno never did have HIV, and Devaraj allowed them to reintegrate with the community. The next morning, they received places of honor next to Hasya at the very front of the Rajneesh Mandir crowd for Bhagwan's discourse. For the first time since July, they were allowed to sing and clap to the music alongside all the other commune members.

During his lecture, Bhagwan revealed the false diagnoses to the crowd. Megha and Zeno would be smothered in lingering hugs and surrounded by laughter as soon as the discourse ended.

But before that could happen, Bhagwan took the opportunity to excoriate the eight HIV-positive disciples sitting in the back of the hall. They had not been so fortunate as Megha and Zeno. Their diagnoses were accurate. Rather than extend any empathy to his devoted sannyasins, Bhagwan ridiculed the Desiderata Canyon residents and described them as pampered and self-righteous. "They started becoming dictators. They started asking for Havana cigars, Mexican cigars, champagne," he announced to the hall. "As if by bringing AIDS here, they have brought a great contribution to the commune. I was trying to respect their humanity, but they were not only AIDS patients, they were idiots, too."

The fact that eight people still had HIV at the commune perhaps came as a relief to Bhagwan, since he could continue using them as a weapon. Outraged to learn that some disciples had stopped following the commune's AIDS-prevention protocols since Sheela left—the condoms, gloves, wiping, no kissing—Bhagwan threatened to unleash the HIV-positive sannyasins into the community so that within two years the entire community would become infected. "Either you take all the precautions," he fumed, "or drop all the precautions and go to hell."

All of the remaining Desiderata residents would be dead within the year.

40 | ALMOST A QUEEN

THE WORLD HAD CHANGED during Sheela's twelve-hour journey to Switzerland. While her Swiss husband, Dipo, helped her aides gather all their luggage from the carousel at the Zurich airport, back in Oregon Bhagwan was on stage revealing to his disciples how Sheela had betrayed him. As she slept that night in the Zurich Rajneesh Meditation Center, Bhagwan told the international press corps all the heinous crimes his former secretary had committed against him. By the next morning, the meditation center leaders had received instructions from Rajneeshpuram to evict Sheela and her gang and lend her no further support.

Dipo's sannyasin friend in Freiburg, just over the Swiss border in West Germany, offered to put them up. Sheela arrived there with her retinue, including her husband Dipo, nurse Puja, commune president Vidya, investment corporation president Su, erstwhile assassin Shanti B, and nearly two dozen others from her Jesus Grove community. Over dinner that night, their host revealed that the Oregon commune had sent out word that sannyasins who offered any assistance to Sheela or her group would be excommunicated. They would have to go somewhere else.

Dipo found a guesthouse large enough to host the entire flock in the Black Forest village of Häusern, West Germany—less than a thirty-minute drive from the Swiss border. There, isolated from the sannyasin world for the first time in years, surrounded by little but trees and sky, Sheela's crew had time to decompress. Shanti B and some of the other former leaders felt nearly catatonic, unable to do much except lie on their beds or wander through the woods. They were in a bewildered state of transition. Some still wore their mala necklaces with Bhagwan gazing out from the central medallion.

As Sheela tells it, the biggest concern eating at her in those early weeks was not the spiraling criminal allegations Bhagwan was making against her, but how she could support herself and her friends now that they had been severed from the Rajneesh financial pipeline. Among his many allegations against Sheela in mid-September, Bhagwan claimed that she pilfered somewhere between $43 million and $55 million. The commune's remaining accounting staff launched an investigation, as did their independent auditors, and they almost immediately assured the press and outside law enforcement that they found no evidence that any money was missing.

Savita's right-hand man in the accounting department, Swami Svarga, who was not part of Sheela's inner circle, laughs when disciples still ask him where "all the money" at the commune went after Sheela left. "There was no money! We poured $60 million into that place and walked away with nothing."

Among the various ideas for how they could support themselves, Sheela's favorite was to purchase a hotel they would operate together. As she started looking into financing, reporters from a leading German newsmagazine, *Stern*, asked if Sheela would be willing to sell her story. In exchange for exclusivity, the magazine would pay the group's living expenses while the article was being prepared, plus a generous fee. By late September, Sheela and her crew had relocated to Juist, a tiny vacation island in the North Sea, just eleven miles long and about half a mile wide, and settled into the Hotel Pabst, which would serve as their secret hideout for the coming weeks while *Stern* reporters interviewed and photographed Sheela and prepared her story for publication.

Sheela's escape from Rajneeshpuram and her master's ensuing fury had made international news, particularly in Germany, which was home to many sannyasins. Even on remote Juist, the locals couldn't help but put two and two together when they saw the mismatched foreigners dressed in orange and red skipping barefoot up and down the island's cobblestone boardwalk in the rain, clapping and singing inane circus songs, led by an arresting Indian woman. An NBC news crew arrived on the island the day before the *Stern* story was set to run and captured Sheela browsing a local clothing store with Vidya and Dipo, Sheela dining with the entire Jesus Grove retinue at a local restaurant, Sheela ambling down the boardwalk with her hands jammed into her khaki pants pockets, a burgundy jacket draped over her shoulders, her mala sliding across her red cable-knit sweater. The former Queen of Rajneeshpuram had a vacant smile and heavy-lidded eyes, while the women around her exuded a forced exuberance, as if they were thrilled to be holed up on a misty island while being pilloried by the community they had built and the master they had served.

The day after the *Stern* story ran in late September, the press surrounded the Hotel Pabst and begged Sheela to come out. She swanned onto the balcony in a pink sweater, purple turtleneck, and enormous sunglasses to give her first televised comments since leaving Rajneeshpuram.

"Are you afraid of Bhagwan?" a reporter called out.

"At times."

"What causes that fear?"

"Too much knowledge that I have about Bhagwan." Indeed, over the next month, Sheela would say repeatedly that she feared that some "crazy sannyasin"—or even an assassin directed by Bhagwan himself—would try to snuff her out, given all the dirt she had on him.

"Where's all the money?" another reporter asked.

"In my pocket!" she said, to laughter from the crowd below.

Sheela revealed that she was looking for work and had lots to offer after running her master's domain for the past five years. "My experience was as valuable as Einstein's theory of relativity. How can I hide it? Impossible to hide such a revelation."

Hours later, Sheela and her loyal aides climbed into covered wagons in the basement of the Hotel Pabst and made a clandestine escape to the airport across the island, while the press corps remained outside her balcony begging for more. After a detour to picturesque Siena, Italy, they returned to the Black Forest in West Germany to plot out their next steps.

Stern continued interviewing Sheela and putting out articles revealing her perspective on her inscrutable master and his allegations against her. With Vidya acting as her press agent, Sheela also gave interviews to other European outlets and *60 Minutes Australia*.

Throughout these interviews, Sheela flatly denied all the crimes Bhagwan accused her of—the poisonings, the murder plots, the wiretapping, the embezzlement—treating them like the ludicrous rantings of a jilted lover. She fired back with her own allegations against the now-ascendant Hollywood Group and Lao Tzu residents, her sworn enemies throughout her time running

Bhagwan's empire. The press learned about the suicide plans that Bhagwan had supposedly concocted with his doctor, Devaraj. Sheela described how Bhagwan would threaten to take his own life unless she bought him Rolls-Royces and other expensive items. She also claimed that the Hollywood Group had been smuggling ecstasy onto the ranch and holding fundraising parties where they would dose food and drinks with it to encourage large donations for Bhagwan.

It was this discovery that led her to finally leave Rajneeshpuram, Sheela would explain in interviews. Using an illegal drug to manipulate people was a step too far. And she felt powerless to stop it, because the people committing this atrocity were the same people showering Bhagwan with luxury goods and cars. Their power was growing and hers was waning, so she decided it was time to go.

"I said, 'Sheela, it's time to look at yourself,'" she told a news reporter. "'Are you ready to compromise and have a comfortable life, or are you ready to rough it?' I said, 'There's no way I'm going to compromise my integrity. It's time to go.'"

After a *60 Minutes Australia* reporter taped an interview with Sheela, he traveled to Oregon and played portions of the video for Bhagwan to get his response. When she accused him of exploiting people, he said, "She's drugged. She's on hard drugs," to laughter from the sannyasins sitting on the floor of the commune's press room. The reporter had in fact asked Sheela about Bhagwan's own drug use. He played an excerpt in which she accused him of taking up to sixty milligrams of Valium each day.

"She has no dignity," Bhagwan said. "All dignity that she thinks she has was given by me. She was just a hotel waitress and I made her almost a queen. I have never made love to her. That much is certain. Perhaps that is the jealousy. She always wanted, but I have made it a point to never make love to a secretary."

When reporters asked Sheela about her future plans, she said she was writing a book about her experiences and searching for a hotel in the Black Forest that she and her friends might run together. Indeed, on October 6 the group purchased a hotel for 3.9 million deutsche marks, with a DM 50,000 down payment—using a loan, Sheela would later say, that her husband, Dipo, had secured.

As for the criminal allegations, Sheela claimed she would willingly return to the United States if needed. "They don't have to extradite me. They just have to call me for a court appearance. They should call me, and I would come. Why not? What do I have to hide?"

Bhagwan anticipated a bleaker future for the woman who delivered his New Commune. "She is just going more and more insane before she goes to imprisonment. You just wait. Either she will kill herself, out of the very burden of all the crimes that she has done, or she will have to suffer her whole life in imprisonment."

41 | FLIGHT FROM OREGON

ON FRIDAY, OCTOBER 25, Bhagwan's criminal defense attorney Peter Schey and Swami Prem Niren met with US Attorney Charles Turner in Portland to confront him with a rumor they'd heard that Bhagwan was about to be indicted and arrested on federal charges. Niren had previously assured Turner that Bhagwan would surrender voluntarily if it ever came to that, and he had similarly told the joint task force at Rajneeshpuram that he would accept service of any subpoenas or warrants on his master's behalf. The ranch was already swarming with state and federal law enforcement, not to mention dozens of armed Rajneesh Security. If officers tried to pierce Bhagwan's heavily guarded compound without notice, Niren said he feared there could be a messy, needless confrontation.

Turner assured Niren that the grand jury had not issued any indictments against Bhagwan. He promised to give them advance notice if Bhagwan were charged with any federal crimes. These were lies.

Two days earlier, the federal grand jury over which Turner had presided for the past ten months issued a thirty-five-count indictment against Bhagwan, Sheela, Vidya, and others for a criminal conspiracy to bring Bhagwan to America and to secure permanent residence for him by making false statements to federal officials. The indictment also alleged that the coconspirators organized a sham marriage scheme at the ranch by which they encouraged sannyasins to lie to immigration officials to secure green cards. The Department of Justice attorneys working on the immigration case originally did not plan to indict Bhagwan himself because they felt the evidence connecting him to the fraud was too thin, but Turner had insisted that they include the guru. Around the same time, the Wasco County grand jury had issued its own indictment against Sheela, Puja, and Shanti B for the attempted murder of Devaraj on Master's Day in July. All the indictments were kept under seal so that none of the defendants knew about them.

While Turner was speaking with Niren that Friday, a joint team of state and federal agents was already en route to West Germany to arrest Sheela, Puja, and Shanti B over the weekend. A team in Oregon would then arrest Bhagwan and the other defendants who remained at Rajneeshpuram. The prosecutors needed Sheela's arrest to come first because they worried that if she caught wind of the indictments she would flee across the nearby border to Switzerland, where it would be impossible to extradite her.

Turner and Oregon attorney general Dave Frohnmayer thus insisted on complete secrecy among all members of the task force until the trap could be sprung. They didn't even want Governor Atiyeh's chief of staff Gerry Thompson to call the governor in Taiwan, where he was on a trade mission, to inform him about the arrests, since the call could be intercepted. Thompson insisted on telling her boss that such an important, potentially explosive event was about to take place in Central Oregon. Unable to find a secure line through the federal government, she used a telephone in the apartment above a friend's restaurant in Salem to convey a cryptic message to the governor.

Niren and Schey left their Friday meeting with Charles Turner's assurances that no arrest was in the offing. As Schey flew home to Los Angeles that night, an *Oregonian* reporter called Gerry Thompson to ask if it was true that Bhagwan was about to be arrested.

Thompson alerted the feds that they had a leak from inside. The weekend's highly orchestrated arrest plan was already in jeopardy.

The following night, Saturday, October 26, another source gave Niren a credible tip that Bhagwan was about to be arrested. He called Peter Schey and told him to get right back on a plane and meet him in Portland the next day, Sunday, so they could again confront Turner. He also passed the tip about Bhagwan's arrest to the guru's personal secretary, Hasya.

Around dinnertime, a private pilot in Santa Ana, California, received word from her employer, Martin Aviation, that an unnamed customer had requested a Learjet in Rajneeshpuram, Oregon. The pilot was to fly there and wait on-call for the next three days, with no further destinations named.

She and her copilot departed early Sunday morning, arriving at the Rajneeshpuram airstrip at 7:35 AM. As soon as they landed, a team of disciples boarded the plane to clean and disinfect the entire passenger cabin. When the pilots asked, the disciples wouldn't say a word about who might be boarding, or when, or where they might be going.

Hasya would later describe it like an unfortunate coincidence. Her master seemed tired. He was under extraordinary pressure, given all the law enforcement activity swirling around the ranch for the past month and a half. There was talk of the National Guard charging in with guns blazing, even though the *real* criminals were thousands of miles away in Europe. Getting Bhagwan off the ranch for a few weeks until things cooled down seemed like the safest idea.

Without telling her master, Hasya claimed, she made quiet plans to get him out of Rajneeshpuram. She called another wealthy sannyasin, Hanya, who owned a mountain home near Charlotte, North Carolina, that could serve as a perfect retreat. As an alternative option, Hasya also reserved an entire floor of a hotel in Bermuda that could host Bhagwan's entourage and insulate him from the press. Only after making all these arrangements, Hasya claimed, did she mention her idea to Bhagwan and secure his approval.

She and Niren would both claim that Hasya never once communicated her wild idea about squiring Bhagwan away to Niren, the man in charge of Bhagwan's criminal defense, who had been flying back and forth to Portland to talk about the guru's potential arrest with prosecutors amid constant rumors that he would soon be indicted for federal crimes.

On Sunday morning, Hasya chartered a second jet, since Bhagwan couldn't travel without his entourage: his caretaker Vivek, Dr. Devaraj, his personal cook, his cleaner, his laundress, and Jayesh, a shrewd Canadian disciple who would pay for whatever they needed. He also needed his "throne"—the padded easy chair that accommodated his bad back.

Bhagwan held his regular discourse in Rajneesh Mandir that morning, where he answered questions without giving any hint about his plans.

Around lunchtime, disciples loaded some luggage onto the Martin Aviation Learjet. The pilots were told to be ready to go later that afternoon. They still didn't know where they were going.

———————————

At 3:00 PM on Sunday, federal and state agents met to finalize their plans. They would arrest Sheela later that night, at 1:00 AM Portland time. The next day around noon, they would move into the ranch to arrest Bhagwan.

———————————

At the same time the agents were planning the arrests, Swami Prem Niren and defense attorney Peter Schey were in Portland calling Charles Turner at his home—the same home that Sheela's gang had stalked and photographed four months earlier. Schey presented Turner with solid information he had received that Bhagwan had been indicted and would be arrested on Monday or Tuesday, even listing his supposed codefendants. To Turner's horror, Schey said the names in the exact order they appeared on the first page of the sealed federal indictment. Turner realized that the sannyasins either had the secret indictment in their hands or had received very accurate information from a government source.

Schey again asked Turner to allow Bhagwan to voluntarily surrender at the federal courthouse in Portland. Turner would only say that the government wouldn't agree to Bhagwan's voluntary surrender if he were ever indicted. Instead, he would be treated like any other criminal defendant, with no special dispensations for things like a private jet to ferry him into federal custody.

Niren claims that he called Rajneeshpuram around 5:00 PM on Sunday night to report the disappointing conversation to Hasya. After some difficulty locating her, operators finally reached her at the Rajneeshpuram airport terminal.

Bhagwan boarded the Martin Aviation Learjet around 5:00 PM with Vivek, Devaraj, and Jayesh. His household staff took the other plane, along with the throne. Their luggage included the type of clothing and toiletries one would expect for a short getaway, as well as some more unusual items, like the passengers' college diplomas, Devaraj's medical license, a handbag containing a .38 revolver and Teflon-coated bullets, $58,522 in crumpled currency, and jewelry worth about $1 million.

As the passengers settled in, the pilots learned for the first time that their destination would be Charlotte, North Carolina. The small jets did not have enough fuel to make it across the continent, so they stopped to refuel in Salt Lake City, Utah, and Pueblo, Colorado, before the final leg to the East Coast. While on the tarmac in Salt Lake City, Jayesh called the ranch and spoke with Hasya, who had stayed behind. Jayesh would later tell the FBI that Hasya urged them to go to Bermuda instead of North Carolina, since she worried the "press" might be tracking their flight. But the pilots said they wouldn't fly out of the country.

By the time Niren returned to the ranch from Portland that night, the planes had finished refueling and were en route to Charlotte. He claims he was shocked to learn that Hasya had done "the stupidest thing she could have done" by sending Bhagwan out of Oregon, given the impending criminal charges, which of course law enforcement would see as an attempt to escape arrest. Niren says they tried to call the planes and direct them to come back to Oregon, but that the federal government had blocked their ability to communicate with the planes—as if they wanted to ensure that Bhagwan did *not* come back and could thus be arrested for unlawful flight.

But Jayesh would later tell federal investigators that he had no problems making and receiving calls on the jet's telephone. One hour out of North Carolina, he called Hanya, the owner of the mountain home, who had arrived at the Charlotte airport around midnight with her passport and luggage. After the call, she approached a private aircraft leasing agent to ask about chartering a plane to Bermuda for eight people with lots of luggage. No planes were available in Charlotte, but after many calls Hanya located two planes out of Allentown, Pennsylvania, for $5,400 each. She gave her

American Express card number over the phone, saying she needed at least one jet immediately.

Bhagwan's plane was descending toward Charlotte.

———————————

Three weeks earlier, a disciple had submitted a question to Bhagwan about the possibility of his arrest.

"Let them arrest me. I have informed them, if they want to arrest me they should come with handcuffs, because I want the whole world to see my hands with their handcuffs," Bhagwan responded at discourse. "And how long can they keep me arrested? Two hours? I have not committed any crime, but within those two hours they will have destroyed their credibility."

———————————

US Customs agent Ronald Taylor was waiting on the tarmac in Charlotte when the planes landed around 2 AM. Upon learning that Bhagwan had fled the state, a furious Charles Turner had mustered resources to arrest the guru before he could escape the country, while the Federal Aviation Administration monitored the planes' progress across the continent. As Bhagwan would later recount it to the press, officers boarded the planes with guns drawn, shouting without saying what they really wanted, before slapping handcuffs around the passengers' wrists. Bhagwan and Vivek were sitting within arm's reach of a carry-on bag filled with $36,500 in cash. Officers also seized thirty-five watches, four bracelets, two pens, a brooch, seventeen pairs of glasses, bank records, a great deal of medical records, and one padded throne.

They were all taken to the US Marshals lockup in Charlotte and later transferred to the Mecklenburg County jail. Around 5 AM they were notified of the charges against them. Bhagwan had an outstanding arrest warrant based on the secret federal indictment issued five days earlier, and the other passengers were charged with aiding and abetting his unauthorized flight and harboring a fugitive. Niren arrived in North Carolina in time to represent his master at his initial appearance later that day. He argued that the judge should release Bhagwan to a "suitable sterile and cleansed environment," at whatever cost necessary, rather than the stinky, dirty, uncomfortable county jail. Bhagwan had been living in a "bubble boy environment," Niren explained, with constant attention to his asthma, allergies, and back problems.

Bhagwan interrupted and insisted on speaking directly to the judge. She warned him not to. "Your Honor, I say I've been sick the whole night on these steel benches and I have been asking those people continuously—not even a pillow. Sleeping on the steel benches. I cannot sleep on the benches. I cannot eat anything they can give." The judge was unmoved. Bhagwan would remain in county custody pending his detention hearing in three days.

That same day, back in Portland, Charles Turner held a press conference to announce the thirty-five-count federal indictment against Bhagwan Shree Rajneesh, Ma Anand Sheela, and six of their accomplices. He reported that Bhagwan was being detained in North Carolina pending a bail hearing, after which he would be remanded to Oregon to stand trial. If convicted, he faced up to 175 years in prison. Turner left no doubt that the federal government believed Bhagwan had fled specifically because of the indictment, citing the fact that his office had "some negotiations" with the guru's attorneys immediately before he left the ranch. As for Sheela, Turner would only say that he had "unconfirmed reports" that she had been arrested in West Germany.

Back at Rajneeshpuram, the new commune president, a British disciple named Ma Prem Anuradha, convened a large meeting for disciples at Rajneesh Mandir to discuss Bhagwan's arrest, although she had little tangible information to share. Some in the group found solace by turning in the direction of North Carolina and chanting the gachhamis. A roving news crew captured a large group of sannyasins at the Magdalena Cafeteria laughing and trying to downplay any concerns about their master's arrest.

"This is what an enlightened master does," one disciple said. "A real enlightened master pulls strokes like this. This is how you separate the curd from the cream. This is how you get rid of people that aren't really with him."

"Bhagwan is continually surprising us," said another. "This is another small episode."

"Every experience that I've had with Bhagwan, the bottom line has been more and more beautiful," an American sannyasin told a reporter. "How could I not trust that [Bhagwan leaving] also is something that will go better and higher? There's no reason for any mistrust in my heart."

The night of October 28, an NBC news crew talked its way into the lobby of the Haus Sonnhalde guesthouse, deep in the Black Forest of West Germany. A small group of police officers near the entrance tried to eject them, but a shrill South African voice called out, "No, no, let them in! That's the way we treat our guests! If the FBI are allowed in, these people can be our guests."

Ma Yoga Vidya, who until recently had been running the Rajneeshpuram commune, appeared in a hallway in a baggy turtleneck sweater, with her blonde hair a tangled mess and her eyes shooting fire at the dozens of German and American authorities combing through the building. Hours earlier, officers had pounded on the guesthouse door and then poured in, bearing a telex from America that they wouldn't share with the twenty-plus former disciples who lived there. With barely a word of explanation the officers had arrested Sheela and Shanti B. Puja was out running errands, and they grabbed her as soon as she returned. Sheela's first question to the arresting officers had been whether they had clean bedsheets at jail or if she should bring her own.

A full search of the guesthouse had commenced with Vidya's blessing since, she explained to reporters, they had nothing to hide. She invited a news crew to roam freely around the house. Cameras captured the investigators rifling through their luggage, digging through their closets, reading piles of documents, and examining bags full of medical supplies and pharmaceuticals. Among the items that German authorities would seize from the guesthouse were eighty-seven syringes, eighteen bottles of Rohypnol, and bottles of Valium and Demerol.

While they collected evidence, a reporter asked Vidya whether she was worried about getting arrested herself. "No, I'm not frightened because I haven't done anything wrong, and neither have any of the twenty other people done anything wrong." Although she had been one of the eight people named in the federal indictment for immigration fraud, the American authorities had requested to have only Sheela, Puja, and Shanti B arrested. Their crimes— particularly the attempted murder of Devaraj—had the best likelihood of a successful extradition back to the United States.

The *Oregonian* reported that news of Sheela's arrest was "met with almost universal delight" back at Rajneeshpuram.

42 | SUNSET

TEN DAYS AFTER BEING ARRESTED, Bhagwan returned to Oregon via federal correctional transportation. The grueling journey spanned three days with stops in jails, airports, and air force bases in Oklahoma City, Tucson, Phoenix, Long Beach, and Sacramento. Emerging from the airplane in handcuffs, with a trench coat draped over his body and his bald head exposed, Bhagwan looked exhausted and unnerved as he waved at a few supporters before being whisked to the Multnomah County Justice Center in Portland for booking.

Two days later, over the federal prosecutors' vigorous opposition, the court released him on $500,000 bail pending trial. After cleaning up at the Hotel Rajneesh in Portland, Bhagwan walked outside in pristine white robes. A jubilant crowd was there on the sidewalk to serenade him with an upbeat song about his wild love. Among the faces was one that Bhagwan had known for two decades: Laxmi, his former secretary, who remained loyal to him despite all the indignities she had suffered over the previous five years. She had been staying at Rajneeshpuram since the summer festival, living in the bugged Alan Watts A-4 quadriplex. "Pune was the seed, and Rajneeshpuram is the fruit," Laxmi said in an interview before Sheela left. "When a seed blooms into a tree, we never remember the seed. We enjoy the fruit, the flower. So now we are enjoying Rajneeshpuram."

Shaking a tambourine and bobbing up and down on the sidewalk, tiny Laxmi got buried in the crowd. Bhagwan didn't acknowledge her, if he even saw her, as he crossed a path of rose petals to his custom Rolls-Royce limousine.

He and Vivek made the long drive back to Rajneeshpuram to await trial, since he was prohibited from flying.

Six days later, in a move kept secret from nearly everyone at the ranch, Bhagwan returned to Portland to seal his fate in America. His attorneys had struck a deal with federal prosecutors by which he would plead guilty to two counts of immigration fraud (making false statements to a government official and conspiracy to defraud the government), pay $400,000 in fines and costs, and leave the country within five days. Using a legal construct known as an Alford plea, he admitted only that the government had sufficient evidence to convict him at trial, but he did not admit his guilt. Niren would claim at a press conference that Bhagwan had been prepared to stay and fight the charges, but his attorneys persuaded him to leave the country since his frail body couldn't withstand attacks from the entire force of the US government. Charles Turner said he agreed to the deal only because it would obliterate the sannyasin community in Oregon. "We felt that if he left the country, the movement would disband. Sending him to prison would have simply served to cause him to be a martyr."

Bhagwan went straight from the courthouse to a private airport where a leased 727 jet was waiting to take him out of the country. Joining him for this next phase of his work were his secretary Hasya, his doctor Devaraj, his caretaker Vivek, and his household staff. Before climbing the stairs, Bhagwan turned in a slow circle and offered a namaste salutation to the disciples who had gathered on the tarmac to see him off. His eyes were red and clouded, perhaps from exhaustion, perhaps from being overwhelmed with emotion about the way his grand American experiment was coming to a close.

That night he flew to New Delhi, never to set foot in America again.

———

Everybody wanted to know what would happen to Rajneeshpuram. Niren and Dhyan John insisted in press conferences that it would continue to be the primary community for the lovers of Bhagwan Shree Rajneesh, at least until the guru recovered from his ordeal and reconvened his flock somewhere else. But at a private commune meeting in Rajneesh Mandir, a somber Mayor Niren told disciples that they were taking a close look at the commune's finances, and he confirmed news that they would be selling off Bhagwan's collection of ninety-three Rolls-Royces. Although there was some sporadic applause, a state police officer noted that the disciples were generally subdued and unenthusiastic about Niren's presentation, with many leaving while the meeting continued, as if they had lost interest. The officer counted around fifteen hundred to seventeen hundred disciples in attendance. Months earlier, the commune had claimed a population exceeding three thousand.

As he continued to hold community meetings, Niren encountered open hostility from disciples who seemed confused and frustrated by a situation where they were getting scant credible information from the commune's leaders. In mid-November, Bhagwan sent a message encouraging all foreign disciples at Rajneeshpuram to go home. By the next day, buses, vans, and cars were pouring out of the ranch. Commune-owned vehicles and other valuable items began disappearing as well, to the point that all vehicles across the ranch were centralized and kept under guard. The commune leadership also froze withdrawals from currency card accounts, where many sannyasins had dumped all their cash.

On November 22, with only about five hundred people left at Rajneeshpuram, Niren delivered the grim news that the commune would be shut down and the property sold. "The impact of the legal attacks on this community have produced a situation where it's no longer viable economically or emotionally or spiritually or sensible to continue," he said. A reporter asked whether Sheela was to blame for the commune's downfall. "The positions of the state and federal governments were in place and fixed before Sheela began her public level of confrontation, and certainly long before she conducted her criminal activities," Niren said. "In terms of the ultimate impact of this, I blame it squarely on Sheela. It's clear the intent to drive this community out of existence was made long before Sheela took public positions that increasingly added to the atmosphere of confrontation."

By early December, the community was being assailed by outside lawsuits that threatened to wipe out its accounts. The State of Oregon sued twenty-six Rajneesh corporations for civil racketeering, seeking forfeiture of nearly every piece of property the sannyasins owned in Oregon since the state alleged it was used for or acquired by criminal activity. The state also sought $250,000 fines from each of the corporations and an injunction prohibiting them from conducting any future business in Oregon.

Around the same time, a wealthy European former disciple closely allied with Sheela's group forced the commune into involuntary bankruptcy when she tried to collect $800,000 that she claimed the commune had withdrawn from her Swiss bank account without her consent. Just before these lawsuits came in, Dhyan John had managed to sell eighty-four Rolls-Royces to an exotic car dealer from Texas for an estimated $6 million.

The final nail in Rajneeshpuram's coffin arrived on December 10, when a federal judge ruled on the lawsuit Attorney General Frohnmayer had filed two years earlier alleging that the city was a theocracy. Siding with Frohnmayer, the judge voided the city's incorporation as an unconstitutional merger of church and state. Within days of the decision, the ranch population was down to only three hundred people, and the leaders planned to further reduce it to around 130 disciples by Christmas, with those who remained serving in caretaker roles until the property could be sold.

———————

On February 6, 1986, after a complex international legal process played out, Sheela, Puja, and Shanti B were extradited from West Germany and returned to Portland. They each faced a unique combination of charges stemming from the attempted murder and poisoning of Devaraj, poisoning Wasco County judges Bill Hulse and Ray Matthew, setting fire to Dan Durow's office, wiretapping, the salmonella poisoning in The Dalles, and federal immigration charges in the same indictment that had brought down Bhagwan.

Sheela's attorneys entered heavy negotiations with state and federal prosecutors to reach a plea bargain. After striking deals in April, the three defendants pled guilty to some of the crimes for which they were charged and received their sentences in July. Sheela was sentenced to twenty years in federal prison, although her attorney predicted—correctly—that she would be out within three to four years under the parole guidelines. She was also required to pay $469,000 in penalties and restitution and give up her permanent resident status. Upon completing her sentence, she would have to leave the United States immediately and would probably never be allowed to return.

"I hate to hold animosity," Bill Hulse told the *Oregonian* newspaper, "but I think she's getting off lightly."

Krishna Deva finally received his day in court in November 1986, after living in federal witness protection for the previous year. As part of his deal with prosecutors, he had already pled guilty to a state charge of racketeering and a federal charge of conspiracy to defraud the INS by entering a sham marriage, but his sentencing had been deferred until November 24. At the hearing before a federal judge, US Attorney Charles Turner said that KD had "rendered an important public service" in providing information that was critical to prosecuting other disciples and that ultimately led to Bhagwan's community leaving Oregon altogether. Turner made a strong recommendation that the court place KD on probation.

Judge Edward Leavy was unmoved. As he saw it, KD was a highly educated American citizen who had defrauded his own government and needed to pay the price. The judge also considered that second-time offenders who illegally entered the country—often uneducated migrant workers who didn't speak English—were routinely sentenced to two years in prison. To ensure KD received a sentence that was proportionate and fair, Judge Leavy sentenced him to two years in prison, 240 hours of community service, and a $1,000 fine. A reporter described KD as appearing "crestfallen," staring down at the floor, as the judge announced the sentence.

Earlier in the hearing, KD had told the judge that he'd spent the past year trying to get his life back on track. "If there is any good to come out of this, it's that it's finished for me."

For a person driving down the county road at the end of 1986, the first glimpse that Rajneeshpuram had ever existed would be an abandoned guard shack and a hand-painted sign that read, CLOSED. NO HOTEL. NO RESTAURANT. NO TOURS. NO GAS. Driving into the valley, only the county road remained open, with all the private roads the sannyasins had stretched across the property blocked with boulders and chains. Nearly everything that could be moved had already been sold at auction earlier in the year, including furniture, modular trailer units, building materials, heavy machinery, and industrial cleaning supplies. What remained were the many buildings the sannyasins had erected between

1981 and 1983, the only period when they had been allowed to develop their property. Vandals had plastered graffiti across many of them, making obscene references to Bhagwan and the disciples who had once lived there.

A few dozen sannyasins remained at the ranch as a skeleton caretaker crew, residing first in the Hotel Rajneesh and then in Sheela's former home, Jesus Grove. Over the summer the Rajneesh Investment Corporation had quoted a negotiable price of $40 million for the entire ranch and all its improvements. Without a buyer by August, the corporation stopped making mortgage and tax payments on the property. That same month, the State of Oregon reached an agreement with five Rajneesh corporations to settle the racketeering lawsuit. The corporations would pay up to $5 million to compensate the state for its investigative costs and to compensate victims of the sannyasins' crimes, including the 751 people who experienced salmonella or salmonella-like symptoms after eating at restaurants in The Dalles in the fall of 1984. The total amount of the compensation fund would depend on the amount received from the sale of the ranch.

By November, the ranch's asking price was down to $26.5 million, which would get the purchaser the entire ranch property and all the buildings that remained, including the 140-room hotel, 95 townhouses, 42 quadriplex cabins, 200 A-frame cabins, 52 double-wide trailers, and 39 commercial and industrial buildings.

The land was zoned for agricultural use, but Wasco County officials said they'd be willing to discuss other uses with potential buyers.

43 | AFTERMATH

ON A SUNNY MORNING in the waning days of Rajneeshpuram, right after a thick blanket of snow had draped over the craggy hills and the dark wooden buildings, a reporter tracked down Ma Mary Catherine, the *Rajneesh Times* reporter who had also served as one of the early planners for the City of Rajneeshpuram. Earnest and straightforward, the New Englander seemed surprised when the reporter asked her to talk not about Sheela, or salmonella, or Rolls-Royces, or embezzled funds—but about what might have happened at Rajneeshpuram if it had been allowed to continue. Mary Catherine's face relaxed into a dreamy expression as she described the next site that would have been developed, an empty parcel of rolling hills near the commune's entrance known as Buddha Grove.

"As you drove through Buddha Grove, first you would have come to an industrial area, then you would have come to a commercial area like a university town, and then gradually you would have come through the residential area. And then up on the top, where you had the view of the John Day River embankment and could see sunrises and sunsets, would have been the meditation hall. We dreamed of a geodesic dome made of glass, with a prism of light that went down inside.

"But that's on the physical side," Mary Catherine said. "What was here, and what I think Oregonians missed, was such a beautiful healing energy, such a kind and gentle place to be, where people were kind to each other. And never mind the fact that there was a nucleus of people going around poisoning others, which was the best secret in the place. Bhagwan said it was a dream.

It lasted for four years. Some people are saying it was Camelot. 'Here it was, it was beautiful, and people from the outside attacked it and missed what was really going on. It's gone. Goodbye.' We don't regret it."

She tried to explain the intangible aspects of the community to an outsider. "Let's just say, to get up in the morning in a beautiful place where you can hear the birds singing, instead of urban noises, and walk down the hill by the stream, watching the ducks or the herons feeding, and then up the steps to Rajneesh Mandir, take off your shoes and feel really grounded on the earth before you go in. And then dance with the music until Bhagwan came in. And then to sit either in silence with him or to listen to what he had to say . . ." She trailed off, gazing beyond the reporter's shoulder to the shining white hills.

"It was joyful. We are a joyful people. We loved each other. There was the whole feeling that we were in it together. We were cohesive because we loved each other and because we loved Bhagwan, and he loved us in return."

―――――――

"I knew from the beginning that they would fail," reflected the Italian woman formerly known as Ma Prem Deeksha. Upon leaving Rajneeshpuram in August 1981, she had become an instant pariah. Disciples were told not to have any contact with her, since her negativity would inhibit their opportunity to attain enlightenment. Sheela accused her of embezzling hundreds of thousands of dollars—a claim that most old hands found unbelievable. After extracting herself from the movement, Deeksha became a government informant, offering investigators an eyewitness account of Bhagwan's personal involvement in planning to move permanently to America and blessing the fraudulent marriage scheme.

From the outside, she watched as Rajneeshpuram crested and then collapsed. "It was like watching an avalanche in slow motion," she later said. "I had a good grasp of how the law works. I knew you couldn't stray too much. I knew absolutely they would fail. I was kind of sad to see people so excited about building the New Commune, knowing it would never work. How could they survive? They wouldn't produce any wealth. How would they survive? Were they planning to get jobs?"

In recent years, Deeksha has become an outspoken critic of Bhagwan among sannyasin circles online. But she also believes that Sheela manipulated Bhagwan just as much as he manipulated her. "I saw them in a room once doing a dance. Sheela had Bhagwan by the balls, and he had her by the throat. They were both using each other."

———————

Dickon Kent, the boy from England who moved to Rajneeshpuram with his mother, left the commune in November 1985 at age seventeen. He traveled with some other sannyasin kids to California, where they planned to open a disco, without anticipating they would need money to get that done. He never went to school again, but he found work. Living in San Francisco at age twenty, he began hanging out with a large group of young people who were not sannyasins. To his astonishment, he found that they were good people. Throughout his childhood, he had been taught that sannyasins were special and that he shouldn't trust anybody else.

Now in his early fifties, with a teenage son of his own, Dickon has mixed feelings about his time at Rajneeshpuram. "I don't want to deny the darkness, and I don't want to deny the positive. From a child's perspective, most of it was positive. It was like Mr. Toad's Wild Ride. But I know there are plenty of other kids who didn't feel that way, who were really distraught, who didn't see their parents much. It's very much an individual thing." Indeed, the sannyasin community experienced a #MeToo watershed in 2021, when a number of former commune children used private Facebook forums to describe the sexual abuse they experienced at the hands of adult disciples. While several abusers publicly apologized, others responded by minimizing or justifying their behavior without accepting responsibility. Inspired by the commune children, some women who had been adults in Rajneesh communities took to the forums to share their own stories of abuse. As they see it, Bhagwan nurtured an environment where vulnerable people were expected to surrender to the whims of those in power, even when that meant submitting to an abuser's sexual desires. This corrosion started at the very top and seeped down to group leaders and other disciples regarded as close to the guru.

Despite experiencing sexual abuse at the hands of a woman who lived in Bhagwan's household, today Dickon Kent feels conflicted when reflecting on the man at the center of it all. On one hand, he sees Bhagwan as a spoiled, self-indulgent, callous man. "You don't do the things we did, you don't command somebody to be as outrageous as Sheela was, if you have any empathy and compassion for other people on the planet, let alone your neighbors." But at the same time, Dickon understands why people like his mother were drawn to the brilliant guru and his extravagant community. He recoils when he sees current and former sannyasins advocating one extreme or the other: that Bhagwan was either a demon or a saint, that his organization was either wholly corrupt or grievously corrupted. "Why can't we hold both of those things and say they're both true? Because I believe they're both true."

Salmonella victims received financial restitution. Targets of murder and poisoning plots saw their perpetrators serve time in jail. But commune children received no justice. The men and women who sexually abused them—and all the sannyasins who knew it was happening and did nothing to stop it—walked away from Rajneeshpuram without any criminal consequences.

Five years after the fall of Rajneeshpuram, the federal government indicted Sheela, Savita, Vidya, Su, Shanti B, Samadhi, and Anugiten for conspiring to murder US Attorney Charles Turner. These would represent the final criminal charges in the Rajneeshpuram affair, after prosecutors had already secured convictions (mainly through plea deals) against more than two dozen disciples from Sheela's Jesus Grove circle for immigration fraud, wiretapping, and arson.

Federal prosecutors had received a boost in the Turner case when two members of Sheela's inner circle signed plea deals: Rikta, who helped Shanti B purchase the "five easy pieces," and Yogini, who surveilled Turner's home and plotted his murder. By this time, Sheela had been released from prison and moved to Switzerland, from where she could not be extradited. All the others would eventually strike plea deals except Savita and Su, two of Sheela's top lieutenants in the commune's final years. Following a lengthy extradition process from England, the two women stood trial in Oregon federal court in 1995—the first and only criminal trial of sannyasins from the ranch. As a condition of earlier plea deals, coconspirators including Krishna Deva, Ava, Yogini, Rikta, and Anugiten were called to testify against their former friends. The jury found the women guilty, and they were sentenced to five years in prison, although both served only three.

Ma Yoga Vidya, the commune president whose emotional breakdown had served as a catalyst for ending the Jesus Grove murder plots, escaped prosecution while living in her native South Africa until she reached a plea deal in 2002 and served about ten months in American prison. Ahead of her sentencing, she sent a letter to the federal judge praying for his leniency. After apologizing to Charles Turner and the people of the United States for her flagrant violation of their laws, Vidya reflected on her experiences at Rajneeshpuram:

> I have spent twenty long years thinking carefully about the deplorable time in 1985 when a conspiracy was hatched. I expect I will live with this unfortunate time for the rest of my life. I have had to look long and hard at myself in order to accept responsibility for a fundamental inability to counter publicly what was happening at the commune at that time. For this, I formally accept responsibility. . . .
>
> At the time, it was difficult to recognize that disloyalty against Sheela and the commune could be honourable and allegiance wrong. . . . In perfect hindsight, the truth was that the man I had worshipped and his secretary were mad and their purposes destructive. . . .
>
> Ultimately, the story of my life comes down to a few key moments of decision, which signify the difference between a life of achievement versus one of regret.

Sheela has long denied her involvement in nearly every crime of which she has been accused, including the plots to murder or poison people on or off the ranch. In 1986, she pled guilty to the following crimes:

- Conspiracy to defraud the US government to move Bhagwan and other foreign disciples permanently to the United States, remain illegally, and obtain permanent resident status
- Conspiracy to intercept wire communications to and from Rajneeshpuram via the wiretapping system established behind the Socrates building

She pled guilty to these additional crimes using the Alford plea construct, by which she admitted that prosecutors had sufficient evidence to convict her at trial, but she did not admit her guilt:

- Attempted murder of Devaraj at the July 1985 Master's Day celebration
- First-degree arson of Dan Durow's office
- First-degree assault for the poisoning of Judge Bill Hulse during his August 1984 visit to Rajneeshpuram
- Second-degree assault for the poisoning of Judge Ray Matthew on the same occasion
- Conspiracy to tamper with consumer products for the September 1984 salmonella poisoning in The Dalles

An anonymous benefactor paid about half of Sheela's $469,000 fine, but the remainder was never collected and the judgment expired. After serving less than three years in prison, she returned to Europe and married Swami Dipo—Urs Birnstiel—again. This time it stuck, although Dipo died in 1992 of AIDS-related complications. She now operates two nursing home facilities in Switzerland for people with mental and physical disabilities.

After pleading guilty and leaving America in November 1985, Bhagwan Shree Rajneesh embarked on a calamitous six-month world tour that brought him to more than twenty countries, all of which denied him entry or deported him before he could settle in. In 1987, he finally returned to his old ashram in Pune, where he would remain for the next three years before dying of an apparent heart attack in January 1990 at age fifty-eight. Some people within the sannyasin community suspect that Bhagwan, who was suffering from very poor health, asked his loyal doctor Devaraj to assist with his suicide, or that he was perhaps murdered by his top lieutenants who were eager to seize control of his valuable empire.

His caretaker Vivek preceded him in death by forty-one days, from an apparent overdose of sleeping pills. Hasya stayed with her master until the end, after which she returned to America and opened mystery schools for spiritual growth in Los Angeles and Sedona, Arizona. She died in 2014 after a long battle with Parkinson's disease.

Just before he died, Bhagwan adopted a new name, Osho, by which sannyasins presently refer to him. Ashram leaders had him cremated within an hour of his death being announced, and his remains were interred in a memorial near the porch of his home, where he had once hosted small audiences. A marble plaque marked the spot, with an epitaph he had dictated:

Osho
Never Born
Never Died
Only Visited this Planet Earth between Dec 11, 1931–Jan 19, 1990

When former sannyasin attorney Swami Deva Bhakti saw this inscription, his mind went back to the fate of his beloved home in Oregon. As the legal strategist had expected, the sannyasins had lost their church/state case when the federal judge ruled that Rajneeshpuram was null and void from the moment it was created. The city was never born, Bhakti thought, just like Bhagwan was never born.

He also recalled a song that some disciples at the commune had written about Rajneeshpuram that included the line "Welcome to the city that will never die . . ." Bhakti doesn't believe that any sannyasins took this sentiment literally. Rajneeshpuram was a mystery school created by an extraordinary, enlightened master to wake up his disciples and people on the outside. Bhagwan had said in Pune that mystery schools by definition were supposed to remain a secret, and that outside forces would smash them into oblivion as soon as they were discovered. When that scenario played out in Oregon, Bhakti saw it as the natural completion of a cycle that his master had long anticipated. The New Commune was never supposed to last.

Deva Bhakti reads Bhagwan's epitaph as a meditation on the impermanence of physical being, but also as an accurate description of the shimmering, volatile community that the guru and his loyal disciples had once tried to create from the mud up.

Rajneeshpuram. Never born. Never died.

ACKNOWLEDGMENTS

I WILL NEVER FORGET the moment when I was walking the streets of Chicago with my husband and I finally mustered the courage to say that I wanted to create a podcast about Bhagwan Shree Rajneesh. The concept had been percolating in my head for weeks, after I had fallen down a rabbit hole reading nearly every memoir and investigative record about Rajneeshpuram that I could get my hands on. I knew there was a story about the sannyasins and their extraordinary community in Oregon that had not yet been told, and the more I chewed on it, the more I convinced myself that I should at least try to tell it.

I waited for him to say that I was a lunatic. I knew nothing about podcasting and didn't even own a microphone. But—I should have known—he supported me without a moment's hesitation. With his encouragement and assistance, I created the podcast series *Building Utopia: Bhagwan Shree Rajneesh* and then this book. So, first and foremost, I acknowledge the unflagging support of my husband, the brilliant and hilarious Bryan Liberona, whom I have loved since I first met him twenty years ago at the Plaza Tavern in Madison, Wisconsin. This book would not exist if he hadn't been so willing to go on an adventure with me. I also thank my son, Wesley, for reminding me to get out of the 1980s and remain present.

Luis Liberona, my father-in-law, passed away while I was working on this book. Even when his health was failing, he encouraged me to keep all my interview and research appointments, to just keep working at it. He was a beloved father and an absolutely doting *ito* to his grandchildren, and we miss him every day.

My deepest thanks go to the former commune members who were willing to share their experiences with me. Every person I interviewed had a fascinating story, and I marveled at their willingness to tell intimate, sometimes unflattering tales to an outsider from a different generation to help him understand.

311

Most of their personal stories do not appear in this text, unfortunately, but their spirit is woven into every page. I extend a special thank you to Satya Franklin (formerly Ma Satya Bharti), who wrote the most beautiful memoir about her time with Bhagwan and who spent many hours helping me fill in some gaps in my research, and also to Toby Marshall for allowing me to use his tremendous photographs of the commune's early days and answering all my many questions. One source, who has asked to remain anonymous, was instrumental in arranging some of my most important interviews, and I thank her for trusting me enough to share me with her people. Another source, whose name has been changed to Ma Anand Sarabi in this book, spent dozens of hours on the phone with me when I was first beginning to write and was a major inspiration for much of the color and description about day-to-day life on the ranch. She deserves a book of her own.

Thanks to the staff at the Chicago Public Library, Mary McRobinson and the staff at the Oregon State Archives, the University of Oregon Libraries Special Collections and University Archives, and Matthew Cowan at the Oregon Historical Society Research Library.

My agent, Jim McCarthy, believed in me and my ability to tell this story. Thank you to Jerry Pohlen, Devon Freeny, and everyone at Chicago Review Press for helping transform this thing from concept to book.

My outstanding beta readers provided invaluable feedback and encouragement. Thank you to Jessica Crews, Toni Schroeckenstein, Amy Cook, Andrea Wise, Abby Hymen, and my brother Robin King. Carrie Compton not only provided comments on the manuscript but also helped to edit my podcast series—*and* she introduced me to my husband. Thanks to Karen Schirm and Michael Liberona for their laboratory wisdom, and to Anna, Cody, and everyone in the Accio writing group for stoking my enthusiasm about both spaceships and beer.

Finally, a huge thank-you to my parents for inspiring me to love reading and writing, and especially to my mother, Judi King, who has always been my first editor.

NOTES

Prologue

"free-wheeling sexual behavior": Michael Corey, "Rumors and Concerns Continue to Shroud Rajneesh Mountain Castle," *Verona-Cedar Grove (NJ) Times*, June 25, 1981.

"I saw girls kissing": Lisa Shepard, "Indian Commune's Sexual Beliefs Cause Concern," *Hanford Sentinel*, December 26, 1981.

"Yes, we're tolerant": Shepard, "Sexual Beliefs Cause Concern."

"Do not let them": Corey, "Rumors and Concerns."

1. The Godman of Mumbai

"Meditation is the key": Osho, "The Last Testament, Volume 2" (unpublished interviews), PDF file, chapter 7, 129.

"It was always ABC": Osho, *The Book of Wisdom: The Heart of Tibetan Buddhism; Commentaries on Atisha's Seven Points of Mind Training* (Mumbai: Osho Media International, 1990), chapter 6.

"a great love affair": Bhagwan Shree Rajneesh, *Far Beyond the Stars: A Darshan Diary* (Pune: Rajneesh Foundation, 1980), chapter 6.

"go totally mad": Bhagwan Shree Rajneesh, *Meditation: The First and Last Freedom* (Cologne, Germany: Rebel Publishing House, 1988), 47.

I've been waiting: Franklin, *Promise of Paradise*, 26.

2. Oasis in Pune

I can't take sannyas: Interview with Satya Franklin, July 6, 2020.

When the time comes: Franklin, *Promise of Paradise*, 47.

"a very insecure type": Swami Prem Chinmaya, letter to family, February 25, 1973, private collection.

"I have a fatal illness": Swami Prem Chinmaya, letter to grandmother, March 2, 1978, private collection.

"the card-playing, lime-sipping": Milne, *Bhagwan*, 127.

"Bhagwan, you are calling": Bhagwan Shree Rajneesh, *The Goose Is Out* (Rajneeshpuram, OR: Rajneesh Foundation International, 1982), chapter 3.

"I looked into his eyes": Interview with Hugh Smith (Avinasha).

"an abomination": Richard Price, letter to *Time* magazine, January 21, 1978, Rajneesh Legal Services Corporation records (hereafter cited as RLS Records).

"whether you are running": Richard Price, letter to Krishna Prem, February 23, 1978, RLS Records.

"Surrender to me": Bharti, *Death Comes Dancing*, 21.

"Your votes will never": Bhagwan Shree Rajneesh, *The Diamond Sutra: Discourses on the Vajrachchedika Prajnaparamita Sutra of Gautama the Buddha* (Pune: Rajneesh Foundation, 1979), chapter 8.

"Deeksha is crazy!": Bhagwan Shree Rajneesh, *The Book of Books*, vol. 1 (Rajneeshpuram, OR: Rajneesh Foundation International, 1982), chapter 6.

Multiple disciples have alleged: See, e.g., Milne, *Bhagwan*, 154–55; Sheela, *Don't Kill Him!*, 158; Franklin, *Promise of Paradise*, 95; Interview with Deeksha, August 10, 2020; Department of Justice report of investigation, October 19, 1983, Rajneeshpuram Case Files, Oregon Department of Justice (hereafter cited as Rajneeshpuram Case Files).

3. The New Commune

"dry, dull, dead": Bhagwan Shree Rajneesh, *The Heart Sutra: Discourses on the Prajnaparamita-Hridayam Sutra of Gautama the Buddha* (Pune: Rajneesh Foundation, 1978), chapter 4.

"You call me": Shanker Bhatt, "Prime Minister Morarji Desai Has Nothing but Contempt for 'Bhagwan' Rajneesh," *Indiascope*, November 30, 1978.

"orange people": Rajneesh Foundation, "Bhagwan's Message to Kutch: Get Ready, I Am Coming!," news release 125, September 20, 1980, RLS Records.

While Laxmi often tried: See, e.g., Franklin, *Promise of Paradise*, 85, 115; Interviews with Deeksha; Interviews with Satya Franklin; Department of Justice report of interview, Ma Prem Geeta, September 24, 1985, Rajneeshpuram Case Files.

"Just accept it": Bhagwan Shree Rajneesh, *The Further Shore: A Darshan Diary* (Pune: Rajneesh Foundation, 1980), chapter 24.

"I do think about": Chinmaya, letter to sister, June 18, 1974, private collection.

"Now it is time": Bhagwan Shree Rajneesh, *Tao: The Golden Gate*, vol. 1 (Rajneeshpuram, OR: Rajneesh Foundation International, 1984), chapter 2.

"He never wanted": Rajneesh, *Tao*, chapter 2.

He looks gorgeous: Franklin, *Promise of Paradise*, 138.

The abruptness of his death: See, e.g., Franklin, *Promise of Paradise*, 138–39.

"mercy killing": FBI interview summary, David Berry Knapp (Krishna Deva), November 15, 1985, Rajneeshpuram Case Files (hereafter cited as KD FBI Interview, November 15, 1985).

This chapter is finished: Sheela Birnstiel, interview in *Wild Wild Country*, directed by Chapman Way & Maclain Way (Netflix 2018), part 1.

4. Exeunt

Life is so much easier: Interview with Deeksha, September 8, 2020.

"It is obvious that": Bhagwan Shree Rajneesh medical records, May 18, 1981, RLS Records.

"At the rate it's going": Sheela Silverman, transcript of interview with Immigration and Naturalization Service, October 14, 1982, RLS Records (hereafter cited as Sheela INS Interview).

"Nonsense": Scotta Callister, Jim Long, and Leslie Zaitz, "Guru's Uncertain Health Improves En Route to Oregon," *Oregonian*, July 5, 1985.

According to Deeksha: Interview with Deeksha, March 12, 2021.

5. Foundations in the Desert

"No fucking": Interview with Toby Marshall, August 17, 2020.

"second underlying and false motive": David Knapp (Krishna Deva), trial testimony, 1995, RLS Records.

"This ranch has been abused": Scotta Callister, "Followers of Indian Guru Work to Turn Ranch Green," *Sunday Oregonian*, August 30, 1981.

6. The Mirage

Where are all the trees?: Sheela, *Don't Kill Him!*, 236.

"a specially chartered aircraft": Sandeha, letter to Sheela, August 20, 1981, RLS Records.

Sheela denies: Interview with Sheela Birnstiel, March 14, 2021.

"ultimate darshans": Interview with Deeksha, March 12, 2021; Gordon, *Golden Guru*, 79–80; Milne, *Bhagwan*, 118; Scotta Callister, Jim Long, and Leslie Zaitz, "Bhagwan Shree Rajneesh: Small-Town Boy Makes Guru," *Oregonian*, July 1, 1985.

An American disciple: Interview with Deeksha, September 8, 2020.

7. Between a Rock and Antelope

"Women stand in one group": Callister, "Followers of Indian Guru."

"We didn't want to go": Interview with Subhan Schenker.

"We can easily be": Russell Chandler and Tyler Marshall, "Guru Brings His Ashram to Oregon," *Los Angeles Times*, August 30, 1981.

You know, Jim: Oregon State Police, information report, "Investigation of Alleged Crimes/Rajneeshpuram" (interview with Jim Comini), October 16, 1985, Rajneeshpuram Case Files.

8. BETTER DEAD THAN RED

"incongruous and unsightly": Margaret Hill, memorandum to Property Owners of Antelope, October 18, 1981, RLS Records.

"will not stand by": Sheela, letter to Margaret Hill, December 1, 1981, RLS Records.

residents had correctly guessed: Report of interview, Swami Krishna Deva, Oregon Department of Justice, November 25, 1985, Rajneeshpuram Case Files (hereafter cited as KD ODJ Interview, November 25, 1985); United Press International, "Guru's Hordes Overwhelm Antelope," *San Francisco Examiner*, April 16, 1982.

"little loophole": Sheela Birnstiel, interview in *Wild Wild Country*, part 2.

Krishna Deva employed: Milne, *Bhagwan*, 241; Interview with Toby Marshall, August 17, 2020; "Town Hall: Fight for a City," May 1982, via YouTube, https://youtu.be/PG8Yw7zz3HA, 56:44.

"The city has lost": United Press International, "Guru's Hordes."

"very explosive": Kathleen Harbaugh, memorandum to Paul Phillips, April 21, 1982, Rajneeshpuram Collection.

"extremely agitated": Bob Oliver, memorandum to Gerry Thompson, April 29, 1982, Rajneeshpuram Collection.

"never perceived such": Oliver to Thompson, April 29, 1982.

"It would seem to me": Atiyeh on Rajneeshpuram sound recording, Rajneeshpuram Collection.

9. A Small Farm Town

A former disciple later told reporters: Scotta Callister, Jim Long, and Leslie Zaitz, "Rajneeshees: From India to Oregon," *Oregonian*, June 30, 1985.

Why not place: Robert E. Harvey and Glenda Joyce Harvey, transcript of taped conversation, November 3, 1983, Rajneeshpuram Case Files.

the result had been preordained: Swami Krishna Deva, affidavit, November 22, 1985, Rajneeshpuram Case Files; interview with Sheela Birnstiel, March 7, 2021.

10. Making It Legal

"[Bhagwan] and/or his closest": US Department of Justice, Immigration and Naturalization Service report of investigation, November 19, 1981, Rajneeshpuram Case Files.

"They have not established": Associated Press, "80 Foreign Members of Commune Told to Leave U.S.," *Corvallis (OR) Gazette-Times*, March 24, 1982.

"How do you define": Associated Press, "80 Foreign Members."

"Marriage is a three-ringed": "Sheela Weds Couple with Love and Laughter," *Rajneesh Times*, September 10, 1982.

"any commitment for": Bhagwan Shree Rajneesh, transcript of interview with Immigration and Naturalization Service, October 14, 1982, RLS Records.

Among sannyasins, there was little: See, e.g., Franklin, *Promise of Paradise*, 62–67; KD FBI Interview, November 15, 1985; Daniel Hoarfrost, letter to U.S. Attorney's Office, November 6, 1985, Rajneeshpuram Case Files.

"Don't fuck with immigration": Interview with Deeksha, September 8, 2020.

Don't worry about: Interviews with Deeksha, August 10 and September 8, 2020.

"What color is your": George Helland (Sharan Ananda), trial testimony, 1995, RLS Records.

"find itself flooded": US Department of Justice, Immigration and Naturalization Service report of investigation, November 19, 1981, Rajneeshpuram Case Files.

11. Bhagwan Takes a Trip

"Flowers?": Master Video 1, October 14, 1982, KGW Rajneeshpuram Video Collection, Oregon Historical Society Research Library (hereafter cited as KGW Collection).

"My master gets nothing": Master Video 1, KGW Collection.

"Did you like": Sheela INS Interview.

"I took a chance": Sheela INS Interview.

"When you visited": Sheela INS Interview.

"She said he was": US Department of Justice, Immigration and Naturalization Service report of investigation, April 28, 1982, Rajneeshpuram Case Files.

"No, I said my husband": Sheela INS Interview.

12. Truth and Consequences

"I had been expecting": "Immigration Officials Turn Down Bhagwan's Petition as Religious Worker," *Rajneesh Times*, December 24, 1982.

13. Religion at Its Highest

"The senate will be": Senate audio recording, March 23, 1983, Legislative Floor Proceeding Audio Records, Oregon State Archives.

"In the name of": Senate recording, March 23, 1983.

"Love is prayer": Senate recording, March 23, 1983.

"I go to the feet": Senate recording, March 23, 1983.

"lending credence and": Russell Sadler, "Bhagwan's Followers Sow Legislative Ill-Will," *Oregonian*, April 4, 1983; Associated Press, "Reps Protest Guru Prayer," *Albany (OR) Democrat-Herald*, March 31, 1983.

"corpse of religiousness": Osho, *Come, Come, Yet Again Come* (Mumbai: Osho Media International, 2013), chapter 13.

"the future of the world": Sheela INS Interview.

OK, Sheela: Interview with Sheela Birnstiel, March 7, 2021.

"I don't need to": "Greetings from Sheela and the Family," *Rajneesh Times*, July 8, 1983.

his *"living religion"*: "Greetings from Sheela."

"making the only": *Rajneeshism: An Introduction to Bhagwan Shree Rajneesh and His Religion* (Rajneeshpuram, OR: Rajneesh Foundation International, 1983), 56–57.

"That's how you": Interview with Sheela Birnstiel, March 14, 2021.

"Ours is the only": Callister, Long, and Zaitz, "Small-Town Boy."

"just a gesture": James, *Osho*, Chapter 26.

As FitzGerald put it: FitzGerald, *Cities on a Hill*, 357.

"We will fight": Jim Hill, "Papers Filed by Attorneys for Bhagwan," *Oregonian*, August 5, 1983.

14. Children of the Commune

He also encouraged: Interview with Erik Hochheimer; interview with Satya Franklin, June 11, 2020; Strelley, *The Ultimate Game*, 151–52; Sheela, *Don't Kill Him!*, 173.

"The child need not": Bhagwan Shree Rajneesh, *Sufis: The People of the Path*, vol. 2 (Pune: Rajneesh Foundation, 1980), chapter 12.

"That's what we'd": Interview with Bhasha Leonard.

"It was very common": Interview with Dickon Kent.

"It's hard to say": Interview with Dickon Kent.

Next door to: Interview with Satya Franklin, June 11, 2020.

Dickon felt it: Interview with Dickon Kent.

"Make the place": Osho, *From Death to Deathlessness* (Köln: Rebel Publishing House, 1990), chapter 32.

"make love a festive": Osho, *From Death*, chapter 32.

"There was a feeling": Interview with Satya Franklin, June 11, 2020.

"It is not certain": Osho, *From Death*, chapter 32.

"If my own children": Interview with Satya Franklin, June 11, 2020.

15. Horse Trading

"We'd love to leave": "Antelope Levy Approved, but Rajneeshees Offer to Leave," *Rajneesh Times*, May 20, 1983.

to present a "scenario": Bob Oliver, memorandum to John Williams, May 20, 1983, Rajneeshpuram Collection.

"an offer by someone": Oliver to Williams, May 20, 1983.

"blatant offer of trade": Associated Press, "Atiyeh Mulls Tax-Hike Veto," *Corvallis (OR) Gazette-Times*, June 2, 1983.

"If the Oregon State": Jayananda, letter to Keith Mobley, May 30, 1983, Rajneeshpuram Case Files.

"fairness, courage, and respect": "LCDC Says: All Cities Should Be Treated Equally," *Rajneesh Times*, June 3, 1983.

"Are rules created": LCDC meeting transcript, July 14, 1983, RLS Records.

"The [land-use] goals": LCDC meeting transcript.

"Thousand Friends should": "LCDC Adopts Anti-Rajneesh Rule on New Cities," *Rajneesh Times*, July 15, 1983.

16. Room 405

"taken off as one": "Nightclub Takes Off," *Rajneesh Times*, January 21, 1983.

Your hotel just exploded: City of Portland Bureau of Police, special report, case no. 83-61349, August 2, 1983, from FBI File of Bhagwan Shree Rajneesh (PDF), accessed at https://archive.org/details/BhagwanShreeRajneesh (hereafter Rajneesh FBI File).

Help! Please help me!: City of Portland Bureau of Police, special report, case no. 83-61349, July 30, 1983, Rajneesh FBI File.

described as "demolished": Portland Bureau of Police, special report, July 30, 1983.

Get me out of this building!: City of Portland Bureau of Police, special report, case no. 83-61349, August 15, 1983, Rajneesh FBI File.

There is nothing planted: Portland Bureau of Police, special report, July 30, 1983.

The commune had sent disciples: Interview with Erik Hochheimer (Megha).

"bomb workshop": United Press International, "Bomber Convicted," *Coos Bay (OR) World*, October 3, 1985.

"Religion became a": Associated Press, "20-Year Term in Bombing of Hotel Rajneesh," *Escondido (CA) Times-Advocate*, November 10, 1985.

reportedly still provides explosives training: Associated Press, "20-Year Term"; "United States: The Jamaat al-Fuqra Threat," Stratfor, June 3, 2005, https://worldview.stratfor.com/article/united-states-jamaat-al-fuqra-threat.

"the product of": "The Product of Prejudice," *Rajneesh Times*, August 5, 1983.

17. God Versus the Universe

"Congratulations on screwing": "Ross Screws Rajneeshees—Changes Advice After Two Years," *Rajneesh Times*, September 30, 1983.

"Quite simply stated": United Press International, "Rajneeshees Threaten to Sue Wasco, Officials," *World*, October 28, 1983.

"known and assumed facts": Oregon Department of Justice, memorandum no. 8148, October 6, 1983, Rajneeshpuram Case Files.

"I believe this is": Don Jepsen, "Rajneesh City Declared Illegal," *Oregonian*, October 7, 1983.

"never attempted to influence": Sheela and Krishna Deva, affidavits, October 1983, Rajneeshpuram Case Files.

"They don't know": Video 8109, KGW Collection.

"control what little bit": Richard Hughes, "Intervention Urged for Antelope Schools," *Salem (OR) Statesman-Journal*, September 29, 1983.

"I tell you one": Video 8109, KGW Collection.

"Calling a spade": Video 5855, KGW Collection.

"I'm an honest person": Video 5855, KGW Collection.

"Answer from the board!": Video 8109, KGW Collection.

"From the tone": Bob Oliver, memorandum to Gerry Thompson, November 14, 1983, Rajneeshpuram Collection.

"The whole state wants": Associated Press, "Bhagwan's Aide Claims Injustice," *Salem (OR) Statesman-Journal*, December 16, 1983.

18. The Spook

"Nobody is going": Scotta Callister, Jim Long, and Leslie Zaitz, "Rajneeshees Establish Security Forces, Large Armory," *Oregonian*, July 9, 1985.

Bhagwan was aware: Osho, *From Bondage to Freedom: Answers to the Seekers of the Path* (Köln: Rebel Publishing House, 1990), chapter 2; Department of Justice report of interview, Diane Langhoff (Sagun), November 6, 1985, Rajneeshpuram Case Files; KD ODJ Interview, November 25, 1985.

19. The Enemy Inside

"I had a bank account": Swami Dhyan John, "The Girl with the Golden Touch," *Rajneesh Times*, March 9, 1984.

"Well, we didn't want": Swami Dhyan John, grand jury testimony, October 24, 1985, Rajneeshpuram Case Files.

"Now here's a woman": Dhyan John testimony.

The Hollywood Group: Dhyan John testimony.

"If anyone needed": KD FBI Interview, November 15, 1985.

"a nice guy": Interview with Erik Hochheimer (Megha).

"I did not want": Sheela, *Don't Kill Him!*, 28.

"directives and scoldings": FitzGerald, *Cities on a Hill*, 319.

"like a cocktail party": James, *Osho*, chapter 20.

"Everybody hated her": Swami Shunyo, grand jury testimony, October 16, 1985, Rajneeshpuram Case Files.

"Puja is a very": Ma Prem Isabel, grand jury testimony, October 23, 1985, Rajneeshpuram Case Files.

"Serving Sheela was": Swami Devaraj, grand jury testimony, October 15, 1985, Rajneeshpuram Case Files.

"full blown Turkish": Tape_015, KGW Collection.

I tried everything: KD FBI Interview, November 15, 1985.

20. Sharpening the Sword

"still pending": Associated Press, "INS Gives Guru Preferred Immigration Status," *Spokane (WA) Spokesman-Review*, February 16, 1984.

"While the lawyers are": "Oregon Court Shifts into Reverse," *Rajneesh Times*, June 29, 1984.

"They are most welcome": Master Tape 6-5747, KGW Collection.

"crushed very easily": Bhagwan Shree Rajneesh, *The Rajneesh Bible*, vol. 2 (Rajneeshpuram, OR: Rajneesh Foundation International, 1985), chapter 20.

"Cash-free is care-free!": "Rajneesh Currency Card Heralds Move to Cash-Free Community," *Rajneesh Times*, January 20, 1984.

"He definitely is going": Master Tape 8-5754, KGW Collection.

"hit her hard": Bhagwan Shree Rajneesh, *The Last Testament*, vol. 1 (Boulder, CO: Rajneesh Publications, 1986), chapter 3.

"I had to teach her": Osho, *Bondage to Freedom*, chapter 1.

Voter fraud, voter fraud: David Berry Knapp (Krishna Deva), FBI interview summary, November 13, 1985, Rajneeshpuram Case Files (hereafter cited as KD FBI Interview, November 13, 1985).

He told her to brainstorm: Sandhu, *Nothing to Lose*, 239.

According to meeting notes: KD FBI Interview, November 13, 1985.

Shanti B similarly recalled: Stork, *Breaking the Spell*, chapter 17.

"once-in-a-lifetime": "Press Release: An Open Invitation to All Americans," *Rajneesh Times*, August 3, 1984.

21. The Chinese Laundry

What if people had the shits: KD ODJ Interview, November 25, 1985.
You don't want to: KD FBI Interview, November 13, 1985.
Let's have some fun: KD ODJ Interview, November 25, 1985.
"What I see here": Win McCormack and Bill Driver, "Rajneeshpuram: Valley of Death?," *Oregon Magazine*, September 1984.
Isabel, what is this?: Ma Prem Isabel, grand jury testimony, October 23, 1985, Rajneeshpuram Case Files.
What a gracious lady: Ma Prem Isabel, grand jury testimony.
Ava would later tell: Ava Avalos, FBI interview summary, October 22, 1985, Rajneeshpuram Case Files (hereafter cited as Ava FBI Interview, October 22, 1985); Department of Justice report of interview, Ava Kay Avalos (Ma Ava), October 7–8, 1985 (hereafter cited as Ava ODJ Interview, October 7–8, 1985).
Krishna Deva heard a similar story: KD FBI Interview, November 15, 1985; KD ODJ Interview, November 25, 1985.

22. How to Win an Election

During the first week of September: Report of interview, Department of Justice, October 17, 1984, Rajneeshpuram Case Files.
Sheela says it was KD: Interview with Sheela Birnstiel, March 14, 2021.
Most commune members: FitzGerald, *Cities on a Hill*, 264.
"I walked with my eyes": Video 5884, KGW Collection.
"When a man is": Bhagwan Shree Rajneesh, *The Discipline of Transcendence: Discourses on the 42 Sutras of Buddha*, vol. 3 (Pune: Rajneesh Foundation, 1978), chapter 10.
"We don't believe": Master Tape 14-5776, KGW Collection.
"change their habits": Video 24-5852, KGW Collection.
"I never thought of it": Video 5768, KGW Collection.
"Nobody will touch": Video 5773, KGW Collection.
"I didn't even have": Video 5773, KGW Collection.
"They're going to show": Video 5806, KGW Collection.

23. Something in the Water

If there is a choice: Ava FBI interview, October 22, 1985.
"lots of places": Ava FBI Interview, October 22, 1985.

It's best not to: KD FBI Interview, November 13, 1985; KD ODJ Interview, November 25, 1985.

Krishna Deva, however, had no doubt: KD FBI Interview, November 13, 1985.

751 people who ate: Thomas J. Török et al., "A Large Community Outbreak of Salmonellosis Caused by Intentional Contamination of Restaurant Salad Bars," *Journal of the American Medical Association* 278 (August 6, 1997): 389–395.

Puji, you've done: KD FBI Interview, November 13, 1985.

"freaked them out": KD ODJ Interview, November 25, 1985.

24. Desperate Times

"Because I have reason": Video 20-5822, KGW Collection.

"maybe just on": Norma Paulus, oral history interview, Sound Recording 21, October 5, 1999, Oregon Historical Society Digital Collections.

"They're setting themselves": Hasso Hering, "Paulus Decries Anti-Guru Vote Plan," *Albany (OR) Democrat-Herald*, September 11, 1984.

"If thousands of": Eric Mortenson, "Guru Opponents May Still Vote in Wasco County," *Albany (OR) Democrat-Herald*, September 20, 1984.

"Recall! Recall!": Tom Gorman, "Rajneesh Foes Meet on Voting," *Salem (OR) Statesman-Journal*, October 2, 1984.

"The clerk of the county": Video 19-5820, KGW Collection.

"Sue Proffitt said that": Video 19-5820, KGW Collection.

"We were just shocked": Video 8106, KGW Collection.

"We will celebrate": Video 8106, KGW Collection.

"I have a contract": Associated Press, "Wasco Clerk to Challenge All New Voters," *Albany (OR) Democrat-Herald*, October 10, 1984.

"This was the last": Video 5821, KGW Collection.

"in effect declared": Ron Blankenbaker, "This Was the Week That . . . ," *Salem (OR) Statesman-Journal*, October 11, 1984.

"could have been elected": Clifford N. Carlsen, Norma Paulus, Judge Edward Leavy, and Greg McMurdo, conversation transcript, August 14, 1995, Oregon Historical Society.

"That means we've won": Associated Press, "Wasco Clerk."

"We had to figure": Paulus oral history, October 5, 1999.

"So she got her": Carlsen, Paulus, Leavy, and McMurdo conversation, August 14, 1995.

25. Sannyasin Hospitality

"ticket back to the big tent": Oregon State Police, person report (William Henry Allen), October 18, 1984, Rajneeshpuram Case Files.

Sheela now admits: Sandhu, *Nothing to Lose*, 240.

Bhagwan directed Sheela to eject: Stork, *Breaking the Spell*, chapter 17.

"liquidate" the Share-a-Home program: Gerry Thompson, memorandum to Governor Atiyeh, October 15, 1984, Rajneeshpuram Collection.

"space cadets": Gerry Thompson, memorandum to Governor Atiyeh, October 19, 1984, Rajneeshpuram Collection.

"This is privileged": Video 5841, KGW Collection.

"The state Board": Video 8038, KGW Collection.

"Clearly he is": Associated Press, "Angels Plan to Protest Rajneesh, Atiyeh," *Salem (OR) Statesman-Journal*, November 3, 1984.

"Nobody was taking": Associated Press, "Angels Plan."

26. The Election of 1984

No, no, no: Carlsen, Paulus, Leavy, and McMurdo conversation, August 14, 1995.

"all American flags": Carlsen, Paulus, Leavy, and McMurdo conversation, August 14, 1995.

"We are following": Video 20-5833, KGW Collection.

"Why are you allowing": Alan Gustafson, "Voter Checks Go Smoothly," *Salem (OR) Statesman-Journal*, October 24, 1984.

all but two of the 207: Jeanie Senior, "Rejections of Two Registrants Spark Confrontation," *Oregonian*, October 24, 1984.

"You just put your": Video 5834, KGW Collection.

"I have been misunderstood": Videos 7981 and 21-5836, KGW Collection.

"very protective": Videos 7981 and 21-5836, KGW Collection.

"You never know!": Video 7981, KGW Collection.

Hey, hey, what do you say?: Video 23-5849, KGW Collection.

"for eternity": Video 24-5852, KGW Collection.

"The seed has been": Video 24-5852, KGW Collection.

27. The Lost Discourse

"Bhagwan, why do you call": Bhagwan Shree Rajneesh, *The Rajneesh Bible*, vol. 1 (Rajneeshpuram, OR: Rajneesh Foundation International, 1985), chapter 1.

"So I have a very": Video 5841, KGW Collection.

"The picture I have": Rajneesh, *Rajneesh Bible*, vol. 1, chapter 1.

"I am no more": Bhagwan Shree Rajneesh, deposition transcript, August 19, 1984, RLS Records.

Isn't organization: Rajneesh, *Rajneesh Bible*, vol. 2, chapter 20.

"Politicians are dangerous": Rajneesh, *Rajneesh Bible*, vol. 1, chapter 7.

"Sannyasins can have": Rajneesh, *Rajneesh Bible*, vol. 2, chapter 20.

Bhagwan tried to demonstrate: Interviews with Toby Marshall; interview with Michel Bisson.

"reconstructed with the": "Bhagwan Shree Rajneesh Speaks: The Rajneesh Bible," *Rajneesh Times*, January 11, 1985.

he claimed awareness and control: Interviews with Toby Marshall; interview with Michel Bisson.

Bhagwan wanted Bhakti: Interview with Deva Bhakti; KD ODJ Interview, November 25, 1985; Stork, *Breaking the Spell*, chapter 17.

28. Desperate Measures

Are you up for: Ava FBI Interview, October 22, 1985.

As I drove past: Swami Sharan Ananda, grand jury testimony, October 17, 1985, Rajneesh-puram Case Files.

"prime asshole": Ava FBI interview, October 22, 1985.

"little old lady": KD FBI interview, November 15, 1985.

"destroy the records": KD FBI interview, November 15, 1985.

"They've done an excellent": Video 11-5762, KGW Collection.

they had blocked Durow's progress: Department of Justice report of interview, Diane Langhoff (Sagun), November 6, 1985, Rajneeshpuram Case Files (hereafter cited as Sagun ODJ Interview, November 6, 1985).

"violently ill" after drinking: United States House of Representatives Subcommittee on Mining, Forest Management and Bonneville Power Administration, Committee on Interior and Insular Affairs, "Enforcement of Regulations Concerning Access to Mining Claims and Public Land Permit Areas in Central Oregon," November 27, 1984, Center for Legislative Archives, National Archives and Records Administration.

"We don't engage": Associated Press, "Rajneeshees Dispute Claim of Poisoning," *Spokane (WA) Chronicle*, November 28, 1984.

"It is proof enough": Rajneesh, *Rajneesh Bible*, vol. 2, chapter 3.

"explosive response": Dan Durow, memo to Fred Hawkins, December 20, 1985, Rajneesh-puram Case Files.

"All I hear this afternoon": Video 5795, KGW Collection.

"They're not the least": Video 5795, KGW Collection.

"*The festival speaks*": Video 5795, KGW Collection.

"*so that should*": Video 5793, KGW Collection.

"*Congressman Bob Smith said*": Video 5793, KGW Collection.

"*I demand that you*": Video 5793, KGW Collection.

29. Downward Spiral

"*Check that your weapon*": Tape_018, KGW Collection.

"*Why are we here today?*": Tape_018, KGW Collection.

recently aired public concerns: Video 5786, KGW Collection.

"*You think I'm crazy*": Video 6246, KGW Collection.

"*We are not going*": Video 6246, KGW Collection.

"*all the way up*": Krishna Deva and John Mathis, audio recording of conversation, September 22, 1984, https://commons.wikimedia.org/wiki/Category:Federal_Bureau _of_Investigation_audio_files_on_Rajneesh_movement.

marriages were "phony": "INS Memo Calls Marriages Phony," Oregonian, August 5, 1984.

"*a witch hunt*": "INS Memo," Oregonian.

30. The Turning Point

The situation doesn't feel: Ava FBI interview, October 22, 1985.

"*do her in*": Ava FBI interview, October 22, 1985.

"*led to fury*": Alma Peralta (Yogini), trial testimony, 1995, RLS Records.

"*bump her off*": Ava FBI interview, October 22, 1985.

I'm sick and tired: Alma Peralta (Yogini), trial testimony, 1995, RLS Records.

If there is a choice: Ava FBI interview, October 22, 1985.

If ten thousand people: Stork, *Breaking the Spell*, chapter 20.

Life is meaningless: KD FBI interview, November 15, 1985.

Why not include: KD ODJ interview, November 25, 1985.

"*hit team*": Ava FBI interview, October 22, 1985.

That's OK: KD FBI interview, November 15, 1985.

"*Indian sun poisoning*": KD FBI interview, November 15, 1985.

Just like Devaraj?: KD FBI interview, November 15, 1985.

"*five easy pieces*": KD ODJ interview, November 25, 1985.

31. Internal Affairs

"*They thought of themselves*": Sheela, *Don't Kill Him!*, 205.

Bhagwan brokered a truce: Franklin, *Promise of Paradise*, 207.

It became an obsession for Sheela: KD ODJ Interview, November 25, 1985; Ava FBI Interview, October 22, 1985; Sagun ODJ Interview, November 6, 1985.

If Bhagwan is killed: Ava FBI interview, October 22, 1985.

he confronted Sheela: KD FBI Interview, November 15, 1985; KD ODJ Interview, November 25, 1985.

Bhagwan talked for more than ten minutes: Ava Avalos, trial testimony, 1995, RLS Records; KD ODJ Interview, November 25, 1985; Joint Task Force log of events, September 23, 1985, Rajneeshpuram Collection (hereafter cited as Task Force Log).

put on planes to Europe: Ava FBI Interview, October 22, 1985; KD FBI Interview, November 15, 1985; Jay Shelfer (Jayananda), trial testimony, 1995, RLS Records.

The list of potential murder targets: Ava FBI Interview, October 22, 1985.

Julian asked him to install: Interview with Michel Bisson.

32. The Garden of Epicurus

"Nazi camp guard": Interview with Erik Hochheimer (Megha).

According to Sheela: Interview with Sheela Birnstiel, March 14, 2021.

washing "scrupulously": "Vision of Bhagwan Shree Rajneesh: AIDS Will Kill Two Thirds of the World's Population," *Rajneesh Times*, March 9, 1984.

"Friends and lovers": "AIDSFREE," *Rajneesh Times*, August 30, 1985.

"place a beautiful bowl": "AIDS Precautions: An Interview with Ma Anand Puja," *Rajneesh Times*, August 30, 1985.

"the ideal city for": "Gays of America," *Rajneesh Times*, July 22, 1983.

"the religion of Bhagwan": "Gays Welcomed," *Rajneesh Times*, July 15, 1983.

"As a homosexual": Osho, *Bondage to Freedom*, chapter 16.

"deprogramming": Bhagwan Shree Rajneesh, "Press Conferences" (unpublished), PDF, chapter 5, September 30, 1985, 68.

"We don't want homosexuals": Rajneesh, 68.

"trying to destroy": Rajneesh, *Last Testament*, vol. 1, chapter 25.

"more positive" than others: Swami Anand Megha, grand jury testimony, November 13, 1985, Rajneeshpuram Case Files.

"As I see it": Osho, *From Death*, chapter 9.

33. Master's Day 1985

she played a tape: KD ODJ Interview, November 25, 1985; KD FBI Interview, November 15, 1985; David Knapp (KD), trial testimony, 1995, RLS Records; Stork, *Breaking the Spell*, chapter 18; Video 5931 (Sheela interview), KGW Collection.

I will do it: Stork, *Breaking the Spell*, chapter 21.

"Sannyas is renouncing": "And the Flowers Showered," *Rajneesh Times*, July 12, 1985.

What's wrong with you?: Jane Stork, interview in *Wild Wild Country*, Part 4.

Shanti B has poisoned me: Oregon State Police, information report, "Rajneeshpuram Investigation of Alleged Crimes: Attempted Murder/Conspiracy to Commit Murder," September 20, 1985, Rajneeshpuram Case Files.

I've been injected: Oregon State Police, information report, September 20, 1985.

Oh shit: Stork, *Breaking the Spell*, chapter 21; KD ODJ Interview, November 25, 1985; KD FBI Interview, November 15, 1985.

Bhagwan had called her: KD ODJ Interview, November 25, 1985; KD FBI Interview, November 15, 1985; Stork, *Breaking the Spell*, chapter 21.

"general freak out": KD FBI Interview, November 15, 1985.

Sheela told her crew: KD ODJ Interview, November 25, 1985; KD FBI Interview, November 15, 1985.

34. Catharsis

"Catharsis can be negative": Bhagwan Shree Rajneesh, *Won't You Join the Dance: Initiation Talks Between Master and Disciple* (Rajneeshpuram, OR: Rajneesh Foundation International, 1983), chapter 15.

Vidya was at least aware: KD ODJ Interview, November 25, 1985.

Members of Sheela's inner circle: Ava Avalos, trial testimony, 1995, RLS Records; James, *Osho*, chapter 27.

"short-circuited": Ma Yoga Vidya, presentencing statement to the court, Rajneeshpuram Case Files.

Oh Sheela: James, *Osho*, chapter 27.

"nervous breakdown": Ma Yoga Vidya, presentencing statement to the court, Rajneeshpuram Case Files.

I can't do this!: Richard Langford (Anugiten), trial testimony, 1995, RLS Records.

I can't do this either: Langford, trial testimony.

OK . . . That's fine: Langford, trial testimony.

35. Plan B

Sheela went back to Mexico City: Ava FBI Interview, October 22, 1985; Department of Justice report of interview, Ma Prem Geeta, September 24, 1985, Rajneeshpuram Case Files.

finally obtained a backdated divorce: KD ODJ Interview, November 25, 1985.

"Beloved KD": FBI report, October 15, 1985, Rajneeshpuram Case Files.

"Beloved Bhagwan": Sheela, letter to Bhagwan, September 13, 1985, RLS Records.

What about AIDS?: Department of Justice report of interview, Cliff, September 24, 1985, Rajneeshpuram Case Files.

36. Collapse

"Puja's salmonella maker": KD ODJ Interview, November 25, 1985.

37. Glad News

She served as a monitor: Ava FBI Interview, October 22, 1985; Sagun ODJ Interview, November 6, 1985; Allen Thomas Gay (Swami Rajesh), FBI interview summary, December 31, 1985, Rajneeshpuram Case Files.

helped to steam open: KD FBI Interview, November 15, 1985.

"scum"... "get rid of them": Department of Justice report of interview, Ma Prem Geeta, September 24, 1985, Rajneeshpuram Case Files.

"Just today I have": Osho, "The Last Testament, Volume 2," chapter 25.

"I spent three years": Video 7976, KGW Collection.

"My mind is in shock": Video 7976, KGW Collection.

"I have been silent": Rajneesh, "Press Conferences," chapter 1, September 16, 1985.

"I have called you": Rajneesh, "Press Conferences," chapter 1.

38. Cracks in the Dam

"Damn near mass hysteria": Task Force Log.

"It is finished": Rajneesh, "Press Conferences," chapter 4, September 24, 1985.

designed to shape their testimony: Daniel Hoarfrost, letter to United States Attorney's Office re: "Proffer of information concerning potential witness ('X')," November 6, 1985, Rajneeshpuram Case Files; Roberta Ulrich and Jeanie Senior, "Fear of 'Armed Confrontation' Recalled by Police," *Oregonian*, November 16, 1986; interview with Erik Hochheimer (Megha).

"It is the feeling": Task Force Log; Charles E. Pritchard, memorandum to William F. Gary re: "October 19, 1985 Staff Re: Assessment of Whether State Should Enter into Guilty Plea Agreement with David Berry Knapp, aka Swami Krishna Deva," November 6, 1985, Rajneeshpuram Case Files.

"I'm doubting a lot": Video 62-5903, KGW Collection.

"Whatever happened in": Osho, *Bondage to Freedom*, chapter 9.

"I'm here to be": Video 32-5923, KGW Collection.

"pope robes": Videos 5971 and 36-5970, KGW Collection.

Hasya said Bhagwan was concerned: Interview with Mahendra (Deva Ananya).

"a great deal of danger": "David Knapp: Past History, Present Activities, and Future Goals," November 1986, Rajneeshpuram Case Files.

"Notwithstanding a mountain": "David Knapp: Past History."

39. A Revelation

"Dr. Shunyo has sent": Video 5898, KGW Collection.

Thank you: Interview with Erik Hochheimer (Megha).

"They started becoming": Osho, *Bondage to Freedom*, Chapter 6.

"Either you take all": Osho, "The Last Testament, Volume 3" (unpublished), PDF, chapter 22, 386.

dead within the year: Interview with Erik Hochheimer (Megha).

40. Almost a Queen

"all the money": Interviews with Edwin Kelley (Svarga).

"Are you afraid": Video 7993, KGW Collection.

"crazy sannyasin": Video 5930, KGW Collection.

"Where's all the money": Video 7993, KGW Collection.

"I said, 'Sheela'": Video 5931, KGW Collection.

"She's drugged": 60 Minutes broadcast, November 3, 1985, transcript, Rajneeshpuram Case Files.

"She has no dignity": 60 Minutes Australia transcript.

"They don't have to": Tape_011, KGW Collection.

"She is just going": 60 Minutes Australia transcript.

41. Flight from Oregon

Thompson insisted: Interview with Gerry Thompson.

"the stupidest thing": Swami Prem Niren, memo to Myles J. Ambrose, November 2, 1985, RLS Records.

"Let them arrest me": Osho, *Bondage to Freedom*, chapter 21.

"suitable sterile": *United States of America v. Bhagwan Shree Rajneesh et al.*, initial appearance hearing transcript, United States District Court for the Western District of North Carolina, October 28, 1985, RLS Records.

"Your Honor, I say": *Rajneesh*, initial appearance hearing transcript.

"some negotiations": Video 45-6030, KGW Collection.

"unconfirmed reports": Video 45-6031, KGW Collection.

"This is what an": Video 45-6031, KGW Collection.

"Bhagwan is continually": Video 45-6031, KGW Collection.

"Every experience that": Video 45-6031, KGW Collection.

"No, no, let them in!": Video 6076, KGW Collection.

"No, I'm not frightened": Video 6076, KGW Collection.

"met with almost universal delight": Roberta Ulrich and Jeanie Senior, "Bhagwan Followers Still Merry," *Oregonian*, October 29, 1985.

42. Sunset

"Pune was the seed": Video 5873, KGW Collection.

"We felt that if": Janet Davies, "Plea Bargains Save, AG Says," *Salem (OR) Statesman-Journal*, July 23, 1986.

"The impact of the legal": Video 53-6147, KGW Collection.

"The positions of the state": Video 53-6147, KGW Collection.

"I hate to hold animosity": Joan Laatz, "Sheela Sentenced to Prison," *Oregonian*, July 23, 1986.

"rendered an important": Associated Press, "Ex-Mayor of Rajneeshpuram to Go to Prison," *Corvallis (OR) Gazette-Times*, November 25, 1986.

KD was a highly educated: US District Court of Oregon Historical Society, *Edward Leavy: An Oral History* (Portland: US District Court of Oregon Historical Society, 2013).

"crestfallen": Associated Press, "Ex-Mayor of Rajneeshpuram."

"If there is any good": Associated Press, "Ex-Mayor of Rajneeshpuram."

43. Aftermath

"As you drove": Video 6201, KGW Collection.

"I knew from the beginning": Interviews with Deeksha.

"I don't want to": Interview with Dickon Kent.

"I have spent twenty": Ma Yoga Vidya, presentencing statement to the court, Rajneeshpuram Case Files.

SELECTED BIBLIOGRAPHY

Archival Sources

Governor Vic Atiyeh Collection, Pacific University Library Digital Exhibits. Forest Grove, Oregon.

KGW Rajneeshpuram Video Collection. Oregon Historical Society Research Library. Portland, Oregon.

Rajneesh Artifacts and Ephemera Collection. University of Oregon Libraries, Special Collections and University Archives. Eugene, Oregon.

Rajneesh Legal Services Corporation records, 1981–1985. University of Oregon Libraries, Special Collections and University Archives. Eugene, Oregon.

Rajneeshpuram Case Files, Oregon Department of Justice. Oregon State Archives. Salem, Oregon.

Rajneeshpuram Civil Suit Records, Oregon Secretary of State (Elections Division). Oregon State Archives. Salem, Oregon.

Rajneeshpuram Collection, Pacific University Library Digital Exhibits. Forest Grove, Oregon.

Rajneeshpuram Correspondence, Oregon State Offices for Services to Children and Families (Human Resources Department). Oregon State Archives. Salem, Oregon.

Books

Carter, Lewis F. *Charisma and Control in Rajneeshpuram: The Role of Shared Values in the Creation of a Community.* New York: Cambridge University Press, 1990.

FitzGerald, Frances. *Cities on a Hill: A Journey Through Contemporary American Cultures.* New York: Simon & Schuster, 1986.

Franklin, Satya Bharti. *The Promise of Paradise: A Woman's Intimate Story of the Perils of Life with Rajneesh.* Barrytown, PA: Station Hill Press, 1992.

333

Gordon, James S. *The Golden Guru: The Strange Journey of Bhagwan Shree Rajneesh.* Brattleboro, VT: Stephen Greene Press, 1987.

James, Maneesha. *Osho: The Buddha for the Future.* Pune: Osho International Foundation, 2018.

Joshi, Vasant. *The Awakened One: The Life and Work of Bhagwan Shree Rajneesh.* New York: Harper & Row, 1982.

Ma Anand Sheela. *Don't Kill Him! The Story of My Life with Bhagwan Rajneesh: A Memoir.* New Delhi: Fingerprint!, 2012.

Ma Satya Bharti. *Death Comes Dancing: Celebrating Life with Bhagwan Shree Rajneesh.* London: Routledge & Kegan Paul, 1981.

Milne, Hugh. *Bhagwan: The God That Failed.* New York: St. Martin's, 1986.

Sandhu, Manbeena. *Nothing to Lose: The Authorized Biography of Ma Anand Sheela.* New Delhi: HarperCollins, 2020.

Stork, Jane. *Breaking the Spell: My Life as a Rajneeshee and the Long Journey Back to Freedom.* Sydney: Macmillan, 2009.

Strelley, Kate. *The Ultimate Game: The Rise and Fall of Bhagwan Shree Rajneesh.* New York: Harper & Row, 1987.

Periodicals

Callister, Scotta, Jim Long, and Leslie Zaitz. For Love and Money twenty-part investigative series. *Oregonian*, 1985.

Rajneesh Times weekly newspapers, 1982–1985.

Original Interviews

Abrahamson, Robert (Abhiyana), March 7, 2020.

Bhakti, Deva (fictionalized name), October 26 and December 7 and 14, 2020.

Birnstiel, Sheela (Ma Anand Sheela), March 3, 7, and 14, 2021.

Bisson, Michel, December 9, 2020.

Deeksha, August 10 and September 8, 2020, and March 12, 2021.

Franklin, Satya, June and July 2020 and February 2021.

Grealy, Stephen (Saten), March 10 and April 13, 2020.

Hochheimer, Erik (Megha), June 8, 2020.

Kelley, Edwin (Svarga), February 25 and March 2, 2020.

Kent, Dickon, March 17, 2019.

Kirsch, Walden, April 15, 2020.

Leonard, Bhasha, August 31, 2020.

Mahendra (Deva Ananya), December 28, 2020, and April 22, 2021.

Marshall, Toby, August 17 and 19, 2020.

Sarabi, Anand (fictionalized name), March and April 2020.

Sarito, Anand, March 4, 2020.

Schenker, Subhan, April 24 and May 14, 2020.

Smith, Hugh (Avinasha), February 26 and March 5, 2020.

Steck, Peter, March 6, 2020.

Thompson, Gerry, May 28, 2020.

And additional sources who asked to remain off the record or confidential.

INDEX

Italicized page references indicate illustrations